Robert G. Hamerton-Kelly is Senior
Research Scholar in Ethics and Lecturer in
Classics and International Relations at the
Center for International Security and Arms
Control, Stanford University. He is the author
of *God the Father: Theology and Patriarchy
in the Teaching of Jesus.*

Sacred Violence
Paul's Hermeneutic of the Cross

ROBERT G. HAMERTON-KELLY

Fortress Press   Minneapolis

For Rosemary
praeter sacrum dilecta

SACRED VIOLENCE
Paul's Hermeneutic of the Cross

Copyright © 1992 Augsburg Fortress. All rights reserved. Except for brief quotations in critical articles or reviews, no part of this book may be reproduced in any manner without prior written permission from the publisher. Write to: Permissions, Augsburg Fortress, 426 S. Fifth St., Box 1209, Minneapolis, MN 55440.

Interior design: Karen Buck
Cover design: Patricia Boman

Library of Congress Cataloging-in-Publication Data

Hamerton-Kelly, Robert.

Sacred violence : the hermeneutic of the cross in the theology of
  Paul / R.G. Hamerton-Kelly.
    p. cm.
  Includes bibliographical references
  ISBN 0-8006-2529-3
  1. Violence—Religious aspects. 2. Girard, René, 1923–
3. Bible. N.T. Epistles of Paul—theology. 4. Christianity and
other religions—Judaism 5. Judaism—Relations—Christianity.
6. Love—Religious aspects. I. Title.
BL65.V55H351992
227'.06—dc20   91-34698
                                                    CIP

The paper used in this publication meets the minimum requirements of American National Standard for Information Sciences—Permanence of Paper for Printed Library Materials, ANSI Z329.48-1984

Manufactured in the U.S.A.   AF 1–2529

96   95   94   93   92   1   2   3   4   5   6   7   8   9   10

Contents

4. Sacred Violence and Original Sin: Adam's Transgression as the Deformation of Desire

5. Sacred Violence and the Jews: Beloved Enemies in the Plan of Salvation

6. Sacred Violence and the Law of Moses: The Prohibition Perverted

7. Sacred Violence and the Reformation of Desire: Eros and Agape

Conclusion

Abbreviations

AGAJU	Arbeiten zu die Geschichte des antiken Judentums und des Urchristentums
AGSU	Arbeiten zu die Geschichte des Spät-judentums und Urchristentums
Bauer	*A Greek-English Lexicon of the New Testament,* ed. William F. Arndt and F. Wilbur Gingrich (Chicago and London: University of Chicago Press, 1979)
BHT	Beiträge zur historischen Theologie
CBQ	*Catholic Biblical Quarterly*
EvTh	*Evangelische Theologie*
ICC	International Critical Commentary
Int	*Interpretation*
IntOrg	*International Organization*
JBL	*Journal of Biblical Literature*
JSNT	*Journal for the Study of the New Testament*
JTS	*Journal of Theological Studies*
KD	*Kerygma und Dogma*
LS	*Louvain Studies*
LCL	*Loeb Classical Library*
MQR	*Michigan Quarterly Review*
NYRB	*New York Review of Books*
NTS	*New Testament Studies*
SNTSMS	*Society for New Testament Studies Monograph Series*
SNTU	*Studien zum Neuen Testament und Umwelt*
StTh	*Studia Theologica* (Lund)
TDNT	*Theological Dictionary of the New Testament* (Kittel)
TheoViatorum	*Theologia Viatorum*
ThZ	*Theologische Zeitschrift*
UNT	*Untersuchungen zum Neuen Testament*

USQR	*Union Seminary Quarterly Review*
WMANT	Wissenschaftliche Monographien zum Alten und Neuen Testament
WUNT	Wissenschaftliche Untersuchungen zum Neuen Testament
ZNW	*Zeitschrift für die neutestamentliche Wissenschaft*

Classical and Patristic

Augustine, *Conf*	Augustine, *Confessions*
Dio Chrys. *Or*	Dio Chrysostom, *Orations*
Epic. *Diss*	Epictetus, *Discourses*
Philo	
Abr	*De Abrahamo*
Cher	*De Cherubim*
Dec	*De Decalogo*
Fug	*De Fuga et Inventione*
Leg All	*Legum Allegoriae*
Opif	*De Opificio Mundi*
Quaes Exod	*Quaestiones et Solutiones in Exodus*
Quaes Gen	*Quaestiones et Solutiones in Genesin*
Quod Lib	*Quod Omnis Probus Liber*
Sacrif	*De Sacrificiis Abelis et Caini*
Spec Leg	*De Specialibus Legibus*
Plato	
Leg	*The Laws*
Phaedr	*Phaedrus*
Tim	*Timaeus*

Jewish

Qumran	
1QS	The Rule of the Community
4QFlor	The Messianic Florilegium
Rabbinic	
Gen Rab	Genesis Rabbah
J Ned	Jerusalem Talmud, *Nedarim*

Preface

It is a pleasure to thank the many friends and colleagues who have assisted me in this work. I am grateful to the friends who support the program in ethics at the Center for International Security and Arms Control at Stanford University, and especially Grace Mortsolf. I am also grateful to the former codirectors of the center, Sidney Drell and John Lewis, and to the current codirectors, David Holloway and William Perry, who have made it possible for me to work as part of a stimulating group and benefit from interdisciplinary discussion.

I thank those colleagues who have read the manuscript as a whole or in part and given me the benefit of their criticism. W. D. Davies and René Girard must be mentioned first in this category. On one memorable occasion I was able to discuss the work with both of them together. I have also had valuable discussions with James Williams, Paul Caringella, Robert Jewett, Burton Mack, Marshall Johnson, and H. J. L. Jensen.

Most of the reaction I have received has attempted to persuade me to soften the criticism of Judaism entailed in my reading of Paul. I have returned again and again to my text in the attempt to remove elements that might offend. The effect of these many rewritings has, however, been to sharpen rather than to soften the reading of Paul's rejection of Judaism. I have tried to nuance my interpretations so as not to give offense, but I could not remove the "offense" that is plainly there, that Paul rejected his ancestral religion because of the violence he perceived in it. So be it.

Thanks to all who have assisted me, especially my wife, to whom I dedicate this work. The responsibility for errors is mine alone.

Introduction

In recent times North American Pauline studies have been dominated by the method of comparative history. The apostle has been interpreted historically by comparison with his Jewish and/or Hellenistic context. Although this method continues to bear fruit, its dominance has driven studies guided by other theories to the margins and has, therefore, hampered progress. Furthermore, it has for the most part been unreflective about its own methodology and has consequently produced some rather doubtful intellectual work, not to mention the accumulation of studies that merely repeat well-known material.[1] We seem to be at an opportune time in the discipline for a methodological revision, which should include a serious reflection on the role of theory.

This study is not another exercise in comparative history but an attempt to use a theory to interpret the thought and experience of Paul. For this reason I must, by way of introduction, establish the nature of theory and clarify the way a theory assists in the process of understanding.

The level of theory is a transcendental level; a theory cannot be arrived at by induction.[2] One cannot formulate a theory by looking at a large number of actual cases, because a theory already guides one in that looking. All observation is theory-laden. This means that for Waltz a theory can only be discovered in a moment of insight. It is an act of "creativity." In support of this view one

---

[1] Recent examples of this, in our opinion, are: P. J. Tomson, *Paul and the Jewish Law,* who argues in effect that since there are moral injunctions in the Pauline material and in the Rabbinic literature the former must be the same as the latter; and A. F. Segal, *Paul the Convert,* who argues that because there is evidence that Paul experienced visions and because there is a tradition of Jewish Merkabah mysticism Paul must have been a Merkabah mystic.

[2] K. N. Waltz, *Theory of International Politics,* 1–17.

might cite Einstein, who describes the discovery of the theory of relativity as a "break" in the continuum of his consciousness. He uses religious language when he says that he believed "nature had revealed herself to me." This "break" was the basis of his belief that the advent of weapons of mass destruction could cause a similar "break" in the continuity of human nature and history and turn the human race away from war.[3] Waltz describes the movement "from law to theory, from the fashioning of hypotheses to the development of explanations of them" not as an induction but as a "leap."[4] This brings me to the next distinction he makes, that between theory and law or hypothesis.

One must distinguish between the level of theory and the level of analysis. On the level of analysis hypotheses are proposed and tested in the search for laws. The logic of a law is the logic of a proved hypothesis, "reliably, if A then B," that is, a reliable correlation between the independent and the dependent variable. A law attests a fact and, therefore, "factuality" obtains at the level of analysis and not at the level of theory (integration).

Theories are tested differently than are hypotheses, not by the reliability of correlations but by their power and elegance. According to Waltz, the power of a theory is its ability to guide our attention to the important phenomena in the field, to enable us to ask the right questions, formulate fruitful hypotheses, stimulate and guide research, and provoke countertheories. The elegance of a theory is the ratio between its complexity and its range of explanation. An elegant theory is a simple one with a wide range. So a critique of theory is a questioning of the power and elegance of the whole theory in its capacity to guide the decision to focus on this or that item in the field and to control the formation of hypotheses for testing. Theory, therefore, orients research and facilitates understanding.

In order to understand the nature of understanding one must analyze the process by which data from the level of analysis are transformed from mere facts into significant facts. I focus, therefore, on the interaction between the two levels, of analysis (law) and integration (theory). Waltz does not pay sufficient attention to the integrating function of theory and thus risks trivializing its role. Theory functions to integrate the results of analysis into a pattern of explanation whose range is in principle universal. On the assumption that we undertake investigations of human activity in order to understand that activity, theory must contribute to that understanding. Understanding takes place by means of the integration of new knowledge into old, the classification of the less known by comparison with the better known. Theory is the guide to this integration.

It is able to guide integration because theory is a series of generalizations based on a wider range of evidence and interpretation than can be taken into

---

[3] R. Rhodes, *The Making of the Atomic Bomb*, 152.
[4] Waltz, *Theory of International Politics*, 8.

account at any one time. Theory enables us to bring in condensed form the results of generations of trial and error, deposited as the tradition of human self-interpretation in the cultural texts and artifacts, and enables us to understand the evidence at hand by comparison with the tradition. Understanding, therefore, takes place as a result of integration by means of comparison at the level of theory, and the act of comparison takes the form of "recognition."

Recognition is the act of identifying something as in some way related to something else. It is the essence of the act of integrative comparison. For the present purpose I describe recognition with reference to two modalities—of time, and of the nature of the comparative relationship—and on two levels—of analysis (comparative history) and of theory. With reference to time, on the level of analysis, recognition is seeing one event as comparable to another in the same historical period (synchronic comparison), while on the level of theory recognition compares events in several periods (diachronic comparison). With reference to the nature of the comparative relationship, analysis identifies events, texts, or structures as parallel or analogous, while theory identifies them according to their significance. (Insignificant comparisons, also known as "parallelomania," are the bane of comparative history.) Significance means that, for existential reasons arising out of the interpreter's experience as extended by theory, events form a cluster of meaning with and for the interpreter. Theory enables the interpreter to extend the range of relevant experience, in terms of which events become significant, so far as to establish their significance for the whole community that shares the tradition on which the theory is based.

The term for the old knowledge into which theory integrates the new is *tradition,* and every field of endeavor has such an accumulation of wisdom, which, it claims, illuminates the general human situation. Theory is a compact statement of the wisdom of tradition. The introduction of tradition does not challenge the claim that theory cannot be reached by induction, but merely denies that theory is either a reflection of the transcendentals of pure reason or the result of a flash of genius of the romantic kind. Theory is the result of a complex process of a critical recognition of the cogency of traditional wisdom, and of the coherence of some of that wisdom with the individual's and the group's vision of the present. The transcendentals of pure reason and romantic inspiration might be parts of the complex process.

The relationship between theory and tradition is not uncritical. Theory, as the deposit of critically sifted traditional wisdom is always open to further critical refinement. This takes place in its interaction with the level of analysis. Since a theory is not factual it cannot be verified or falsified directly or piecemeal. It must be judged as a whole by the criteria of power and elegance. The criterion of power includes two subcriteria, the test of recognition or integrative comparison, and the test of orientation. A theory is confirmed when it is able to integrate all the laws of analysis, and disconfirmed as it fails to do so. It is also confirmed and disconfirmed through the success or failure of a statistically significant number of the hypotheses it has helped to frame by orientation, and its ability subsequently to integrate those laws.

Although this is not a study in comparative history, it is a historical study. I argue that the phenomena I interpret did happen as reported. Allowing for the unavoidable distortions and accretions arising from historical limitations and ideological interests, it is still possible to recover the reliable account of a life from the selection of letters I have at my disposal. It is the life of a zealous Jew whose zeal for the Law of Moses as his community understood it caused him to persecute deviants. He underwent a "conversion," the essence of which is by nature inaccessible to analysis, as a result of which he changed allegiance from his Jewish community to the community of those he had been persecuting. He described this act as a "dying to the Law" that took place, not apart from the Law, but "through the Law," and which was necessary so that he might live no longer for the Law but for God (Gal 2:19). He contrasts life for the Law with life for God, and he attributes his change to something in the Law itself! He came to believe that his Jewish life had not been a life for God but for the Law, that is, an idolization of the Law. This is a historical study, therefore, inasmuch as it seeks to describe the salient features of Paul's experience by a careful reading of the primary sources.

It is, however, more than historical in the usual sense of the term because it seeks generalizations about the nature of individuals and groups based on this historical evidence. In this aspiration it is more like anthropology or sociology than history. I wish not merely to describe Paul's life and thought but to use that description to confirm certain generalizations about human life. Only if my reading illuminates human life in general will it have contributed to this understanding. For this reason I use the theory of sacred violence, based on a wide reading of the religious, anthropological, literary, and philosophical tradition, to integrate Paul's thought and experience into a general pattern of explanation that illuminates human experience in general.

Theoretical understanding in this sense is hermeneutic. It interprets the significance of the evidence in question for all humanity at all times. It makes a claim as near to universal as it is humanly possible to make. Paul's hermeneutic of the Cross, therefore, places the death of Jesus in the widest possible frame of reference. In his time that frame of reference took the form of the themes and images of Jewish apocalyptic literature, for the most part. The theory enables me to widen the frame of reference to include literary and other forms of evidence from many different times and cultures, by going beneath the surface of the texts to the generative mechanism and disclosing it as the same mechanism at work all over the world.

In this post-Cartesian situation one cannot ignore the historical embeddedness of the interpreter. Therefore, in my quest for a theory of interpretation for our time I should ask what the salient elements in our culture are, elements that impinge on me as I attempt to make sense out of this field of investigation, and how these elements might be brought into fruitful connection with the tradition of interpretation. I believe that the overriding fact of our time is violence; therefore a theory that attempts to make sense out of violence is more likely to orient us to the points in the field that are salient for our time. This is relatively easy in the field of Pauline studies, because the tradition of interpretation is dominated by the theory of Luther, which is a theory of violence insofar as it is centered on the Cross. Therefore, there is a congruence between our times, our texts, and our tradition that makes for a powerful interpretive constellation and vindicates my choice of the theory for a new initiative in the field. This constellation is the linchpin of my argument, as will become evident in the course of the interpretation, so I shall not argue it further here. Here I shall merely review the theoretical situation in the field so as to make place for this new theoretical démarche.

This is, therefore, a work of historical theology in the hermeneutical mode, not in the sense of nonfoundational discourse, which is the sense some current writers give to the term "hermeneutic," but in the theological sense of showing the abiding significance of the Pauline text. It claims to show that Paul's experience, which the church has always accepted as paradigmatic for faith, is indeed paradigmatic of the human condition in general. It concludes, therefore, that Paul's criticism of his own culture is still valid as a criticism of ours. The salience of violence in both circumstances is a prima facie reason to accept the possibility that both might be integrated by means of theory into the same pattern of explanation and thus confirm the generalizations about violence and the Sacred that the theory discloses.

The most powerful theory in modern Pauline studies has been the theory of Luther. Luther ranks with Galileo, Newton, and Einstein in the intellectual history of the West. The philosophical canons by which theories are judged, namely, power and elegance, attest the validity of his theory, and it can only be displaced by a theory of comparable force. There have been three serious theoretical challenges to Luther in the history of the discipline, from Albert Schweitzer,[5] Rudolf Bultmann,[6] and Franz Rosenzweig,[7] respectively. Schweitzer formulated a theory from his understanding of the apocalyptic literature, Bultmann from the philosophy of the early Heidegger, and Rosenzweig from his understanding of the Jewish religion. Schweitzer has been revived recently by E. P. Sanders,[8] and Bultmann has influenced the field for

---

[5] A. Schweitzer, *The Mysticism of Paul the Apostle.*
[6] R. Bultmann, *Theology of the New Testament,* vol. 1, 185–345.
[7] F. Rosenzweig, *The Star of Redemption.*
[8] E. P. Sanders, *Paul and Palestinian Judaism: A Comparison of Patterns of Religion.*

three generations. The theory of Rosenzweig has lately made its bid in the work of Gager[9] and Gaston.[10]

It is not my purpose systematically to evaluate these attempts to displace Luther but rather to propose another theory and demonstrate its power, elegance, and beauty. In the course of that demonstration I believe that the implied criticism of rival theories will be evident and the groundwork for a systematic critique of them will be laid. In any case, theories need not be mutually exclusive, as will be readily apparent from a preliminary consideration of the theories mentioned, plus one more that is implied in the work of W. D. Davies.[11]

Davies works with the well-known historical theory of continuity and discontinuity,[12] or, more precisely, discontinuity within continuity, when he argues that Paul retained the form of his ancestral religion but changed the content at critical points. The most critical change was the substitution of Christ for Torah, in the sense that Christ became the focus of divine disclosure and demand in the life of a Pharisee for whom the Messiah had come. That meant that it was not the fact of legal demand that changed but rather the content of the demand. Paul's religion remained formally the same as Judaism in its overall structure while the content was changed. Thus Davies could structure his presentation in terms of antitheses that were both continuous and discontinuous, like "the old and new humanity," "the old and new Israel," "the old and new Torah," "the old and new obedience," and "the old and new hope."

This coheres with my interpretation inasmuch as I too see Paul's theology as a reinterpretation of salient features of Judaism, especially the figure of Adam and the content of the Law. Since Paul understands the significance of Christ to be worldwide, he presents him in terms of Adam, and since he sees the Torah to have been misunderstood by Judaism he argues for a new and different understanding of its content. He does not object to the nature of law as demand or prohibition as such, only to its interpretation in the Jewish context. That there is a divine law for all the human race he does not doubt.

E. P. Sanders revives Schweitzer's apocalyptic interpretation in its broad outline, to the effect that for Paul following Christ entailed a transfer from one community to another, and that membership in the new community entailed a "participation" in the reality of Christ. I accept these two points as fundamental, but describe their substance differently. Whereas for Sanders the transfer takes place for entirely positive reasons unrelated to any dissatisfaction Paul might have felt as a Jew, I see it as the result of a dire discovery of the sacred violence in his ancestral religion, as well as the result of the mysterious experience Paul associates with the resurrection; that is, I see both negative and

---

[9] J. Gager, *The Origins of Anti-Semitism.*

[10] L. Gaston, *Paul and the Torah,* 79.

[11] W. D. Davies, *Paul and Rabbinic Judaism: Some Rabbinic Elements in Pauline Theology*[3] (Philadelphia: Fortress, 1980).

[12] See, for example, D. M. Thomson, *The History of Europe since Napoleon.*

positive reasons for the transfer. I cannot show that he was dissatisfied as a Jew, but I can show that as a result of his conversion Paul discovered a determinative flaw in Judaism that caused him to adopt a dialectical attitude toward it (chapter 5). The problem with Judaism was not only, in Sanders's now notorious epigram, that it was not Christianity, but also that it was, in a phrase to be explained at length below, a sacrificial structure of sacred violence. On the nature of the hitherto vague "participation in Christ" I emphasize the social dimension of participation both in the Jewish and the messianic communities and invoke the still-to-be-explained category of mimesis to understand the precise nature of this social participation.

Bultmann makes the category of self-understanding central to his interpretation, while retaining the Lutheran insistence that what Paul found wrong with Judaism was its demand for legal obedience, which led to self-righteousness and boasting before God, which, in turn, is a betrayal of the creature's dependence on the Creator. There is much to be said for this interpretation, not least because one cannot ignore the frequent references in the text to boasting, but it must be differently nuanced. The fact that Judaism in general was not a religion of "works righteousness" but a "covenantal nomism" constitutes a possible but not necessary refutation of this reading of Paul. It is possible that Paul experienced a form of Judaism that was a "works righteousness" and that his texts constitute a strong testimony to its existence.[13] Recent work on the Pauline texts themselves, however, has shown that the "boasting" occurred in connection not with justification before God but with ethnic exclusionism. He boasted in the fact that he was not a gentile sinner (Gal 2:15) but rather belonged to the holy people, whose ritual boundary markers he zealously guarded.

Bultmann is right that Pauline faith is a new self-understanding. Self-understanding has, however, to be understood mimetically, and that entails more serious attention to the social dimension than Bultmann pays. At this point the work of Käsemann[14] and J. L. Martyn[15] is important, because they include the social dimension. For them Paul experienced a change of self-understanding within the context of a change of Lord or a change of world. This approaches the position of Sanders concerning transference from one community to another, but diverges in the understanding of the new community as a transcendental rather than an historical entity. The significant point

---

[13] Segal, *Paul the Convert,* makes the same kind of argument when he says that the Pauline texts are the only testimony to a Kabbalah-like mysticism in the 1500 years between Ezekiel and the Kabbalah. This fact does not discourage him from accepting their testimony as historically reliable. By the same token Paul the persecutor (cf. Paul the mystic) attests the existence of a violent and xenophobic Judaism.

[14] E. Käsemann, *Perspectives on Paul.*

[15] J. L. Martyn, "Apocalyptic Antinomies in Paul's Letter to the Galatians," 410–24; "Paul and his Jewish-Christian Interpreters," 1–16; "A Law-Observant Mission to Gentiles: the Background of Galatians."

for the Bultmannian project in the work of Käsemann and Martyn is that the change of self-understanding takes place in a socially embedded self as a result of the change of the context in which it is embedded.

The theory of Franz Rosenzweig is that Jesus is only the Messiah of the Gentiles, carrying to them the blessings of the covenant that Jews enjoy already. There are two covenants, one for the Jews and one for the gentiles. Some such theory is implicit in Sanders's attempt to show that Paul found no specific fault with Judaism. Paul, however, can be fitted to this theory only by ignoring some of his central concerns, and his attitude to Judaism is dialectical rather than univocal as this theory implies.

This brings me to Luther himself. Luther's insight must be approached in the spirit of Davies's "discontinuity within continuity." One cannot avoid Luther's fundamental conviction that Paul saw something wrong with his ancestral religion—whether while he was still within it or as a result of his conversion is not important—and made a decisive break with it. Even if he retains the forms of its discourse he fills them with significantly different content. Paulinism is emphatically not "Moses for the masses" as the theory of Rosenzweig holds; it is a new and different take on the old religion and is in deep disagreement with Moses. Luther thought that the disagreement was to be lodged against the legal nature as such of the Torah, but it is at this point that subsequent work shows Luther to have been somewhat in error. It is not simply the legality of the law that Paul objects to but the way that legality has been deployed by the Jewish community to exclude the gentiles and to glorify itself, which is, in turn, a clue to the fact that the Jewish community has distorted the basic intention of the Law. Paul sees the basic intention of the Law restored when it is transferred from the Jewish context to the context of the community of the new creation, which on the hermeneutical level means: when it is read through the lens of the Cross.

Paul's problem with Judaism became clear to him as a result of his conversion, and it is unnecessary to speculate about the psychological harbingers of his change of mind. His problem was caused not by the alleged "works righteousness" of Judaism but by its exclusionism, expressed in the laws of circumcision, Sabbath, and diet. He saw this exclusionism as a sign of what was wrong with Jewish communal life, and took it as the basic reason for leaving the Jewish community and joining another. Through the lens of my theory I see this exclusionism as a thread which leads to the primitive Sacred. The primitive Sacred is a context in which the Law of God, expressed for Paul most emphatically in the primal prohibition (Gen 2:16-17) and the command to love the neighbor, is distorted to the service of violence. Paul experienced his Jewish way of life, specifically his zeal as a persecutor, as the historical counterpart of the primitive Sacred. Jewish religious life seemed to Paul to be a context in which the Law of God was made to serve violence, and the clearest sign of this fact was the crucifixion of Christ and the exclusion of the Gentiles. The justification of this reading comes later, but here one might say that from this theoretical point of view Paul was right in this estimate of his ancestral religion and that in this regard it was representative of all religion to the extent that in religion the primitive Sacred is operative. Exclusionism is a sign of the presence of the Sacred.

In terms of my theory Luther was wrong to make the demand-nature of Law the problem rather than the sacral context in which the demand was deformed to the service of violence. He was, however, not far from the truth in his basic theological point concerning the proper relation of the creature to the Creator. In his terms the fundamental sin is the pride of desiring to be equal with God, while in my terms it is the pride of trying to get the better of God in the game of mimetic rivalry. Thus, while for him the essentially wrong attitude is self-sufficiency, for me it is mimetic rivalry, which is the essence of violence. Violence, therefore, is the original sin, as I attempt to show in chapter 4.

Luther was, however, right again in generalizing his criticism of Judaism to all religion, which in his context was represented by the late medieval church. The negativity that Paul saw and rejected in Judaism, Luther and subsequent Lutheran exegesis saw and rejected in Catholicism. However mixed the motives for this enterprise—and E. P. Sanders subjects it to relentless criticism—its instinct is sound. The insight should be generalized, because the great negativity that the Pauline gospel lays bare is in all religion. The primitive Sacred, present in all religion to a greater or lesser extent, is a sacrificial, exclusionary, scapegoating violence. The fatal flaw of the Lutheran attack on Judaism and Catholicism is its self-righteousness, and so it is hoist on its own petard, because it fails to turn against itself the criticism it levels at others. All such criticism should be in the first person plural. I hope to show that in this regard the apostle is better than his Lutheran epigones.

The greatest gift a writer can receive is the attention of a careful reader, but the state of the field is such that one must prepare for cursory readings. I hope, therefore, that a summary of these salient conclusions will help to make it easier to follow the argument, and forestall misplaced criticism.

1. The sacred violence Paul discovered in Judaism is present in all religions, including Christianity. Paulinism is, therefore, in respect of this negative element, an indictment of all religion, and, for that matter, all institutions and structures of "this age." My statement of the nature and function of theory makes clear that sacred violence is a general category of interpretation applying in principle to all religions and all institutions.

2. Paul did not reject the authority of Torah as such but only a certain Jewish interpretation of it. A proper reading of Torah reveals its essence to be the command to love the neighbor (Lev 19:18) and the primal prohibition to avoid mimetic rivalry (Gen 2:16-17). Paul is no Marcionite, and repeatedly appeals to the revelation in the Torah to support his theology. He believes his theology to be "according to the scriptures," and ranks Jesus with the prophets

(1 Thess 2:14-15). However, in order to see grace in the Torah one must read it by the hermeneutic of the Cross.

3. Therefore, Paul's argument with his Judaism is essentially a controversy about how to interpret the Torah. When read through the lens of the Cross the Torah reveals the nature of Adam's sin and the perpetuation of that sin in the Mosaic interpretation.

4. In Paul's usage "Law" is a metonymy for the Jewish community, and that is why he sometimes sounds as if he rejects the Law when in fact he rejects certain salient practices of the community based on its misinterpretation. "Works of Law," in Pauline usage, means the Jewish way of life, especially its exclusionary aspects, and not the individual's *cursus honorum* on the way to God.

5. The clearest sign of that misinterpretation was the exclusion of the gentiles from the community, which Paul compares to the crucifixion of Christ and thus integrates into a theory. It showed that the misinterpretation of the Torah had made at least that part of the Jewish community represented by Saul the persecutor into an instance of the primitive Sacred.

6. Paul, therefore, saves the divine authority of the Law by rejecting the way of life based on its misinterpretation. He saves the Law at the expense of Judaism. Only when it is taken out of the Jewish context does the Law function properly, to restrain violence rather than to foster it.

7. Paul's gospel is, therefore, a Jewish self-criticism, and the community based on it claims to be not the new Israel but the true Israel. Paul uses the doctrine of the remnant, which he inherits from the prophet Isaiah, to give structure to this conviction. The true Israel is the remnant that includes both Jews and gentiles.

8. Paul did not understand the new community to be a sect rivaling Judaism. It was for him an instance of the "new creation" beyond the forces of mimetic rivalry.

9. Paul concentrates on the Jewish role in the killing of Jesus and links it to the tradition of the rejection of the prophets (1 Thess 2:14-15). In this he was consistent with his own experience as a Jewish persecutor of Christians. His discovery of the violence in himself, which occurred while he was persecuting Christians, caused him to interpret that violence as of a piece with the violence that killed Jesus and scapegoated the gentiles (Gal 2:19). It was, for him, the violence of the Jewish community misusing the Law as a weapon of exclusion and persecution. Since obedience to the Law as interpreted in his Jewish community made him a persecutor, Paul was in a position to understand the violent implications of that interpretation. The experience I call his "conversion" enabled him to see this violence in himself and connect it with the religious structures he had served.

10. In doing so I believe he was correct, because religious communities in general, under the influence of the Sacred, produce such people and encourage such violence. In view of sound theoretical considerations and solid historical

evidence it is impossible to argue that the Judaism of that time was immune to the process linking violence and the Sacred.

11. Historically speaking, the Jews and the Romans together were responsible for the death of Christ. Although crucifixion is a Roman form of punishment, it is a priori unlikely that the Romans alone were responsible. It is more probable that the temple establishment collaborated in this death as they had in many other ways. The claim that the Romans alone were responsible entails the dire corollary that the Gospels and Paul were either woefully ignorant or maliciously anti-Jewish. If the latter is the case then our theory could be applied to expose the Gospels and Paul as myth-makers of sacred violence, and the Christian religion as a prime example of the primitive Sacred. While I do not deny that it became in time an example of this kind, I do not see historical warrant for this estimate of its origins. The temple priesthood was a sordid establishment of collaborators and quislings, quite capable of feeding victims to the Roman terror.

12. Theologically speaking, in crucifying Christ the Jews and the Romans acted representatively for all the human race. The essence of anti-Semitism with respect to the crucifixion is to pretend that only the Jews are responsible and not all of us gentiles too, that is, to scapegoat the Jews. The mirror image of this, that it is only the gentiles who are responsible, is equally an act of scapegoating. According to mimetic theory it is an example of the way mimesis makes the rivals into doubles. The Jews who claim innocence are the mimetic doubles of the Christian anti-Semites. Jews and Romans together are responsible, as representatives of all the human race in its violence against the divine. Thus I indict scapegoating as such and not just another scapegoat.

13. Paul does not entirely break free of the coils of sacred violence. The most portentous instance of this failure is his clinging to the category of election with regard to the role of Israel in the plan of salvation (chap. 5). Because he cannot give up the idea that Israel, even in its rejection of Jesus, must be playing a central role in the plan of salvation, he comes up with the perilous notion that Israel, like the Pharaoh of the Exodus, makes a positive contribution by playing a negative role. This means that Israel was chosen by God to produce and then reject the Messiah, with the corollary that it remains God's beloved enemy until the day of salvation when it will be included among the blessed.

The reasons for Paul's inability to cut the links clearly between the old and the new religion arise from the fact that Jesus, and Paul, and many of his coworkers were Jews, and the term "God," therefore, referred primarily to the God of Jewish scripture and tradition. This entailed that the break with Mosaic Judaism could ever only be a qualified one, taking in this case the form of a sharp difference concerning the principle of interpretation and producing a different kind of community, but remaining focused on the same divine revelation as the Mosaic Jews.

The category of election, under which the Jews were chosen by God to reject the Messiah and so reveal sacred violence, is itself a myth of sacred violence. It is the other side of the coin of special privilege that Paul criticizes for having killed Christ and expelled the gentiles. Had he been consistent in the use of the hermeneutic of the Cross, Paul would have abandoned the category of election altogether and viewed the Mosaic Jews as simply an instance of sacred violence like all other scapegoating groups. In that case there would have been nothing special about their deed, and the category of sin would not, like the category of salvation, have ranked "the Jew first and then the Greek" (Rom 1:16; chap. 4).

There is, however, an indication in Rom 8:28-30, if election there is interpreted inclusively rather than exclusively,[16] that in Christ all who love God are elected to salvation. God's choice is that all should be saved, the realization of that choice depends on the loving concurrence of human beings. Read in this way the category of election is demythologized, in the sense of being delivered from the scapegoating principle. If this reading of Rom 8:28-30 is permissible, one may draw two conclusions: first, that in the case of the election of Israel powerful personal factors (Rom 9:1-5) caused Paul to maintain the category in its mythological rather than its demythologized (inclusive) form; it was a case of nostalgia overwhelming his judgment; and, second, that for the sake of a modern theology, the criticism of sacred violence should be continued until the category of election is done away with altogether; to do so would be to fulfil Paul's project, which he was kept from doing by his nostalgia.

The resurgence of ethnic and nationalist conflict in our time has replaced the threat of the weapons of mass destruction as the salient instance of violence. The threat from these weapons has not disappeared but it has been eclipsed for the time being by the recrudescence of ethnic violence in Europe and Africa, and its dreary continuance in the Middle East. My theory shows that Paul focused his thought and experience on a form of this kind of violence as it took shape in his context, namely, religiously justified exclusionism and chauvinism. In pursuing the analysis, therefore, I hope that my theory will enable us to understand not only Paul in his time but also the enduring truth of his interpretation of the crucifixion of Jesus. It was a crime of ethnic violence of the kind we now often witness; the in-group scapegoated Jesus. By analyzing the powerful explanation Paul gave of this deed we can learn something of the structures that generated it then and continue to generate similar deeds now.

---

[16] Cf. Karl Barth, *The Epistle to the Romans*, 321: "Who then are those that love God?— They—'who are called according to his purpose.' Not, that is, these men or those men; not indeed men considered as a whole: for we are forbidden to give a quantitative answer to the question.... Rightly understood, there are no Christians: there is only the eternal opportunity of becoming Christians—an opportunity at once accessible and inaccessible to all men."

1

Sacred Violence, Deformed Desire, and Generative Scapegoating
The Theory of René Girard

Algernon. You don't seem to realise that in married life three is
    company and two is none.
Jack (sententiously). That, my dear young friend, is the theory that
    corrupt French drama has been propounding for the last fifty
    years.
Algernon. Yes; and that the happy English home has proved in half
    the time.
Oscar Wilde, The Importance of Being Earnest, Act 1.

La vie monte aux orages sur l'aile du refus.
St. John Perse, Pluies 6

The threat of violence has become overwhelming in our time. George
Steiner says we are living in Bluebeard's castle.[1] Behind the door of our common consciousness are the bodies of our victims. Not since Tamerlane has a
culture had the murder of so many people on its conscience. Stretched between
Auschwitz and Hiroshima the tenor of our times is a travesty of biblical faith.
In the Bible to have faith is to live in hope, remembering past deliverances and
looking forward to a consummation. We, however, live in forgetfulness and
dread the future, not in faith but in fear.[2] We may indeed ask, as Steiner does,
what sort of culture is possible in such an atmosphere, whether all we have
left is music because there is nothing to say.

---

[1] G. Steiner, *In Bluebeard's Castle.*
[2] These lines were penned before the Berlin wall came down. The end of the cold war makes
the threat of weapons of mass destruction slightly less urgent, but only slightly.

13

Susan Sontag tells how when first she saw photographs of the Nazi death camps they moved her to appreciate not only the power of photography but also the plight of our culture.[3] So we have photography as well as music; but both are wordless, just the pointing and the cry, sights and sounds, but no sense. No one can view that horror without experiencing a surge of doubt about both religion and humanism.[4] Its cultural aftermath forces us to doubt even the capacity of language to comprehend reality, and reason to guide policy.[5] Our confidence in the reliability of representation and the capacity of reason has been shaken. We have lost the rational umbrella of epistemology and are left with nonfoundational hermeneutics.[6] Philosophy can no longer provide convincing justification, only relative certification.

These laments are well known, even hackneyed, but they do frame our concern. The crisis of reason in our time is the crisis of violence, at last come to light in a form that cannot be ignored. If in the past we could sweep the brute facts of battle under the rug of euphemism, glorify the profession of arms, and sanctify the warriors, we can do so no longer, because of the weapons of mass destruction. We might have lost confidence in representation,[7] but we cannot deny the prospect of limitless violence.

Nonviolence is an integral part of the gospel message, because its basic teaching is the absolute value of love. There are the injunctions in the Sermon on the Mount to love one's enemies, not to take revenge but to turn the other cheek (Matt 5:38-48). There is the blessing of the peacemakers as children of God (Matt 5:9) and the instruction to be reconciled before offering sacrifice (Matt 5:23-26). There is the "great commandment" to love God with all one's heart and to love one's neighbor as oneself (Mark 12:28-34). More than these specific injunctions there is the example of Jesus who resisted calls to defend himself violently, and went unresisting to his death. The tradition of Christian pacifism bases itself on the literal interpretation of these themes in the Gospels.

---

[3] Susan Sontag, *On Photography*.

[4] Compare the well-known bon mot: "Of Auschwitz, religion asks, Where was God? Humanism asks, Where was man?"

[5] S. E. Shapiro, "Failing Speech: Post-Holocaust Writing and the Discourse of Post-Modernism."

[6] R. Rorty, *Philosophy and the Mirror of Nature*, 315–94.

[7] See Jacques Derrida, "No Apocalypse, Not Now (full speed ahead, seven missiles, seven missives)" in *Diacritics,* Summer 1984 (on "Nuclear Criticism"), 20–31. "The hypothesis of this total destruction watches over deconstruction, it guides its footsteps; it becomes possible to recognize, in the light, so to speak, of that hypothesis, of that fantasy, or phantasm, the characteristic structures and historicity of the discourses, strategies, texts, or institutions to be deconstructed." The nuclear age is also the age of literature, in that literature is shown to have a radically precarious and radically historical existence. "But at the same time, literature gives us to think the *totality* of that which, like literature and henceforth in it, is exposed to the same threat, constituted by the same structure of historical fictionality, producing and then harboring its own referent" (27). The *totality* is, however, more than literature, and exposed to a threat that cannot be confined to literature. The bomb is not a literary device. Text is not all; there are the human relations that the text merely represents with more or less verisimilitude. See R. Girard, *Things Hidden,* 62.

All Christians see them teaching that love is the antidote to violence, and by the same token, that violence is humanity's great affliction.

The Cross is a symbol of violence to a victim, and Christian theology has made the interpretation of the Cross a central task. How might this task be undertaken today in the light of the burning children of Auschwitz and Hiroshima? Since Christianity has been compromised by its relative failure to side with the Jews during the Holocaust, this question is especially pressing for Christian theology. Irving Greenberg argues that all subsequent theological thought must take place in the light of the burning children of Auschwitz.[8] Recent philosophical reflection on the nuclear threat converges with Greenberg's emphasis on the children. Russell Hardin and John Mearsheimer write:

> Perhaps this is the most important lesson moral philosophers offer for the debate over nuclear policy: the popular view of the Soviet-American conflict as us against them and of nuclear retaliation as an act of vengeance cannot be squared with the threat of immolating tens of millions of children.[9]

The notions of "we against them," of the right of vengeance, and of the appropriateness of surrogate victims like the children, are all part of the structure of what I shall call the system of sacred violence.

René Girard's theory enables us to expose this violence and to quarrel creatively with our founding texts.[10] He has also given us examples of how the interpretation should work, and has contributed new insights into the meaning of texts selected mostly from the Old Testament and the Gospels.[11] Raymund Schwager has provided a programmatic essay on the possibilities of the Girardian theory in the field of biblical interpretation.[12] Robert North has given us a useful evaluation of its impact thus far and a guide to the literature on Girard and the Bible.[13] North also exemplifies the indignation of the professional biblical scholar at this invasion of the field by an outsider.

The modern quest for an understanding of human desire can be traced to Hegel's *The Phenomenology of Mind* (1807).[14] Freud made the strategies of desire central to psychoanalysis, and Sartre to the project of existentialism. The

---

[8] I. Greenberg, "Cloud of Smoke, Pillar of Fire," 7–56.

[9] Russell Hardin and John J. Mearsheimer, *Nuclear Deterrence*, 5.

[10] R. Girard, *Deceit, Desire, and the Novel: Self and Other in Literary Structure; Violence and the Sacred; The Scapegoat; Things Hidden Since the Foundation of the World*, with J.-M. Ourgoulian and G. Lefort; *Violent Origins: Walter Burkert, René Girard, and Jonathan Z. Smith on Ritual Killing and Social Formation; Violence and Truth: On the Work of René Girard.*

[11] *The Scapegoat* contains a series of hermeneutical probes into texts from the Gospels; book 2 of *Things Hidden* is a treatment of biblical texts, and there are scattered brief treatments in *Violence and the Sacred.*

[12] R. Schwager, *Must there be Scapegoats?*

[13] R. North, "Violence and the Bible." See also *Semeia*, 33, 1985, "René Girard and Biblical Studies," ed. Andrew McKenna.

[14] See J. P. Butler, *Subjects of Desire.*

nature of desire was a major concern of French thought after World War II. In the context of that concern, René Girard, who had been influenced by Sartre, turned his attention to the nature of desire. Since he is not a philosopher but a literary critic, he did not pursue his project in conversation with these philosophers, but was oriented to the problematic of desire by the general trend of thought.

Girard's thought also stands in a tradition of the human sciences. He proposes a general theory of society and culture that has religion at its center, and thus continues the tradition of Emile Durkheim. He makes sacrifice central to his understanding of religion and thus continues the emphasis of Henri Hubert and Marcel Mauss. Furthermore, he makes imitation a pivotal element, and that recalls the thought of Durkheim's antagonist Gabriel Tarde. Girard is, therefore, the heir of a rich tradition in the human sciences, and his theory must, therefore, also be located in the context of that tradition. The methodological question is fiercely debated in anthropology[15] and the procedure of the French school will not be universally accepted by current practitioners in the field. Nevertheless, Daniel O'Keefe has recently given us a fine example of the use of this French tradition in formulating a general theory of magic.[16]

Durkheim's fundamental insight is that religious feeling is the individual's awareness of the group. The experience of group excitement or group solidarity, of esprit de corps, is a response to the presence of a power greater than the individual. The empirical basis for this theory in the history of anthropology is the sense of the Sacred among the Melanesians, described by Codrington in 1878 and called mana.[17] Mana is the source of religion and magic because it is the first human recognition of society. It is "a feeling of circumambient power"[18] that is then symbolized by objects that become sacred in the process. Religion crystalizes around these sacred objects. Religion is, therefore, a projection of the feeling that the group arouses in its individual members, a feeling that is shared by all and communicated by means of symbols.

The terms "crystalize" and "projection" are used by O'Keefe, and are an accurate account of Durkheim's position; they are not, however, for that reason clear. Indeed, they are intensely metaphorical; a less poetic account of the way that religion comes out of the group is possible.[19] Mana, I shall argue, is the transfigured violence of the primitive Sacred and the god is the transfigured

---

[15] Marvin Harris, *The Rise of Anthropological Theory*. On the current methodological disorder in the field, see Louis A. Sass, "Anthropology's Native Problems."

[16] D. O'Keefe, *Stolen Lightning*.

[17] G. van der Leeuw, *Religion in Essence*.

[18] O'Keefe, *Stolen Lightning*, 166.

[19] Jane Harrison, *Themis*, 30–49, in discussing the myth of Zeus and the Curetes, argues that the god comes out of the crowd as the daimon of the crowd, the projection of the greatest of the Curetes. She treats this myth as a myth of initiation. Girard makes much of it as a myth of mob murder (*The Scapegoat*, 66–75).

victim whose death makes community possible. The feeling of the "uncanny" is the awareness of the threat of violence in the form of the possibility that mimetic rivalry could break out again. Thus Girard's theory explains the precise nature of the overarching authority of mana, as well as the relationship between the quasi-ontological "social fact" of Durkheim and the individually based "social fact" of Tarde.

Tarde held that imitation is the essential social characteristic of human beings. It is neither a biological nor an "intramental" phenomenon but rather "intermental," a way in which a human being is influenced by other human beings. Durkheim resisted the notion that a social fact could have a psychological basis, insisting that the social whole is other than the sum of its parts, and that social facts have a "structural origin." Tarde called these facts Durkheim's "ontological Phantasmagoria" and, by contrast, called himself a "philosophical nominalist." The whole, for him, is nothing more than the sum of its parts.[20]

Girard is able to explain why the "social fact" is experienced as "that which [is] exterior to the individual and imposed on him through a sort of constraint" (Durkheim),[21] as well as its rootage in imitation, as Tarde held. Tarde's imitation is more conscious and deliberate than Girard's, however, despite the fact that he insisted that it "flowed" from the inner to the outer person. Tarde's understanding does not allow for the spontaneous nature of imitation rooted in the hominization process in the way that Girard's theory does. Tarde was also less concerned with origins, despite his use of the comparative method; he was more synchronic in his approach than Girard. Nevertheless, despite these differences, Tarde's thought does provide an early analogue to the thought of Girard and entitles us to locate the latter in the tradition that flows also from Tarde.

Girard's particular contribution is the identification of violence as the energy of the social system. Durkheim, Hubert and Mauss, and Tarde provide precedents for the Girardian description of the structure of the system, but the insight that mimetic violence and surrogate victimage actually drive the system we owe to Girard alone. This insight is the missing piece in the puzzle and once it is in place we are able to account for all the imponderables. We can explain the emergence of the primordial religious institutions with sacrifice at their center, the relationship between the individual and these institutions, and the ongoing energetics of the system as a whole.

Girard's theory begins with desire. He was alerted to the triangular nature of desire by the Anselmo and Lothario episode in *Don Quixote,* where Anselmo urges Lothario to seduce his fiancée. Anselmo needed Lothario's desire for the woman to confirm his own desire for her. To explain this Girard followed the evidence of literary and ethnological texts to the Bible, where he claims to

---

[20] Terry N. Clark, *Gabriel Tarde,* 16–17.
[21] Ibid., 16.

have found the answer plainly set forth. Beginning with triangular desire he elaborated a theory of the Sacred that explains the role of religious institutions in the generation of culture and provides a hermeneutical theory to interpret both religious texts and cultural formations.

It is a poststructuralist theory in the sense that it assumes the gains of structuralism, precisely the insight that there are generative patterns or structures beneath the surface of the texts that supercede the intention of the author and control the action of the narrative without the author's conscious collaboration. Something speaks in the text that transcends the consciousness of the author and leads one to the depths not just of the author's unconscious but of the culture itself. The generative energetics and mechanics of the social system can be discovered by those who penetrate its disguises. The energy is violence, the mechanism is the Sacred, and society is a system of sacred violence.

I shall present a straightforward account of the theory here, with some preliminary critical evaluation in Appendix I. I cannot evaluate the literary and ethnological evidence exhaustively, and in any case the best test of the theory's validity is the pragmatic one. Use it and see how it succeeds or fails in elucidating the phenomena.[22] The energetics of the system of sacred violence might be called generative scapegoating[23]; the mechanics might be called the founding mechanism.

Girard's hypothesis has two dominant and closely related parts: mimetic rivalry, and the surrogate victim.[24] He develops it in a series of books published during the last twenty years, and it is necessary to follow this development from book to book if one is to grasp the theory. To each of the major moments there corresponds a major book. *Deceit, Desire, and the Novel* (1961, E.T. 1965) expounds the foundational notion of mimetic desire. *Violence and the Sacred* (1972, E.T. 1977) expounds the role of sacrifice and the surrogate victim in the formation of society. *Things Hidden from the Foundation of the World* (1978, E.T. 1987) applies both ideas to the interpretation of anthropology, psychology, and the Bible. *The Scapegoat* (1982, E.T. 1986) summarizes and defends the category of the surrogate victim and applies the theory to further texts of persecution and texts from the gospels. *Job, the Victim of his People* (1985, E.T. 1987) uses it to give a new interpretation of the book of Job.

---

[22] For examples, see R. G. Hamerton-Kelly, "A Girardian Interpretation of Paul," "Sacred Violence and the Curse of the Law," "Sacred Violence and 'Works of Law,' " and "Sacred Violence and Sinful Desire."

[23] The best composite statement of the theory is *Things Hidden*, 3–138. B. Mack gives a brief account in "Introduction: Religion and Ritual," in *Violent Origins*, 1–70. See also Girard's "Generative Scapegoating" and the discussion of it in *Violent Origins*, 73–145; See also E. Webb, *Philosophers of Consciousness*, 183–225.

[24] Jean-Pierre Dupuy, *Ordres et Desordres*, 125.

The Nature of Desire (Acquisitive and Conflictual Mimesis)

The starting point of the theory is a quality of desire called mimesis, which is integral to a system of desire that operates autonomously.[25] Girard begins the analysis of mimesis in *Deceit, Desire, and the Novel* by treating mimetic desire, and in *Things Hidden* he uses the terms "acquisitive and conflictual mimesis" to refer to the same phenomenon. I shall focus my discussion on these two works, with some attention to *Violence and the Sacred*.

Hegel distinguishes between "the sentiment of self" at the level of animal life and "self-consciousness" at the human level.[26] Animal needs persist at the human level but are not to be called desire. Schwager draws the distinction between animal needs and human desire in terms of the specificity of the former and the generality of the latter; the desire that is subject to mimesis is "that fundamental desire that forms and defines the total behavior of the human being," which is to be distinguished from hunger or the need for sleep.[27] While assuming an etiology that leads back to the animal level, Girard picks up the discussion at a point where human desire has already come into being.

Desire is imitative and acquisitive. It operates by copying someone else's desire for an object. Girard calls the model of desire the "mediator." Desire automatically copies the mediator's desire for an object—that is, it desires the object because the mediator desires it.[28] All the great novelists understand this "intuitively and concretely, through their art."[29] Don Quixote, for instance, "has surrendered to Amadis the individual's fundamental prerogative: he no longer chooses the objects of his own desire—Amadis must choose for him. This model, Amadis, is the mediator of desire."[30] Madame Bovary desires through the heroines of the second-rate fiction she reads, and one of Stendahl's *vaniteux* "will desire any object as long as it is already desired by another person whom he admires."[31] Proust's snob is the prisoner of those he wishes to be like, and their disdain of him lashes his admiration of them to greater

---

[25] The best introduction to this part of the discussion are books 1 and 3 of *Things Hidden;* Roel Kaptein and Pieter Tijmes, *De Ander als Model en Obstakel;* Jean-Pierre Dupuy, *Ordres et Desordres;* Henri Atlan and Jean-Pierre Dupuy, "Mimesis and Social Morphogenesis," 1263–68. The last two references emphasize the "systems theory" aspects of the Girardian theory. They see it as a self-generating, autonomic system of mimesis. As such it might also be compared with the account of the social system as a system of communication given by Niklas Luhmann, *Soziale Systeme.*

[26] See Appendix II.

[27] Schwager, *Scapegoats?,* 235, n. 9.

[28] Ibid., 35–37. Dupuy (*Ordres et Desordres,* 133) distinguishes Girard's position as *un désir selon l'Autre* from Hegel's as *un désir du désir de l'Autre.*

[29] *Deceit, Desire, and the Novel,* 3.

[30] Ibid., 1.

[31] Ibid., 6.

intensity. Such characters reveal the mimetic nature of desire, since they can only value objects that others already value, and the essential autonomy of the system of desire, since they have no other option than to copy the desire of others.

The configuration of desire is triangular, therefore, running from the subject through the mediator to the object. The angles at the base of the triangle can be large or small; the larger they are the farther the distance between the plane of the subject and the plane of the mediator, and vice versa. When the distance is relatively far the imitation is relatively untrammeled by rivalry; Girard calls this the state of "external mediation." When the distance is relatively near the imitation becomes rivalrous; Girard calls this "internal mediation." As the plane of the mediator approaches the plane of the subject, rivalry grows with an intensity inversely proportionate to the diminishing distance. Eventually the mediator becomes an obstacle and the subject shifts attention from the object to the mediator/obstacle. Thus mimesis becomes mimetic rivalry. What was an imitative aspiration for the object becomes a direct rivalry between the imitators.

Therefore, not all acquisitive motivation is actually rivalrous although all is mimetic.[32] Desire in the form of mimetic acquisitiveness is more or less rivalrous depending on the distance between the planes of the subject and the mediator.[33] It is only when the planes coalesce that mimesis inevitably becomes mimetic rivalry and desire inevitably violent.

Violence is therefore the relationship between desire and the mediator-becoming-an-obstacle in the process of the development of mimetic rivalry, which is the process of the movement of the planes of the mediator and the subject with respect to one another.

When the mediator arrives on the same plane as the subject, he or she stands between the subject and the object, and thus the instigator of desire is the obstacle to its fulfillment. At this point the subject wishes to destroy the obstacle, but cannot do so without destroying the instigator of desire and thus its own reason for being. The desire of the mediator created the value in the first place and thus called forth the subject's desire; therefore in order to

---

[32] Jean-Marie Domenach ("Voyage to the End of the Sciences of Man") complains that Girard gives no place to free will, attributing all action in the development of culture to mimesis. Mimesis operates too mechanistically. Girard does not, however, eliminate the role of free will, but sees it for the most part to be more or less constrained by mimesis, depending on the size of the angles at the base of the triangle.

[33] There are, however, times when Girard speaks as if desire were always rivalrous. "Desire is what happens to human relationships when there is no longer any kind of resolution through the victim.... Desire is the mimetic crisis in itself: it is acute mimetic rivalry with the other which occurs in all the circumstances which we call 'private,' ranging from eroticism to professional or intellectual ambition.... We might well decide to use the word desire only in circumstances where the misunderstood mechanism of mimetic rivalry has imbued what was previously just an appetite or need with this ontological or metaphysical dimension" (*Things Hidden,* 288, 296).

maintain itself desire must maintain the mediator as obstacle. Desire needs a rival to survive, because its fulfillment is its end.

Thus rivalry is built into the structure of desire, and this we call the "scandal" of desire. Etymologically the scandal is that which causes one to stumble. In its developed meaning, the stumbling block is the hindrance that one loves, the obstacle that gives painful purpose to one's ever-frustrated and thus ever-renewed desire. Scandal is the essence of unquenchable desire, the necessary void at the heart of eros.

As the mediator changes from model to obstacle, he or she fills the horizon and obscures the object entirely. At this point the conflict itself becomes more important than the object, and any of several more or less trivial objects could be an excuse for conflict. As Nietzsche said, "You say that a good cause makes a good war, but I say that a good war makes a good cause" (Zarathustra). This detachment of desire from the original object of rivalry gives violence a quasi-metaphysical status and explains how surrogates come to play a decisive role in the process.

Violence, therefore, is the actualization of desire's mimetic propensity as rivalry, through the process of the mediator becoming the obstacle. Violence is the whole range of this deformation of desire—from the beginning in rivalry to the climax in the killing of surrogate victims—not just the obvious physical coercion. It is the driving energy of the social system. It has many forms more subtle than physical force. On the level of attitude it is envy and the strategies by which desire attempts to possess itself in the other and the other for itself. It is the sadomasochistic transgression of the other as obstacle that cultivates the obstacle so it can continuously overcome it and be overcome by it. Thus violence is more inclusive than aggression, which all species need to survive, and more general than physical coercion. Violence describes the deep strategies of deformed desire in pursuit of its ends in all the modalities of culture.

The triangularity of desire means that the human being is structured with reference to transcendence; desire is structured through mediation from without, not from within. Human being is constituted relationally—that is, transcendentally—and the state of mimetic rivalry is the pathology of a "deviated transcendence," of a desire that should be aroused from a truly transcendent spiritual source but instead is aroused by the immanent neighbor. The biblical name for this is idolatry; its antidote is faith in the unseen God. Its ethical expression is eros, whose antidote is agape. So when we describe desire as deformed, we make a theological judgment in the light of the grace of agape.

The autonomous nature of the system of mimetic desire is theologically the bondage of sin into which the idolator falls. Within the system the only transcendence is the enslaving transcendence of the system itself, which shifts the locus of autonomy from the subject to itself and thus robs the subject of its freedom. The subject becomes a function of the system or of the intersection of several systems (biological, cultural, social), rather than a center of free initiative in an interactive relation with the system.[34]

The dissolution of the subject through enthrallment to the system of desire is a modern counterpart to the Pauline experience of religion.[35] I shall argue that the famous passage on the bondage of the will in Romans 7:14-21 is an account of this experience of enthrallment to the system and that the system in question there is the system of sacred violence. This system still operates through the power of mimetic desire and the mechanism of the surrogate victim.

The subject, understood as desire, cannot, however, be saved from enthrallment to the system by simple self-assertion. Humanism asserts the stable, self-sufficient subject instead of the triangular relational subject. Girard calls this the "romantic lie," that desire is self-generated and not mimetic. Postmodernism, however, as represented for our purposes by Borsch-Jacobsen,[36] records the collapse of this heroic self by its inner contradictions into a phantasm of violent alterity. This is the nemesis of Prometheanism, or the judgment of God on the proud. When the relationship with God is broken, the self falls back into the "deviated transcendence" of mimetic rivalry with the human other in the cycle of violence. It obscures the fact of this violence by means of the myth of the heroic self. The real escape from violence is to renew the relationship of true transcendence and loving mimesis, which is the ultimate form of external mediation, of the creator who is external to all human systems and relationships, and beyond the possibility of rivalry. The rage of the postmodern critics to become their own progenitors is the rage against true transcendence and thus just one more turn in the spiral of violence.

Desire is imitative and acquisitive; it does not desire the desire of the other directly but only as mediated through the imitation of the other's desire for an object. Only as mimesis progresses toward conflict does desire begin to lose sight of the object and to focus on the other with the extreme outcome of the mimetic crisis in which the object is lost altogether. Thus it becomes the desire not merely to possess what the other desires but to possess the being of the other. This movement takes place in three stages: First, desire imitates the desire of the other for the object; secondly, the self replaces the object in the desire of the other; thirdly, by replacing the object the self seeks to possess not only the desire of the other but its own desire as it finds it mimetically in the other, because the self and the other have become each other's doubles. The result of these three stages is that the mediator and the subject become doubles and mediate each other's desire, each believing the other to have the "substance" (prestige) that it needs for fulfillment. Girard calls this category

---

[34] In this theological sense, efforts like Luhmann's to think the system without the subject are efforts to imagine a thoroughgoing consequence of sin, the total domination of the system of mimetic desire over the subject.

[35] See Appendix I on the Freudian subject.

[36] Ibid.

"metaphysical desire" because it is rooted in the subject's lack of being and the conviction that the mediator can supply that lack.

So the rivals come to resemble each other more and more as the differences between them are progressively erased. What started as a one-way imitation becomes a two-way imitation, each copying the desire of the other until they are identical. The appearance of doubles in a text, the erasure of difference, as for instance in the characters of Dionysus and Pentheus in Euripides' *Bacchae,* is a sign that mimetic desire has reached this crisis stage. Distinctions are blurred, human identities melt together, and monsters appear. This is the moment of the "sacrificial crisis."

The process of internal mediation is, therefore, an oscillation in which the generative ground of desire is located in the "between" rather than in any one of the players. It is too simple to say that we learn desire from the other, as if we came empty to the other. Desire brings to the other its image of the other's desire, which it forged out of the awareness of its own desire to which it was alerted by the desire of the other. It attributes mimetic rivalry to the other because it intuits it in itself and then it realizes its own intuited mimesis by miming the other's. Desire imitates itself as it sees itself in the other; but the self that it sees in the other is neither only the self that the other in fact sees, nor only the self that the self imagines the other sees, but some combination of the two which, therefore, exists only in the "between" of the oscillation. The forms of desire, being thus mimetic, are irreducibly communal, and the subject can find self-realization only in the community of desire.

Mimetic desire is infectious. It is the "hunger for the envy of the other." Fashion is driven by mimesis, so is the arms race, and so are the stock and real estate markets. The intrinsic value of a stock or property is negligible compared to the exchange value. Marx used this insight to criticize capitalism for rendering us psychologically incapable of enjoying the intrinsic value of anything. We buy art for its investment potential and we write books for the market. The market defines our likes and dislikes rather than the other way around; there is very little free about the "free market system"; it is a network of bondage to one another's imagined likes and dislikes, an essentially fantastic web of servitude to the phantoms of desire.

The mimetic and subsequently rivalrous structure of desire is a fundamental characteristic of human nature. Girard first recognized it in European novels, Greek tragedies, and certain ethnological sources, and then expanded it into a fundamental anthropology. The question of the nature of human nature remains alive, for him, and is to be asked and answered in the "domain ... of the origin and genesis of signifying systems," which in the life sciences is the process of hominization.[37] Thus mimetic theory becomes a theory of origins that links current human relations with traditional societies and animal behavior.

---

[37] *Things Hidden,* 6–7.

The mimetic nature of human desire is shared with the higher primates. There is a developmental connection between animal mimicry and human imitation, and the point of hominization might be plotted with reference to the change in this activity. Animal mimicry is also acquisitive and goes through the same process of escalating rivalry as human mimesis. However, animals have instinctual braking mechanisms that prevent the rivalry from becoming group-destroying violence. The weaker animal surrenders and patterns of dominance are established; subordinate animals now imitate dominant ones without acquisitiveness. Animal mimesis is closely tied to the object and does not develop the metaphysical dimension of the struggle. The human capacity for metaphysical desire might be correlated with the growth of the brain and the extraordinary length of infantile dependency. Humans have more mimetic energy than animals and press the rivalry to the point where the object disappears and the rivalry becomes metaphysical and murderous.

Thus the moment of hominization occurs with the disappearance of the contested objects in the midst of conflict and the spontaneous emergence of the surrogate victim.[38] In Girard's terms, hominization occurs when acquisitive mimesis becomes conflictual mimesis. The rivals become to each other both the model to be imitated and the obstacle to be overcome in a struggle not for any object but for pure prestige. The violence thus generated converges upon a victim.

> If acquisitive mimesis divides by leading two or more individuals to converge on one and the same object with a view to appropriating it, conflictual mimesis will inevitably unify by leading two or more individuals to converge on one and the same adversary that all wish to strike down.[39]

We have arrived at the second fundamental human characteristic upon which the social system is based, the surrogate victim mechanism.

The Double Transference

The banal "French triangle" is the clue that leads to the discovery of mimetic desire; the equally banal tendency to transfer blame to others leads to the surrogate victim. These characteristic human behaviors are omnipresent and require no special insight to see. Girard shows that they are common because

---

[38] Frans de Waal, *Peacemaking among Primates*, 57–79, gives a vivid account of protosacrifice among chimpanzees who collaborate to kill a victim. This evidence suggests that not only mimesis but also the surrogate victim mechanism has its roots in the prehuman stage of phylogeny. The behavior that de Waal describes suggests that at the prehuman stage the device of the surrogate victim occurs in a vestigial form that develops into the full mechanism at the point of hominization.

[39] *Things Hidden*, 26.

they represent fundamental truths about human nature and that we have made them banal by our inattention to their significance. It is a strength rather than a weakness of the theory that it is founded on facts that we usually consider banal.

The Surrogate Victim

The surrogate victim is a spontaneous psychological mechanism.[40] It can be observed synchronically in the everyday tendency to make scapegoats bear the brunt of violence that cannot be contained or vented on a target that can avenge itself. In the diachronic development of humankind it is the conflictual mimesis that happens when rivals converge no longer on the object that divides them but on the victim that unites. The most significant other clue to its existence is religion—that is, the primitive Sacred in its manifestations of prohibition, ritual, and myth. In taking the institutions of religion this seriously, Girard stands in the tradition of Durkheim, especially as it is represented by the English school of social anthropology, pioneered for religion by Jane Harrison and the Cambridge school of Greek historians.[41]

Mimetic rivalry in its advanced stages can easily change its object. Violence has the capacity to substitute one object for another. There are two factors at work in this substitution. One is the obscuring of the object in the advanced stages of rivalry, the detachment of the rivalrous energy from any particular object by its submersion in the subjective conflict; the other is the spontaneous agreement of the mutually intimidated rivals to transfer violence to a vulnerable substitute. This is formally a rediscovery of the object, now as something to be destroyed rather than possessed. The conflict reaches the point at which the rivals, now doubles, find that they share the desire to destroy each other, but since they are mutually intimidated and identical, they cannot proceed. Then they rediscover the object pole and deflect the destructive energy from one another onto a substitute. Thus the surrogate victim appears from within the process of mimetic rivalry as the temporary resting place of desire. The mechanism of the surrogate victim is, therefore, a sociopsychological mechanism that occurs as the organizing moment in the human social system.

We might imagine the originary scene as follows. In the beginning the representative "primal horde" was wracked by mimetic violence. This violence

---

[40] Girard uses the term "surrogate victim" only for the spontaneous psychological mechanism by which we transfer violence to a victim, and not for ritual transference (*Things Hidden,* 33). His essay "Generative Scapegoating," in *Violent Origins,* is the best explanation of the surrogate victim mechanism.

[41] See F. M. Turner, *The Greek Heritage in Victorian Britain,* 116–34, cited by Albert Henrichs, "Loss of Self, Suffering, Violence." Henrichs describes the Cambridge school as "a small circle of historians of Greek religion at the turn of the century who transformed Greek myth and tragedy into a blood-drenched hunting ground for cannibals and ritual murderers and who saw a human substitute for the dying Dionysus in each tragic hero on the Attic stage." J. G. Frazer, of *The Golden Bough* fame, is an important influence behind the school. He was Jane Harrison's teacher.

increased until it reached a crisis point, at which the surrogate victim mechanism automatically "kicked in." This was the point of hominization. First one pair of rivals, then another rediscovered the object pole of the mimetic triangle as the substitute target for their rage at each other. Some discovered it spontaneously; most would have discovered it by imitating the discoverers. Mimesis broke out in a new form, acquisitive mimesis became conflictual mimesis—in the sense that the desire was no longer to acquire the object but to destroy it—uniting rather than dividing the community, as all cooperated mimetically in the killing of the victim. Not all could acquire the victim but all could kill it. Thus unanimous victimage played the same role in human community as the surrender of the weaker animal plays in the establishment of dominance patterns among the higher animals.[42] It enabled the group to find unity by dealing with mimetic acquisitiveness.

The story of Solomon's judgment (1 Kings 3:16-28) is a good example of this. The two harlots both wish to acquire the child, and Solomon proposes the standard sacrificial solution, to unite them in conflictual mimesis against the child. He proposes that the child be cut in two. The real mother refuses the unanimity of the sacrifice and thus proves her motherhood. Solomon understands that acquisitive mimesis can only be overcome by conflictual mimesis or by renunciation of mimetic rivalry. Thus we have an early example of how the Bible understands the dynamics of primitive religion and moves to expose it.[43]

Gazing at the victim's corpse the mob's stupefaction turns to awe as it realizes that it has just experienced its first moment of unanimity. This reconciliation must have come after a mimetic crisis so severe that the sudden resolution at the expense of a single victim seemed like a miracle. "The experience of a supremely evil and then beneficent being, whose appearance and disappearance are punctuated by collective murder, cannot fail to be literally *gripping*."[44] Thus occurs the primal misunderstanding: the mob misidentifies the cause of unanimity. It is in fact mimetic rivalry and the surrogate victim mechanism acting in the group, but they think it is the victim. The victim is at most a catalyst and at least only the passive object of the mechanism, rather than the cause of the violence and unanimity. The mob, however, makes the victim the cause, and by so doing obscures its own violence from itself by thus transferring it to the victim. The first illusion is, therefore, "the illusion of the supremely active and all-powerful victim";[45] it makes the victim a god, placing the victim above the group as the transcendent source of order and repository of disorder.

This is the critical moment of the *double transference,* of both the cause of violence and the cause of peace from the mob to the victim. The transference is

---

[42] *Violent Origins,* 129.

[43] A. McKenna, "Biblical Structuralism: Testing the Victimary Hypothesis," 71–87; *Things Hidden,* 237–45.

[44] *Things Hidden,* 28 (italics added).

[45] Ibid., 52.

double because the mob's violence has two parts: mimetic rivalry and surrogate victimage, corresponding to the moments of disorder and order, respectively. The mob transfers its own violence to the victim by the simple misattribution of the cause of unanimity. This transference is the critical step from the victim to the social system. It is the creative response of the human group to the "creativity" of its own deformed desire in spontaneously generating the surrogate victimage solution to the problem of its violence. Violence was not repressed and cast off into the unconscious, but was detached and transformed into culture by being transferred to the victim.[46]

Thus the catalyst became the cause, and the victim became the sign of the two valences that correspond to the two stages of violence. These two parts of the mob's violence work through the victim and transform the victim into a god, because of the power the victim now mediates. The victim is full of mimesis that can break out as vengeance on transgressors of the taboo, and is full of the power of order that must be renewed by ritual sacrifice. Thus we transfer to the victim not only our mimetic violence but also the deflecting mechanism of our surrogate victimage; in theological language, we make the victim bear both our sins and the sin of making the victim bear our sins. It is not we who threaten vengeance and demand victims; it is the victim! Thus the double transference is the foundational lie of culture and the original act of bad faith.

The double transference also makes the victim *the transcendent signifier*. The cadaver is the first object of a non-instinctual attention because of the miraculous peace that attends the death. The difference between the victim and the mob is the beginning of all differentiation, by the logic of the exception or the "short straw." Structuralist topology demands at least two signs at the beginning, because signs only signify with reference to each other; the logic of the victim differentiates by means of the one who stands out from the many, the exception, the representative. The mob and the victim are the two poles of signification.[47] The form of the first verbal response to the surrogate victim is the myth that tells the story from the point of view of the perpetrators of the crime, a fiction of the double transference.

The social system, as a system of sacred violence, comes from the surrogate victim, therefore, by way of the double transference. The victim is the cause of mimetic disorder and of surrogate-victim order. The victim's living must have caused disorder if dying brought order. In the form of a god, the victim reflects these two misunderstandings back as the imperatives for prohibition and ritual, respectively, and thus controls behavior. The victim determines human behavior, however, not by means of what really happened but through the *interpretation* of what happened that the community transfers to the victim

---

46 *Violence and the Sacred,* 136.
47 Ibid., 100–101.

and that the victim in turn represents to them, in the form of prohibition, ritual, and, in addition, myth. For this reason, hermeneutic stands at the origin of all culture, since it is not what really happened but the (mis)interpretation of what happened, as re-presented by the victim, that controls behavior. Culture comprises the misinterpretation of the killing of the surrogate victim that takes the form of prohibition, ritual, and myth. The victim is the primary signifier, and the signified "constitutes all the actual and potential meaning the community confers on to the victim and, through its intermediacy, on to all things."[48] The victim is the sign of the double valency of disorder and order that all prohibition, ritual, and myth seek to represent. The summary term for the sign is the Sacred. The Sacred sign, however, is a lie.

The Sacred

The Durkheimian tradition in which Girard stands sees religion as the primary expression of the power that forms society, and ritual as the essence of religion. A major alternative view, represented in our time by Eliade, sees religion as a response to the experience of the a priori Sacred, understood as ontologically prior to the individual or society, and sees myth as the essence of religion.[49] Myth and ritual are human responses to the manifestations of the Sacred. Thus the word precedes the deed and myth goes before ritual. Against this Girard argues, like Durkheim, that the Sacred is itself a product of society. The group generates the Sacred through the double transference onto the victim, and the Sacred in turn mandates prohibition, ritual, and myth. The social crisis of violence is absolutely prior, to the Sacred, to prohibition, to ritual, and to myth. The impact of these moves on the general conception of religion is to place ritual at the center of the general description, and to see religion as the product of social forces. It represents the triumph of Durkheim over Freud and Eliade.

The Sacred is the transcendental pole of primitive religion. It has been understood either as an invention of the superstitious mind to provide pre-scientific explanations, or a mysterious real presence apprehended in the religious attitude. Girard tells us that it is a mendacious representation of human violence; it is "the sum of human assumptions resulting from collective transferences focused on a reconciliatory victim at the conclusion of a mimetic crisis."[50] The element of "the overwhelming" defines the Sacred; it includes the experience of tempests, fires, and plagues, but its primary content is violence understood as being, like these catastrophes, outside normal human control. "Violence is the heart and secret soul of the Sacred."[51] The

---

[48] *Things Hidden*, 103.
[49] Mircea Eliade, *The Sacred and the Profane*.
[50] *Things Hidden*, 42.
[51] *Violence and the Sacred*, 31.

Sacred is violence misrepresented by the double transference. The dangerous quasi-substance polarized around the victim[52] is reified violence, which constitutes the polluting power of the holy, and the prestige of kings, priests, and mythic heroes. All institutions are initially attempts to use this prestige to reproduce the moment of reconciliation; they and their hierarchies are sacrificial structures of violence.

Prohibition, ritual, and myth are the three imperatives of the Sacred. They are impositions of the Sacred rather than conscious or unconscious functional strategies of the group. The interdiction of mimicry, or the ritual regulation of vengeance, for instance, are not primarily unconscious judgments of a functional kind but rather responses to and representations of the Sacred's monopoly of violence. To say that they are not functional does not mean that they are not rational, but only that the rationality is mediated through the Sacred, as responses to its threat and promise in the form of prohibition, ritual, and myth, respectively.

The first two imperatives of the Sacred are curiously contradictory. Prohibition in essence means that one should not repeat any aspect of the original crisis, while ritual requires that one repeat the whole thing with great care. Prohibition interdicts mimicry, contact with former antagonists, acquisitive gestures toward the objects that caused rivalry, and anything that might reactivate the crisis. Ritual deliberately reactivates it, organizes orgies of transgression, and immolates new victims in ways that are thought to repeat the original action. This is because prohibition corresponds generally but not exclusively to the mimetic rivalry element in the Sacred, while ritual similarly corresponds to the surrogate victim. Prohibition focuses on the negative side of the process, the mimetic rivalry that caused a crisis, while ritual focuses on the positive side, the surrogate victim that reconciled the adversaries. They, along with myth, are the cultural counterparts of the products of the double transference.

The Transformations of the Sacred

The double transference transforms the surrogate victim into the Sacred with two valences and a narrative justification, which are respectively prohibition, ritual, and myth. They are the basic components of the social system, and each undergoes its own further transformations. Their respective lines of development sometimes intersect and so the lines of exposition will intersect also.

---

[52] *Things Hidden*, 48.

Prohibition and Ritual

I shall first follow the line of prohibition and then the lines of ritual and myth respectively. Prohibition emerges from the mimetic rivalry pole of the double transference. The transformations of the prohibition, beginning with the presacral stage are: mimetic violence, which is the same as uncontrolled vengeance; transformed (by the transference) into a) the prohibition sanctioned by the vengeance of the god[53]; b) expressed as ritually controlled vengeance in the sacrificial system; and c) finally becoming rationally controlled vengeance in the legal system. The transformations of the prohibition are therefore the history of the emergence of the legal system. They are of particular interest for our purpose because so much of Paul's theology is concerned with the Mosaic Law. It is critical for the Pauline understanding of that Law that the first emergence of law in culture takes the form of the prohibition on mimetic violence sanctioned by the vengeance of the god. The idea of law, therefore, contains the idea of the divine vengeance at its core.

The mimetic nature of vengeance is superficially obvious. The principals imitate each other's violent acts in an apparent display of the well-used category of reciprocity. Reciprocity is normally understood either economically or legally. Economically it is a form of fair exchange for mutual benefit, but vengeance poses an insoluble problem for the economic interpretation, because it is a reciprocity of loss, the classic instance of the fallacy that two wrongs make a right, and is frequently undertaken to the detriment of the avenger. So it cannot be based on a rational calculation of advantage except in terms of the sacred intangibles that are impenetrable to economic logic.

Vengeance is the basis of retributive justice, but since the law is rooted in the sacred prohibition, the relationship between law and vengeance can be understood only by means of an analysis of the generative role of the Sacred. Vengeance is mimetic violence transformed into retributive justice by the Sacred.

Prohibition and the Vengeance of the God

Prohibitions exist to prevent mimetic rivalry.[54] They generally pertain to objects that the community cannot divide peacefully—food, weapons, and the best places to live. The value of such objects is constituted not by scarcity alone but also by their prestige in the game of mimetic rivalry. The common sanction of all sacral prohibitions, therefore, is fear of mimetic rivalry transformed by the detour through the Sacred into fear of the vengeance of the god.[55]

---

[53] Ibid., 14.
[54] Ibid., 14 and 19.
[55] Ibid., 76.

Having been the catalyst of the conflictual mimesis that united the group, the victim/god becomes the sign of the prohibition on anything that can disrupt that unity. No member of the mob can reach out to possess the victim/god without causing the rivalry to start again. The victim/god is not to be approached, not to be touched, not to be possessed. It occupies a place beyond reach and a line of distinction is drawn between it and every other place. Thus the first prohibition and the first differentiation are the same; they are the distinction between the victim/god and the group, the Sacred and the profane. This fundamental prohibition is the essence of the concept of law and the concept of transcendence.

Thus the god is possessive, reserving certain persons, places, and things to itself. The possessions of the god are prohibited. In this role the god is the transformed model-obstacle, the great rival, a point that I shall emphasize in the interpretation of Paul's reading of the Adam story as the process of the idolization of God by turning God into the great rival. This divine possessiveness expressed as the threat of vengeance generates the system of ritual law characteristic of the next transformation.

Ritually Controlled Vengeance
—the Sacrificial System

The sacrificial system is the whole structure of prohibition, ritual, and myth, and it controls vengeance in two ways. It uses the prohibition pole to generate a system of sacred rules to keep people in their proper non-mimetic places, and it uses the surrogate victim pole to keep violence in its proper ritual channels, and myth to re-create both moments verbally.[56] Ultimately, however, the same energy flows in all three subsystems. I shall return to myth later; here I concentrate on the elements of prohibition and ritual.

Before the prohibition became law in the legal sense, it was law in the ritual sense of the prescriptions guarding the sacred precinct. These are the laws of priestly purity and the protocols governing the offering of sacrifice. They give structure to the transcendence of the Sacred, and provide the channels within which violence flows to sustain the sacral order. Sacrifice renews the therapeutic effect of the surrogate victim mechanism, by providing a core to which the violence is ritually attracted and from which it flows out again in proper channels. These channels are the rules of ritual purity that keep the various parts and persons of society in their "proper" places. As this law extends its control into the profane community, it organizes the community as a structure of sacred violence centered on the place of sacrifice. Thus the

---

[56] "By ritual retelling of the Creative Acts (gesta), the society believes it can make present once again the powerfully creative dynamics of that primal period and so recharge the energies of the present" (William G. Doty, *Mythography*, 141).

phenomenon of the holy people ruled by the law of the god and centered on the temple is generated by sacred violence.

Contravention of the rules causes pollution and the polluting agent is not dirt but violence. Dirt is a rationalization of violence. In these matters biblical scholars usually invoke the authority of Mary Douglas,[57] and her designation of dirt as that which is out of its proper place. This is too rationalistic a definition and, besides, it begs an important question. It does not explain how or why the notion of a "proper" place came about in the first place. It assumes that the logical order of thought can be attributed univocally to the order of society. Such attribution is at best metaphor and at worst anthropomorphism. The essential ingredient in all ritual pollution is violence.

The "proper" place is any place that is so located as not to cause unnecessary rivalry. Thus the proper place of family members in the subsequent generation is another family, because siblings are too close to each other to avoid mimetic rivalry; and so the laws of incest are part of the sacrificial strategy to channel violence. The incest taboo functions sacrificially in two ways: it drives out those who are drivable—that is, those who are weak and least likely to be able to defend themselves—and it prescribes the limits of proximity of family members. It provides for sacrificial deflection of old violence onto victims that will bear it away, and for differentiation that prevents new violence from occurring. Brides, therefore, were victims and scapegoats before they were commodities. Incest pollutes because it breaches the dikes against mimetic rivalry and lets violence flow outside the proper ritual channels into the profane area of the family.

For the sacred order to be maintained there must be a way of keeping violence within the proper channels. Any threat to that confinement must be appeased. The prohibition demands appeasement and the surrogate victim provides it, in a clear instance of the interaction of the two poles of the Sacred. The prohibition demands two kinds of appeasement, one propitiatory and the other prophylactic, to repair the damage done by transgression and to forestall future transgression, and the surrogate victim provides both through the ruse of sacrificial deflection.

Propitiatory appeasement is simply the deflection of the justly incurred vengeance of the god onto a surrogate. Prophylactic appeasement is the controlled release of excess violence from the social system. Violence demands to be activated and this demand must be appeased; "if left unappeased, violence will accumulate until it overflows its confines and floods the surrounding area."[58] The release of violence must be controlled if it is not to provoke counter-violence. Ritual sacrifice, as the controlled transgression of the prohibition on violence, is the way to express violence without incurring vengeance.

---

[57] Mary Douglas, *Purity and Danger.*
[58] *Violence and the Sacred,* 10.

It works by deflecting the reciprocating violence from its target onto victims that cannot retaliate and have no one to avenge them. Thus it provides ritual channels along which violence flows out of the group. Sacrifice is controlled transgression.

The prophylactic function of the sacrificial deflection ruse is evident in the way some primitives deal with vengeance. Girard has observed that among the Chukci the fear of reciprocal violence is so great that they do not allow vengeance to be taken on the one who commits the outrage, but rather on someone else belonging to the cognizant group. In this way they seek to avoid a symmetry that could become an endless reciprocity.[59] The result is two random victims and two killers infected by violence. Nevertheless, it makes perfect sense because it protects the groups in question from falling into a spiral of vengeance. It breaks the symmetry so that the clash is never between violence and violence—the avenger and the murderer—but always between violence and a victim. Because victims come from outside the interchange, they can draw off the violent energy and carry it away from the groups. In this way the current of violence is broken, and the power fizzles dangerously but fruitlessly into the social space made for it, the space of the surrogate victim. The two infected parties are kept from contacting each other and so the possibility of an epidemic of violence is reduced.

Rationally Controlled Vengeance
—the Legal System

Law is the myth of vengeance: it conceals its origin in sacred violence. Law in the ritual sense is the order of "good violence," running in the channels carved for it by sacrifice; it is ritually controlled vengeance. Law in the legal sense is good violence flowing in the no longer evidently ritual channels of the legislature and the judiciary. It is rationally controlled vengeance. Thus we have the following sequence in the transformation of vengeance into law: (1) uncontrolled vengeance, (2) ritually controlled vengeance, and (3) rationally controlled vengeance. Raymond Verdier, the editor of the most thorough recent examination of the phenomenon of vengeance,[60] calls level two "the vindicatory system"(*le système vindicatoire*), by which he indicates that most primitive societies had prelegal, ritual devices for confining vengeance. He sees this as a refutation of Girard's claim that primitive society was subject to the danger of limitless revenge before it discovered the sacrificial mechanism;

---

[59] Ibid., 17–28.

[60] *La Vengeance 1 and 2: La Vengeance dans les sociétés extra occidentales* (ed. Raymond Verdier); *La Vengeance 3: Vengeance, pouvoirs et idéologies dans quelques civilisations de l'Antiquité* (eds. Raymond Verdier and Jean-Pierre Poly); *La Vengeance 4: La vengeance dans la pensée occidentale* (ed. Gerard Courtois). This reference is to Verdier's introductory essay in vol. 1, 13–42.

but his view in fact confirms Girard, in that the sacrificial system is precisely such a prelegal vindicatory system.[61]

The third category of law can dispense with the deflection stratagem, because in the legal stage of social development the institutions of religion and the state have gained a monopoly of violence and so there is no longer the threat of it spiraling out of control. The one who commits the crime is the one who pays for it, and the agency inflicting the punishment is the temple or the state, not a private citizen, not a relative of the deceased. The act of revenge is precisely targeted, and the avenger is impersonalized, thus making reciprocal violence impossible. Furthermore the monopoly of violence by the temple or state means that the avenger is so overwhelmingly strong as to intimidate retaliation.

The institutions of religion and the state make individual guilt and responsibility possible, and this might explain why the consciousness of individuality arose *pari passu* with the development of the city. The city is the triumph of the Sacred (Gen 4:17). Prohibition becomes law in the context of institutions so deeply structured by the surrogate victim mechanism that eventually they no longer need to represent it in periodic sacrifices. They are themselves the reification of the scapegoat ritual, existing in the power of exclusion and deflection that they practice all the time. Prohibition, therefore, is the transformation of the threat of divine vengeance, and law is the myth of that avenging god.

Beginning along the line of the prohibition, having already intersected with it several times along the way, we now follow the line of ritual.

Ritual and Prohibition[62]

The transformations of ritual are: (1) blood sacrifice; (2) religious institutions: priests and temples; (3) politico-military institutions: kings and heroes; (4) scapegoating.

Blood Sacrifice

If the prohibition corresponds to the negative valency of the Sacred (mimetic rivalry), ritual corresponds to the positive (surrogate victimage). Girard reserves the term "surrogate victim" for this general socio-psychological ruse of deflection. When this is ritualized, he speaks of "sacrifice" or the sacrificial victim. Blood sacrifice, therefore, is the primary form of ritual, and the fundamental element in sacrifice is the deflection ruse by which we transfer violence from one target to another.[63] We have seen how the surrogate victim as ritual

---

[61] Mark Rogin Anspach, "Penser la vengeance."

[62] Doty, *Mythography*, is a good account of the state of the discussion in myth and ritual studies. For this section, see *Things Hidden*, 48–83.

[63] *Things Hidden*, 131.

sacrifice propitiates and prevents violence. But propitiation and prophylaxis are merely subsets of the fundamental function, which is to repeat the first killing and so renew the ordering effect of unanimous violence and the power of the transference by ritual repetition. For Girard sacrifice is "a mechanism for diverting violence" that operates by substitution. It is the principal form of ritual and it performs a vital social function by renewing the energies of the founding mechanism. The idea of sacrifice as an exchange between the god and the offerer—the *do ut des* or *quid pro quo* explanation—is a rational transformation of this in the direction of the economic notion of reciprocity.

Girard's theory of sacrifice, we should note, is only one among several.[64] It traces its lineage to Robertson Smith's view that the earliest form of religion was a belief in a theriomorphic ancestor with which the tribe had a blood relationship and which they consumed ritually to assimilate its power. The same theory inspired Freud's proposal that the murder of the father by the sons to acquire the women lies at the dawn of religion, and Jensen's theory that sacrifice is a reenactment of the killing of a primordial divine being from whose body came forth the plants useful for food.

Religious Institutions: Priests and Temples

Hyam Maccoby calls attention to the figure of the "sacred executioner."[65] In him the status of victim is extended to a living member of the group who becomes a liminal figure. He is the priest, a figure that, along with the king and the mythic hero, is especially associated with the Sacred and therefore regarded with deep ambivalence. These figures represent the "beyond" at the center of society. Their precincts are the forbidden cities, temples, places of sacrifice, where violence is processed into power. Prestige and the other intangibles of authority that cling to them are the transformed violence that congeals around the victim and attaches to those who are associated with the victim.

Politico-Military Institutions: Kings and Heroes

Every king and hero, like the priest, is to a greater or lesser extent, by association, the victim and the god, an institution for the processing of violence from bad to good.[66] Thus violence is the essence of primitive leadership. As the incarnate Sacred, such a figure is feared and adored, punished and praised, and his perch is always precarious. The leader's oscillation from god to victim in

---

[64] For a convenient treatment of current theories, see Joseph Henninger, "Sacrifice," in *The Encyclopedia of Religion* 544–57; see *Violence and the Sacred,* 1–67.

[65] Hyam Maccoby, *The Sacred Executioner.*

[66] *Violence and the Sacred,* 104–8.

the public mind takes place suddenly, as many a politician in a sacrificial crisis can attest. The shift from adoration to execration is sudden and swift. Only the double role of the model as model and obstacle, and the double valency of the Sacred, can explain these gyrations of attitude and the extraordinary power of the leader for good and for ill.

Kingship is an institution whose rituals clearly show the working of the founding mechanism. In the beginning the king was probably the victim whose period of preparation stretched until he had so much prestige that the community could no longer kill him. He was originally "a victim with a suspended sentence."[67] Kingship rituals often include the king's transgression of especially strong taboos in a moment of a ritual chaos that is reduced to order by his enthronement, thus enacting the transformation of violence through the death of the victim, and presenting enthronement as the ritual equivalent of sacrifice.

The king is the living god, and the god is the dead king. The king represents the presence of sacred power in this world, while the god represents its presence in the "beyond." The king is correlated with the moment before the death, in which the chosen victim shares the prestige of violence while still alive, while the god is correlated with the moment after the death in which the violence is located in the "beyond."

Scapegoating

Just as the transformations of the prohibition end with the myth of rational law, so the transformations of the ritual end with the myth of the scapegoat. The scapegoat is no longer discernible as the surrogate victim of ritual violence, but all around us the game of blaming others for our transgressions, and loading them with responsibility for our sins and solecisms, goes on con brio and we play along with zest. Racism, nationalism, and anti-Semitism are only the most vulgar examples of this dirty game.

In modern usage the term "scapegoat" designates both a ritual and a more or less unconscious and spontaneous socio-psychological act. It is a technical term in ethnology for a ritual and a term in common usage for a psychological act. Thus the correlation between psychology and ritual has been inscribed in the language; the Girardian theory has been hidden in plain view. The psychological precedes the ritual meaning of the term in that the surrogate victim mechanism is the cause, not the result, of ritual. Therefore, the scapegoat is not a mere metaphor for an inconsequential psychological phenomenon, but the spontaneous surrogate victimage impulse that has been ritualized and

---

[67] *Things Hidden,* 52–53. The point is that the victim had to come from outside the group, but also be identified with it long enough to become representative. During this period the victim would be the living victim, and might garner so much prestige as to forestall actual sacrifice.

mythified. The savage mind's strange idea that guilt can be transferred from one person to another like a physical burden is not the result of an inability to reason, but, on the contrary, a cunning act of rationalization by means of ritual and myth. By the same token, doctrines of substitutionary atonement are mythic.

Myths

"Myths are the retrospective transfiguration of sacrificial crises, the reinterpretation of these crises in the light of the cultural order that has arisen from them."[68] "Mythological elaboration is an unconscious process based on the surrogate victim and nourished by the presence of violence."[69] Myth like ritual represents the founding murder from the point of view of the murderers; only the murderers can make a murder appear a good thing.

Both Lévi-Strauss and Girard see mythology as a representation of the birth and development of differential thought. They also share the conviction that the passage from undifferentiation to differentiation through a "driving out" is a constant feature of myths. Lévi-Strauss interprets the "driving out" as the expression of the logic of elimination and exclusion by which the mind disencumbers a congested field of perception to make space for differential thought. Mythic thought represents this differentiating process metaphorically, but because it is incapable of sufficient abstraction it confuses the process of thought with the process of history and reifies the players. Girard interprets this mythic structure as a sacred misrepresentation of the founding mechanism.

Lévi-Strauss's topological interpretation leaves some critical points unaccounted for. First, one might ask why the generation of something as antiseptic as his immaculately conceived differential thought should so frequently be represented by a violent expulsion. Secondly, if the expulsion is for the purpose of disencumbering a field, the expelled must come from within that field; in the myths the victim comes both from within and from without. Thirdly, his topology cannot account for the conjunction of the chief elements in the structure. Fourthly, it cannot account for the fact that the eliminated fragment at first bears a negative connotation and then a positive connotation. Only the surrogate victim mechanism accounts for all the important phenomena.

Girard does not simply display the same inability for abstract thought as Lévi-Strauss attributes to the myths, confusing the representations with their referents. He does not simply infer the communal murder from its representation, although he like everyone cannot escape the hermeneutical circle. Rather he offers it as a better explanation of the phenomena that both he and Lévi-Strauss observe. Minimally these are: the negative connotation of the

---

68 *Violence and the Sacred,* 64.
69 Ibid., 136.

eliminated fragment, the positive connotation of the elimination as such, and the collective nature of the expulsion. It is precisely the conjunction of these three that the Lévi-Straussian topology cannot explain while the hypothesis of an actual communal murder can.

A full Girardian account of the structure of myth has the following features: the theme of undifferentiation; accusations; collective violence; the founding or refounding of culture; the accusation against the mythic hero taken as an incontestable fact.[70] He also speaks of the "stereotypes" of persecution such as the loss of differences, crimes that eliminate differences, the marks of the victim on the alleged authors of the crimes, and the violence itself.[71] The accusations are transformed into facts because the tellers of the story are the accusers themselves. Mythology's "real project is that of recalling the crises and the founding murder, the sequences in the realm of events that have constituted or reconstituted the cultural order,"[72] and it is always a project of the killers rather than the victim. Therefore demythification consists in retelling the story from the point of view of the victim, exposing the lie, and revealing the founding mechanism. Demythification reverses the double transference.

Girard claims that the Bible for the most part demythifies because it tells the story from the point of view of the victims. Myths have been demythified in the process of history; the great Greek tragedians took the process part of the way, and the Bible brought it to a decisive climax. The Bible is the "essential if not exclusive cause of the dynamic" that sustains Girard's program.[73] Historically, it is the fountainhead of the unprecedented and unparalleled progress of Western civilization away from ritual and myth.

On a spectrum from thorough misrepresentation to complete disclosure, myth stands close to the former pole. With the decay of the sacrificial order, texts come into being that are nearer the mid-point of the spectrum. Girard calls these "texts of persecution." They are especially helpful for identifying the mechanism, since in them it is partially revealed. Texts about the persecution of Jews or witches, for instance, betray their mendacity clearly; they accuse their victims of incredible crimes. Although the texts accept those accusations as true, we know them to be false. We also know the victims and their sufferings to be real. Thus we have an instance of the founding mechanism working before our eyes.[74] In the more or less mythic texts of persecution the mimetic crisis of violence generates the need for victims, who are accused of incredible crimes and executed, and as a result, order returns to the community.

---

[70] *Things Hidden*, 119.
[71] *The Scapegoat*, 24.
[72] *Things Hidden*, 120.
[73] Ibid., 138.
[74] *The Scapegoat*, 1–44.

Because of biblical enlightenment, which, in turn, gave rise to general enlightenment in the West, we can no longer ritualize or rationalize our violence. We are no longer able to produce idols around which to collect and coagulate it. We are thrust into a time of absolute responsibility. Once and for all we know that there is no vengeful god who desires victims, that that god was always only a mask for our own appetite, that there is no god to prohibit us from mimeticism, and consequently that the only barrier between us and violent self-destruction is our own restraint. In the light of this we applaud the deconstruction of all our sacrificial knowledge, the "major liquidation of philosophy and the sciences of man that is currently taking place."[75] But there is too much ceremony about it; the funeral lasts too long. The dead should now be left to bury the dead while we get on with reconstructing a cultural understanding in full acknowledgment of the surrogate victim, and a cultural practice founded on the renunciation of violence.

The theory is primarily an explanation of human relations. The forces of primitive sacred violence are still at work; the chief difference now is that they have been unmasked in the course of the desacralization of culture. We are able now to understand the mechanism. We know how the double transference works and we understand the system of sacred violence. This should enable us to decode texts. In what follows I hope to show how this might be done. The chief utility of the theory for this purpose, therefore, is hermeneutical. I wish to use it to interpret texts, and so I turn to the question of its utility as a hermeneutic, and compare it with other hermeneutical efforts.

---

[75] *Things Hidden,* 135.

2

Sacred Violence
as Hermeneutic
Decoding the Double Transference

La parole a été donnée à l'homme pour déguiser sa pensées.
Talleyrand to the Spanish envoy Isquierdo

Men do not seem to have acquired speech in order to conceal their thoughts...but in order to conceal the fact that they have no thoughts.
Kierkegaard, *Journal*, 1844

The theory of sacred violence posits the founding mechanism that produced prohibition, ritual, and myth, and gave the social system its structure. Since, according to the theory, sacred violence generated these structures, the theory can also be used to interpret them, and since texts are among the generated structures it can function as a theory for the interpretation of texts.

In this capacity it functions *per contra*, by reversing the direction of the double transference. The double transference is an act of misinterpretation by which the victim is transformed into the god by being blamed for the violence of the group. The group does not take responsibility for its own violence but transfers it onto the victim, thereby making it sacred. The theory of sacred violence as a hermeneutical device will simply reverse the direction of the double transference, returning responsibility for violence to its proper place and thus desacralizing the victim. Guile will be met with double guile.[1]

---

[1] Paul Ricoeur, *Freud and Philosophy*, 32–36, coins the phrase "guile will be met with double guile" to characterize the interpretive efforts of the three great "masters of suspicion," Marx, Nietzsche, and Freud. Their basic insight is that the consciousness of meaning does not coincide with the declarations of meaning, and therefore the decipherment of the declarations must match

In this way the theory becomes a deconstructive "hermeneutic of suspicion" in the sense that by exposing the cogs and levers of the sacrificial machine it dispels the mystery and enables us to withdraw cooperation. By categorizing (= accusing)[2] sacred violence, the theory exposes it to public scorn. Simply by pointing it out, drawing attention to it, making it the subject of research and hypothesizing, the theory deconstructs sacred violence. Thus it overcomes the effects of the mechanism without destroying it, subjects it to deconstruction as distinct from destruction.

I can only demonstrate the theory's efficacy pragmatically, by showing how it succeeds in illuminating the texts. Since the criteria of success for a theory are its power and elegance, this raises the question of the precise relationship between the theory and the evidence, the question of what counts for power and elegance in the theory as it confronts the evidence to be understood. The answer to this question must be sought in the interaction between the theoretical and the subtheoretical level—the level of hypothesis and law—and in this interaction the first problem to be faced is the problem of circular reasoning.[3]

The texts attest the theory and the theory in turn interprets the texts. In this case this is not a vicious circle because the theory is not derived from the texts by induction. The texts are merely one kind of evidence among others— from psychology, ethology, and ethnology—which warrant the positing of the theory. Nevertheless, the theory does not entirely escape the circle, loosely defined, because it comes to a specific text as a preunderstanding that allows its adherent to focus on certain features rather than on others. In this way it is more or less self-confirming. More or less, because an honest user of the theory will be sensitive to the danger of forcing the evidence, and willing to allow the exceptions that prove the rule, as well as ready to admit when the exceptions have become the rule and the theory has to be changed or discarded.

Girard's own attitude to the hermeneutical problematic is a curious mixture of Cartesianism and postmodernism. While he insists on the sobriety of "commonsense reality" his understanding of the subject as mimetically constituted is post-Cartesian and so undermines the structure of a "commonsense" subject-object epistemology. Furthermore, he draws heavily on tradition for the justification of his theory and in this regard approaches the position of the hermeneutical philosophy of Gadamer.[4] Nevertheless, he believes that

---

the encipherment by the strategies of social being, the will to power, and the cunning of desire, respectively. Behind the representations of consciousness lurk the puppet masters of money, power, and sex. To these Girard adds violence, the summary term for all three.

[2] Heidegger (*Being and Time*, 70) reminds us that the root meaning of κατηγορεῖσθαι is "to make a public accusation," or "to take to task in the presence of everyone," and thus to let everyone see the Being of the categorized.

[3] On the idea of the hermeneutical circle see the classic passages in M. Heidegger, *Being and Time*, par. 63, 358–64.

[4] Hans-Georg Gadamer, *Truth and Method*.

there is sufficient stability in the subject-object model to allow for a reliable referentiality and a theoretical purchase on reality.

I cannot discuss at length the difficulty that the idea of the mimetically constituted subject raises for the commonsense notion of a stable subject observing a stable object. It is sufficient to accept that the subject and object in the commonsense scientific situation seem to be stable and that much of the evidence gained from such a situation is successful in enabling us to make scientific progress in dealing with nature and society. The mimetic nature of the subject makes no significant difference at this epistemic level.

Furthermore, the hermeneutical circle need not be interpreted radically as in the case of Heidegger and Gadamer. Epistemic circularity does not entail epistemological skepticism or ontological relativism. Natural scientists have long since accepted the theory-laden nature of evidence. Einstein is reported to have said to the young Heisenberg, "It is theory which decides what we can observe," a remark that set Heisenberg on the track that led to the theory of indeterminacy. Niels Bohr coined the term "complementarity" to describe the fact that terms like "wave" or "particle" are abstractions that do not exhaust the reality they designate and, therefore, that different theories can enable complementary rather than conflicting descriptions of the same reality under different circumstances.[5] However, and this is the point, despite this epistemological instability, quantum mechanics succeeds in giving us a purchase on nature. Therefore, it is not necessary to interpret the hermeneutical circle skeptically. The theory we bring to the evidence decides what we can observe, and then the observations decide what theory we can bring, and so on, in a cybernetic reciprocity that is, paradoxically, not self-contained, but related to reality beyond itself.

Scientific Realism and Structuration

I might illuminate the point further by a brief consideration of the debate between empiricists and scientific realists in the philosophy of science. I shall again take an example from the theoretical discussion in the field of international relations as a guide. In a discussion of the old problem of the relationship between the individual agent and the transindividual structure, Wendt argues that the proper balance between the two can best be struck in terms of scientific realism[6] rather than empiricism.

Scientific realism is the view that it is in principle proper to posit the existence of unobservables by "abductive" or "retroductive" inference from

---

[5] Richard Rhodes, *The Making of the Atom Bomb*, 130–33.

[6] Alexander E. Wendt, "The agent-structure problem in international relations theory," 335–70.

observables, if the posited entity can be seen to produce observable effects or if by using it we can intervene with effect in the observable world. Empiricism, on the other hand, holds that only what we can observe by sense-experience can be said to exist. In the field of scientific explanation realism identifies "underlying causal mechanisms which physically generated the phenomenon" while the nomothetic explanation of empiricism subsumes phenomena under some lawlike regularity.[7]

Using the realist permission to posit causal mechanisms and the obligation on social scientific practice to be critical, in the sense of looking for underlying causes, Wendt gives an account of the ontology of social structures that is formally the same as the account we have given of the Girardian generative mechanism. There are generative structures whose effects can be observed in the texts, and they must be searched for by means of a critical interpretive practice.

In terms of the distinction between the theoretical level of understanding and the subtheoretical level of analysis, scientific realism operates on the subtheoretical level. Its abduction of unobservable structures is equivalent to the proposal and testing of hypotheses and the formulation of laws. It is analytic rather than interpretive.

At the theoretical level Wendt classifies his procedure with the work of Anthony Giddens, Roy Bashkar, and Pierre Bourdieu. He calls it "structurationist," using the name coined by Giddens.[8] According to structurationism, social structures—that is, sets of internally related elements within a social organization, like agents and practices—are unobservables posited by individual agents. Therefore, unlike individualism on the one hand and structuralism on the other, structurationism sees structure and agent as mutually dependent. Structure does not exist apart from the agent that perceives and validates it, and the agent is controlled in significant ways by the structure that generates and guides his or her action.

In these terms, the Sacred is a posited structure that can be abduced from a range of observable phenomena by an agent who brings to the phenomena a preunderstanding generated by the theory of sacred violence. This is a circular procedure. Wendt faces the problem of circularity and solves it pragmatically. If the structure is posited on the basis of certain evidence from which it was abduced, the way to avoid vicious circularity is to bring other evidence for the structure from observation of different evidence. In the natural sciences one checks the postulate by working back from the phenomenon to a postulated causal mechanism and then forward again from the postulate to the

---

[7] Ibid., 352–53.

[8] See Anthony Giddens, *Central Problems of Social Theory,* and *The Constitution of Society.* Nigel Thrift ("On the Determination of Social Action") uses the term more generally to include the work of Pierre Bourdieu (*Outline of a Theory of Practice*), Roy Bhaskar (*The Possibility of Naturalism*), and Derek Layder (*Structure, Interaction, and Social Theory*).

phenomenon, within a closed experimental system. Closed experimental systems are harder to find in the social sciences, but bodies of text like the Pauline letters are relatively bounded fields within which a test might plausibly be conducted.

I have called this method of testing pragmatic. Girard, guided by his theory, posited the structures of sacred violence on the basis of certain evidence, and we hope to demonstrate that it can also be posited on the basis of other evidence, thus confirming not only the postulation but also the theory. Positing the causal mechanism of sacred violence is pragmatically justified when it convinces the reader that the interpretation is correct because of its conformity to the usual standards of scientific explanation, as well as its conformity to the reader's sense of reality.

The introduction of the reader's sense of reality means that I must include the subjective experience of recognition in the pragmatic criteria of a successful interpretation. An interpretation succeeds when the reader recognizes it as true both to his or her experience of the world and to the text's experience of its world. To borrow a metaphor from Gadamer, this occurs when the horizon of the reader's experience and the intentional horizon of the text coalesce. In the case of the Pauline narration of the Cross the coalescence takes place in terms of violence. The violence on the horizon of the text coalesces with the violence on the horizon of our times and causes us to recognize our selves in the text and the text in our times.

This brief account cannot do justice to Wendt's argument, but it does indicate that the scientific status of the theory of sacred violence is secure within the context of responsible debate in the philosophy of science. It remains to provide the pragmatic justification from the Pauline texts that will show the theory to be justified by its power to evoke recognition, in addition to the elegance of its internal logic.

Literary Precursors

Girard innovates not only in the field of social theory but also of literature. He is a poststructuralist in both these realms. We have seen how he takes structuralism to a new level of sophistication in anthropology; he does the same in the field of literature, from within the modern French tradition. Wallace Fowlie characterizes that tradition from Baudelaire to the present as a "climate of violence."[9] Beginning with Baudelaire's revolt against the oppressive

---

[9] Wallace Fowlie, *Climate of Violence*. Steiner, *Bluebeard's Castle*, 9–11, reminds us of the phenomenon of ennui named by Baudelaire and others, the longing for heroic action that was frustrated by bourgeois life. "Madness, death, are preferable to the interminable Sunday and suet of a bourgeois life-form." He quotes Theophile Gautier, *plutôt la barbarie que l'ennui*.

violence of the city, and Rimbaud and Lautreamont's celebration of the individual's violent reaction to the violence of society, Fowlie traces the struggle of the literary tradition to safeguard the individual in the face of the group.

The central drama in all this agony is the drama of the individual locked in a mimetic embrace with other individuals and striving to be free, to rise above the web of mimetic involvement into the pure air of solitude and integrity. The end of the line traced by Fowlie is Sartre's *Huis Clos,* which argues that we become what other people see us to be because of the nonessential nature of human being. For Sartre, to allow this to happen is to abdicate our freedom. Paradoxically, he holds that somehow, despite its lack of essence, the self has the power to constitute itself over against the others. Revolution is the supreme example of human freedom, the claiming of the right to invent one's own laws. There seems, however, to be no logical reason, on Sartre's premises, for this power of the self to constitute itself over against the others, unless it be something like the Nietzschean notion of the self as constituted by the will to power.[10]

Girard agrees that literature discloses the human condition, but he is less sanguine about the individual's ability to escape the coils of mimesis by sheer will power. In this he is "confronting"[11] the Nietzsche of Heidegger who argues that in the wake of the collapse of the Platonic Christian worldview, the only possible ground for values is the individual will understood as the power to transcend the self primarily by means of art. In taking literary art seriously, Girard is a postmodern, "post-Nietzschean" thinker; but he makes the opposite choice to Nietzsche, for the Bible and against the primitive Sacred. Nevertheless, in maintaining the mimetic construction of the self, he partakes of the postmodern skepticism about the independent subject and thus necessitates the move to the human sciences and the recognition that the self and its social context are mutually dependent. Therefore, the individual cannot escape from the group by the sheer power of decision. The way out of the coils of group mimesis has traditionally been not the Promethean will but the surrogate victim, and that social embeddedness of the subject still pertains. The only way out of the system of surrogate victimage is faith in response to grace.

Girard maintains the social location of the self, and lays bare the pathology of mimetic violence; but he is not a pessimist or orgiast of violence. He turns to Christianity for a solution to the problem, but not to the Platonic Christianity that has been more or less discredited. Rather he points to elements of the Augustinian tradition that also occur in the work of Claudel, Lacordaire, and Mauriac, and that posit the reality of only one love, the divine. The divine

---

[10] M. Heidegger, *Nietzsche 1.*

[11] This is the word Heidegger uses to describe his approach to Nietzsche. He also uses it to translate *polemos* in Heracleitus B53 and B80. He understands it to mean the lighting or clearing in which beings are present to one another and so can be distinguished from one another.

is the proper transcendental pole of mimesis by relation to whom mimesis is preserved from rivalry and violence. Love is nonviolent mimesis structured by the relation to the truly transcendent. According to the Girardian theory, love is the fundamental human impulse to imitation uncorrupted to violence by immanent mimetic rivalry. Love is a nonviolent mimesis.

Claudel is especially relevant in his description of the phenomenology of love. According to Claudel, since love is love of somebody else, one's true self is in that beloved other. "The real significance of a man's life is in someone else."[12] Love is the void in the self that calls out for the other to fill it, and only the divine other is equal to the task. The notion of love as transcendentally structured nonviolent mimesis is the Christian answer to the problem of the social constitution of the self by mimesis, the way out of perpetual violence and beyond the religion of sacrifice and all its intellectual analogues. The self does not have to be expelled from the group, or to expel itself, or to join the group in expelling someone else, in order to be the self; it can participate in the group by means of the nonviolent mimesis of love. There is no possibility of renouncing mimesis; the artists who scapegoat themselves by setting themselves over against the group merely serve the violence of the group. Only those who attempt to transform mimesis from within do not serve violence.

Postmodernism

Referentiality

Girard is classified as a poststructuralist or postmodern critic. Harari locates him "at the point where anthropology joins classical Greek tragedy . . . at the crossroads of the Derridean and Lévi-Straussian problematics," and says that his theory "maximizes referentiality."[13] The point at issue is referentiality, and there is both a similarity and a difference between Lévi-Strauss and Girard in this regard. For both the signs refer to a structure and to experience, but for Lévi-Strauss, in order to discover the structure "one has to first reject experience, if only to reintegrate it into an objective synthesis devoid of any sentimentality,"[14] while for Girard experience, in the sense of the common phenomena of human relations, is a guide to the structure. Lévi-Strauss's structure is the structure of thought abstracted from experience, while Girard's structure is posited on the basis of experience itself. The symbol of the difference between them is the fact that the former gives priority to myth and the latter to ritual in the theory of religion.

To include Girard among the poststructuralists as Harari does is clearly not to rank him with the postmodernists, because he maximizes referentiality.

---

[12] Fowlie, *Climate of Violence,* 148.
[13] Joshua V. Harari, "Critical Factions/Critical Fictions," 17–72, 56.
[14] Ibid., 21.

Nevertheless, his conception of referentiality is not a throwback but genuinely poststructuralist, and to some extent postmodernist. Since representation arises out of the victim, the crisis of representation in postmodernism is a sacrificial crisis caused by the unveiling of the role of the founding mechanism in the establishment of the categories of representation. Indeed, the term category comes from the Greek κατηγορεῖσθαι (to accuse), and the first act of representation was to accuse the victim by means of the double transference. Representation is accusation within the system of sacred violence; on the level of the text it is mythic misrepresentation. The desacralization of culture is also the deconstruction of sacrificial misrepresentation.

Deconstruction does not destroy the structures of meaning but merely removes from them their ontological underpinning, thus reducing the signifiers to counters in a game without necessary form.[15] By revealing that the structure undergirding signification is sacred violence, Girard in effect deconstructs the signifiers; nevertheless he insists on referentiality. This is not necessarily a contradiction, because he sees no immediate alternative to sacrificial structure, and so continues to work within it. The "good violence" of sacrificial order does make communication possible by holding the signifier and the signified together referentially. The therapeutic process must be a gradual modification of the order of violent referentiality as love replaces violence. In the meantime the present order of referentiality remains provisionally in place.

The crisis of our culture is more than a crisis of thought and representation, however; there were skeptics before Nietzsche. What is unprecedented about our time is unbounded violence, and that is more than a problem of representation; it is a problem of politics and public order. The epistemological status of political discourse is a relatively insignificant question besides the question of the ends of its rhetoric. That question belongs in the realm of ethics, which is not much better off than literature with respect to legitimation and justification. In such a situation one might be forgiven for attempting to revive the ethical function of literary interpretation as a cultural criticism that searches for the "underlying causal mechanisms" that the text might be hiding.

Gynesis[16]

According to the feminist critics, what the master text of Western culture hides is woman. Her absence has enabled that text to perpetuate the violence of univocal truth and absolute morals in the guise of patriarchal metaphor. To include woman in the text of the master narrative provides an element in the conversation that is "somehow intrinsic to new and necessary modes of

---

[15] Cf. Allan Megill's description of the deconstructed conceptual world as "a realm of aesthetic illusion and play" in *Prophets of Extremity,* 53.

[16] A. A. Jardine, *Gynesis.*

thinking, writing, speaking." Jardine calls the process of inclusion "gynesis," and describes it as "the transformation of woman and the feminine into verbs at the interior of those narratives that are today experiencing a crisis in legitimation." These "new and necessary modes" are not new texts or persons, but "a horizon, that toward which the process is tending: a *gynema*. This gynema is a reading effect, a woman-in-effect that is never stable and has no identity."[17]

In Girardian terms, gynesis is the inclusion of the victim. The "nonknowledge" that has eluded and engulfed most of the master narratives has been the suppression of the knowledge of their own generation by violence out of the surrogate victim, the killing and burial of their own violent fathers under the myth of patriarchy. To the extent that gynesis is the return of the victim, it is also the unmasking of mimetic violence, of the Titanic father who devours his children, and the opening up to new postsacrificial meaning. Jardine calls this struggle for communication in our time the struggle to find "new configurations of desire outside of the logic of substitution"[18]—that is, outside the order of sacrificial civilization. Gynesis is the antidote to mimesis.

There is always the danger of substituting one tyranny for another by "naturalizing" woman in the process of gynesis. Jardine suspects certain of the male postmodernists of doing this and so perpetuating the power of the patriarchal metaphor under the guise of woman. This false step has in fact been taken by much American feminist thought; that thought does not deconstruct the patriarchal narrative but rather proposes another narrative that, although it is about women, remains by virtue of its referentiality and ethical concern the same patriarchal narrative that it seeks to replace. The French modernists are more subtle but nonetheless vulnerable to this irony, in that they make too much of woman in the process of gynesis. "Perhaps the inflationary feminocentrism of gynesis . . . has been confronting the breakdown of the paternal metaphor with nothing less than catachresis—sometimes metaphor, sometimes metonymy, the only name for that which is unnamable—God—or, perhaps . . . Woman."[19] To fill the spaces in the master narrative with the feminine is to substitute one tyranny for another—in this case, to idolize woman.

Idolatry and Referentiality

The issue before us now is idolatry, an essential part of the problematic of violence and the primitive sacred. Every nondialectical identification of the object of transcendence is idolatrous and thus violent. The idol is the victim become god by the double transference of the Sacred; the problem is to welcome the return of the victim without idolization. This is precisely what

---

[17] Ibid., 25.
[18] Ibid., 39.
[19] Ibid., 39–40.

the Girardian hermeneutic achieves and in this regard is at one with Jardine's gynesis; but the return of the victim is more than a "reading-effect," it is a memory trace; it is the deconstruction of the patriarchal master text by the remembrance of suppressed sacrificial violence.

Because of the restoration of this memory by the disclosure of sacred violence, we are able to deconstruct its structure by withholding willing cooperation from its violence while we try to replace it with love. In the mean time the structure remains in place because good violence is better than chaos. Taken in this sense the feminism that postmodernism accuses of replacing the patriarchal metaphor with a metaphor that is essentially the same because of its referentiality and ethical concern is justifiable as an attempt to work within the only structure there is, to modify it gradually by changing its dynamic from violence to love, from eros to agape. Thus sacred violence enables a non-idolatrous attitude to signification and referentiality by means of a dialectic that says both no and yes to the structure of good violence.

Susan Handelman argues that traditional Christian hermeneutics idolizes the referent, while rabbinic hermeneutics is anti-idolatrous because its openness to ongoing interpretation relativizes referentiality.[20] Since my inquiry has the debate between Christianity and Judaism so close to its center, we must pay attention to this claim. I shall argue that Handelman interprets the phenomena tendentiously, and that rabbinic interpretation is at least as susceptible to idolatry as the patristic interpretation she accuses. Furthermore, to make Freud, Lacan, Derrida, and Bloom representatives of the rabbinic mode of interpretation in our time is tendentious in the extreme, and to take patristic exegesis as the Christian pole of comparison is anachronistic. Clearly a more relevant pole of comparison for Augustine is the Talmud.

Handelman argues that these modern interpreters represent the rabbinic mode that remains bound to the text by commentary, over against the Greco-Christian mode of referentiality that seeks one general truth in the text that, when found, makes the text obsolete. For Plato the word is only a name, and a name is a vocal imitation of an object; persons are said to name a thing when they imitate it with their voices. The object or idea to which the text refers is the important thing, not the text itself. The truth of a text lies outside the text in the realm of objects, and especially the universal ideas. The Christian counterpart to this view is to transcend the letter of the text in the power of the ultimate referent, the incarnation. As the presence of eternity within time, the incarnation breaks the temporal limits of linear language. "The Word became flesh"—that is, text became a living person. "The end of language is precisely this end of the sign 'stubbornly adhered to by the Jews,' now replaced by its referent, the incarnate divinity," writes Handelman of Augustine's theory of

---

[20] *The Slayers of Moses.*

language.[21] This end of language is also the end of desire, according to John Freccero, since desire and language are both founded on the absence of the object.[22]

The linear temporality of language constitutes the fundamental lack in the human access to knowledge. We are ever able to see only a part of the truth as it unfolds seriatim in language, and are therefore condemned to a perpetually synecdochic relation to reality. However, in the presence of the Spirit this handicap is overcome as the "letter which kills" is left behind, and the text, like John the Baptist, points away from itself to the one who must increase while it decreases. Thus the referent displaces the text.

The rabbinic attitude, on the contrary, "keeps faith with the poor exiled scapegoat, writing."[23] For the rabbis the word (*dabhar*) is more than just an imitation of an idea or object, but is a "thing" itself, and can never be transcended or dispensed with. The primary reality is linguistic; God speaks—that is, God creates texts—and the access to God is always in and through the texts, by means of the commentary. The text is the indispensable mediator of the divine. Scholem writes;

> As opposed to the idea of revelation as a specific communication, revelation which has as yet no specific meaning is that in the word which gives an infinite wealth of meaning. Itself without meaning, it is the very essence of interpretability. For mystical theology, this is a decisive criterion of revelation.[24]

There are two characteristics of the rabbinic method, according to Scholem, and the way he expounds them links Freud, Lacan, Derrida and Bloom; (1) "truth must be laid bare in a text in which it already exists; (2) not system but commentary is the legitimate form through which truth is apprehended."[25]

The depth of meaning in the text, its dark fecundity, suggests the image of a cave. Bloom, who is especially indebted to Scholem, writes that the god of the poets is not Apollo but "the bald gnome Error, who lives in the back of a cave." Alluding to the allegory of the prisoners in the seventh book of the *Republic* he says that knowledge comes not from the light at the mouth of the cave but from the darkness at the back. In a vivid image, Handelman compares Bloom to "a kind of Judas Maccabaeus of criticism, coming forth from the caves to cleanse the defiled Temple (of literature) of its Hellenist conquerors."[26]

The image of the defiled temple poignantly reminds us of the Jew's situation of exile and links the theoretical with the historical. The rabbinic interpretation

---

[21] Ibid., 119. She should, of course, have written "incarnated divinity" because now interpretation points to the resurrected, spiritual, once incarnated, not (still) incarnate Christ.

[22] John Freccero, "The Fig Tree and the Laurel," (cited by Handelman, 119).

[23] Handelman, *Slayers of Moses*, 171.

[24] "Revelation and Tradition," *Diogenes* 80, 164–94 (cited by Handelman, 205).

[25] Handelman, *Slayers of Moses*, 203.

[26] Ibid., 193.

is an interpretation from the point of view of exile. After the destruction of the temple in 70 C.E., the rabbis were expelled from the sacred center, taking with them only their texts. The texts replaced the temple as the locus of meaning; but it was a fragmentary meaning. Meaning lies in ruins with the temple, and there can be no return to the sacred presence. Fragmentariness entails that there can be many equally valid interpretations of meaning; no one true meaning; only the seemingly endless variety and interaction of commentary.

Therefore the Christian idea of the incarnation as the one locus of meaning, the early Christian identification of Christ as the new temple, and the Christian community as the locus of the divine presence, is idolatrous. Since God has turned away the divine face, the believer must be content to wander in the wilderness of broken meaning. Christians, on the other hand, succumb to "the worship of reified signs" of the presence of meaning, which in truth points to "an absence or a signification yet to come." Idolatry is precisely such an attempt to "render presence . . . to evade the temporality inherent in the human condition by reifying signs and thereby externalizing significance in the here and now."[27]

The rabbinic transference of the significance of the temple to their own texts is not idolatrous, however, because the texts are always open to interpretation. The rabbis substituted remembrance and not repetition for the reality of the temple. The contrast of remembrance and repetition comes from Freud. Freud made the murder of the father the constituent factor of the human psyche. He began by identifying the murdered father as the Greek King Laius, who represented the gentile culture that Freud could not enter because of "the stain" of his Jewish birth, and ended by unmasking the more primordial Jewish murder of Moses. These parricides were misrepresentations of Freud's own unconscious parricide of the father that had "stained" him with Jewishness at birth.[28] The strange interpretation of dreams, by which he arrives at these farfetched conclusions, is another form of rabbinic commentary, both part of and a departure from the tradition; it is a "heretic hermeneutic" that both acknowledges and kills the father.

For Bloom the tradition is an "anxiety of influence," which the poet must suffer and overcome, by avoiding repetition. Freud translated repetition into remembrance, calling repetition the regressive death instinct. After the destruction of the temple the rabbis remembered the temple by studying and commenting on the texts that described its ritual; they did not attempt to repeat the ritual at some other place; remembrance rather than repetition replaced the temple for the rabbis, while repetition rather than remembrance replaced it for the Christians.

---

[27] Yehezkel Kaufman as presented by John Freccero, in Handelman, 117. Freccero calls idolatry "the reification of a sign in an attempt to create poetic presence."

[28] Handelman, 135, citing Marthe Robert, *From Oedipus to Moses, Freud's Jewish Identity.*

This is the nub of Handelman's accusation of idolatry against patristic exegesis and her exoneration of the rabbinic. In criticizing her I recognize that her purpose was not so much to accuse patristic exegesis as to identify her modern interpreters as standing within a Jewish tradition. The Jewish tradition in which they stand is, in fact, the mystical tradition mined so effectively by Scholem rather than the tradition of the Mishnah and Talmud. For the rabbis of the Mishnah, the text and its readers became the locus of the divine presence, the new temple. They expressed this by transferring the rules of purity that governed the ritual conduct of the priests in the temple to the conduct of observant Jews in their study of Torah and the conduct of their domestic life. This transference was underway before the destruction of Jerusalem, in the second temple circles of the Pharisees, where the rules of purity and the questions of group membership were of vital concern.[29] These interests became a major issue at stake between the early Christians and their Jewish counterparts, but the issue here is the extent to which in both Jewish and Christian circles sacred violence reasserted itself in the form of the idolization of the referent.

Handelman's account of the Christian hermeneutic needs to be modified because it reads the Christian position too much in terms of Greek philosophy. What may be a just account of Augustine's Neoplatonist hermeneutic is not just for Paul and most of the rest of the New Testament. She treats the incarnation as if it were the primitive Sacred, but the incarnation is conditioned by the crucifixion and that makes Jesuolatry impossible. In Christian thought the Cross is never simply annulled by the resurrection. The elusive nature of the resurrection narratives in the Gospels, and the Pauline insistence that it is only a foretaste of an as yet unfulfilled eschatological promise, prevent us from idolizing the incarnation. The Christian hermeneutic sees the sign of Cross and resurrection pointing forward to eschatological fulfillment in the resurrection of the dead beyond history. As Paul says: "For in this hope we have been saved. Now hope that is seen is not hope. For who hopes for what he sees? But if we hope for what we do not see, we wait for it with patience" (Rom 8:24-25, RSV). The incarnation is the coming of the one who was rejected: "He came to his own home and his own people received him not" (John 1:12, RSV). The Cross is the divine presence-in-absence, the dialectical overcoming of the structure of sacred violence that suffers violence nonviolently, while leaving the violent structure intact until the eschaton.

An eschatologically conditioned Christian hermeneutic begins with the crucified sign, the broken body, the ruined temple (John 2:21-22), the absence of the Lord. "So we are always of good courage; we know that while we are at home in the body we are away from the Lord, for we walk by faith and not by sight" (2 Cor 5:6). We are not at home in the body (neither in the

---

[29] Jacob Neusner, *Judaism.*

text nor in the idea); the text and the system are precisely places of presence-in-absence, and that is why they must be interpreted by faith, "the hidden presence [hypostasis = that which stands beneath the surface] of things hoped for, the evidence of things not seen" (Heb 11:1). It requires courage to interpret faithfully in the dark; courage to resist the temptation to abandon hope and embrace the gnome of darkness, and the temptation to idolize the text as allegedly inexhaustible. There is a limit to textual fecundity as there is a limit to everything human. Only the divine is inexhaustible, and to confuse the two is the essence of idolatry.

The proper response to the absence of the Lord (meaning) symbolized by the destruction of the temple and the crucifixion of Christ is not an alliance with underground error in a conspiracy of misprision, but the hopeful construction of hypotheses, based on the memory of past experience (faith) and the anticipation of the future vindication of the hypothesis by experience (hope). Thus the status of the Girardian proposal as a theory that produces hypotheses corresponds formally to the biblical hermeneutic of faith and hope, and escapes the violent and willful assertiveness of subterranean error. It does not make a virtue of necessity by idolizing blindness, and taking the human condition of limit as a license for misprision. It risks a construction in the spirit of scientific humility, which is also the spirit of Christian faith, hope, and love.

Finally, in the light of Borsch-Jacobsen's exposition[30] one may ask whether Freud can legitimately be classed among the father-slayers. He sacrifices the father on one level, only to have him return on another as the absolute subject who exists prior to sociality and makes the Oedipus complex work. Bloom, on the other hand, although he seems to smuggle the father back in the form of the idolized word, the mystical presence that is more imperious for being unlimited, nevertheless provides a classic instance of conflictual mimesis. His idolized word is not the father but the surrogate victim.

Bloom's wandering chthonic dwarf Error (*errare* = to wander) is the mimetic rivalry of interpretations in search of surrogate victim texts to misprize (sacrifice). No single interpretation can possess the text because of the violence of acquisitive mimesis, but at a point of intense mimetic crisis acquisitive mimesis becomes conflictual and the interpreters agree to kill what they cannot possess. Every interpretation under the guidance of error is a sacrifice of the text to the pretence of interpretation, a mode of the double transference that disguises its hunger for victims as the perpetual openness of the text to interpretation. Thus the same text can be sacrificed again and again, and the unanimity of the mob of error renewed under the flag of freedom. This misprision seems, therefore, to persecute the "poor scapegoated text" more assiduously than Christian interpretation under the guidance of the Spirit.

---

[30] See Appendix I.

The Christian hermeneutic of the Cross has really gone into exile beyond the sacrificial mechanism, to renunciation of violence in the shadow of the ruined temple of Christ's broken body. In faith and hope, and the eschatological incompleteness of love, the Christian hermeneutic is open to the other as the bearer of a fragmentary meaning in this world, and to the great Other of the kingdom of God.

The Hermeneutics of Liberation

Both feminism and Marxism are theories in the service of the liberation of the oppressed. They maximize referentiality. Girard's hermeneutic has been judged by some to be hostile to both these approaches. Hayden White sees Girard continuing the legitimist tradition of De Maistre and De Bonald, arguing in reaction against everything modern, "individualism, democracy, rationalism, naturalism, humanism, progress, enlightenment, and so on."[31] Girard justifies religion on the basis of science, representing, in effect, the antithesis of Marxism. Toril Moi claims that Girard's theory of mimetic desire cannot account for female desire, because it leaves the mother out of the Oedipal triangle.[32] Borch-Jacobsen, however, has shown why the Oedipus complex cannot explain the facts,[33] White's criticism, if ever it was on target, is now quite out of date in the light of Girard's subsequent publications. There are interesting points of convergence and divergence, however, between Girard and representative feminist and Marxist interpreters, which demonstrate how his theory responds to the same needs that they identify.

Feminism

I take biblical interpreters as representative of the feminist hermeneutic. This, I realize, restricts the focus to what may be the least sophisticated ex-

---

[31] Hayden White, "Ethnological 'Lie' and Mythical 'Truth.'" In this review, White, however, seems to miss the point of Girard's view of religion. In describing religion as essential to the order of society, Girard endorses it only provisionally, faute de mieux. Religion has prevented humankind from confronting the truth about its violence. The sacrificial crisis of modernism is, therefore, a good thing, because it unmasks the deceit of religion; we can no longer deal with violence by means of ritual and myth. Girard, far from being a defender of religion as usual, is a severe critic of it. White's misunderstanding is representative of a class of misapprehension of Girard's position as actually advocating the sacrificial solution to the problem of violence; nothing could be further from his intention.

[32] Toril Moi, "The Missing Mother." Moi claims that Girard's description of desire is inadequate because he never discusses the pre-Oedipal stage of experience in which the child is totally wrapped up in the mother, probably unaware of the father's existence. At this stage, she argues, nonmediated desire is formed, which then functions at the later Oedipal stage. This is a version of the instinct/libido theory of desire; it is not pertinent to the description of mimetic desire, because Girard does not deny that there are other forms of relationship.

[33] M. Borch-Jacobsen, *The Freudian Subject*. See Appendix I.

pression of feminist hermeneutics.[34] Nevertheless, these critics do represent the field of biblical studies, which is our chief interest, and they do provide an example of the link between feminist and Marxist theory. Mary Ann Tolbert, in an essay that sounds the key note of an edition of *Semeia*[35] devoted to feminist hermeneutics, makes the spurious objectivity of the dominant interpretations the first target of her criticism. This ploy is well known from liberation theology. "Thus," she concludes, "all hermeneutical perspectives are advocacy positions,"[36] a conclusion that shows the triumph of politics in literary theory.

There are, generally speaking, three feminist approaches to biblical interpretation. One joins liberation theology in arguing that within the Bible there is a prophetic tradition of liberation that forms a canon within the canon and proclaims the liberation of women along with the liberation of all the oppressed, whose side God takes against their oppressors. The prophetic call for the liberation of the oppressed is, for this position, the essence of biblical religion. The second approach seeks out the references in the text to women's action and identifies these references as remnant signs of a much greater presence whose traces have been partially erased by the patriarchal producers of the text. Tolbert calls this the "remnant option." A third approach turns from the text to the historical context and seeks to reconstruct the role of women there. The status of the text is highly problematic on this (non)reading, because it is seen as itself the product of a deceiving patriarchal tradition that strove to conceal the action of women.

All these approaches listen for the faint notes and even the pregnant silences in the text. They pay attention to the gaps and aporiai; they are hermeneutics of suspicion. In this regard Girard's hermeneutic, which looks for signs of the concealed victim and clandestine violence, is comparable. In the case of the feminist hermeneutic, women are the scapegoats; their work and life is driven out, and the violence by which this is done is covered up. In the Girardian hermeneutic the victims include women along with other possible kinds of victim; that is, his range of suspicion is wider and less political than that of feminists; he looks for telltale signs of persecution as such, whoever the victims might be. In this regard he is close to Jardine in her objection to the "inflationary feminocentrism" that, in fact, is the idolization of woman. Girard's thought is, therefore, less political than feminism, although he will surely be accused of serving the interests of the male establishment by his insistence on the transpolitical status of his victims, on the assumption that the "default" position in a patriarchal culture is always chauvinist.

---

[34] *Feminist Studies* 14/1 (1988) is devoted to the problematic role of deconstruction in feminist studies. The problem is that if all reconstructions of the real are arbitrary, feminism as simply one more construction loses its political weight.

[35] Mary Ann Tolbert, "Defining the Problem."

[36] Ibid., 117.

With particular reference to the Bible, Girard says that its texts are texts in travail between myth and the gospel[37]—that is, between the concealment of violence and victimage, on the one hand, and their disclosure, on the other. This view is similar to the first two feminist approaches described by Tolbert, according to which some parts of the biblical text struggle against others for the prophetic message of liberation or the presentation of the remnant feminine presence. The struggle of these voices to come to word is not only a struggle about content but also about genre and style. There is a poetics of violence generating the text, and a competing poetics of love. The question between Girard and the feminists, therefore, is not what procedure should be followed—both are hermeneutics of suspicion that see beneath the surface of the text the generative power of violence—but simply whether to focus the eye of suspicion on the signs of the suppressed feminine alone, or whether to look for every telltale trace of the victim whose voice has been silenced by whatever violence might be operating.

So sacred violence is more inclusive than feminism, at least as the latter is represented by Tolbert. The two are, however, allies. Indeed, a telling feminist interpretation could be mounted on the Girardian foundation to unmask the violence of patriarchy as a transformation of the violence of acquisitive mimesis, and thus link patriarchy and capitalism as partner pathologies.

Marxism

I take Frederic Jameson as a representative of this mode of interpretation.[38] There is a formal similarity between Jameson and Girard. In a review of Jameson's major work, Hayden White explains that Jameson places a text within three concentric frames of interpretation, which function as "distinct semantic horizons." They are (1) political history, (2) the relevant social context, and (3) "history now conceived in its vastest sense of the sequence of modes of production and the succession and destiny of various social formations, from prehistoric life to whatever far future history has in store for us."[39]

The machinery of this last stage "is comprised of nothing more consequent than Desire in conflict with Necessity." Texts must be read within these three "semantic horizons." In order to understand a text one must know its mode of production; in other words, its causality.

Jameson begins with the assumption that there is nothing human that is not social and historical, and that "in the last analysis" everything is political.[40]

---

[37] *Violent Origins,* 145: "We are in a place between the full revelation of the scapegoat and the totally mythical. In history, we are always between the gospel and myth."

[38] Frederic Jameson, *The Political Unconscious.*

[39] Hayden White, "Getting out of History," 2–13.

[40] Jameson, *Political Unconscious,* 20.

This insight entails in turn that "totalizing" thought is necessary and prior.[41] That brings up the question of how the influence of the whole on its parts is to be understood. Althusser attacks the problem by presenting three historical forms of causality ("effectivity" in his jargon), two from traditional philosophy and one Marxist. (1) The mechanistic system in which causality was a direct, transitive effectivity of the whole on its parts (Descartes); (2) the Leibnitzian-Hegelian concept of "expression" according to which the whole can in principle be reduced to an inner essence, which is then expressed phenomenally in its parts; and (3) the Marxist concept of *Darstellung* according to which the whole is immanent in the parts, and the parts imbedded in the whole.

The problem of causality in this regard is the problem of understanding how the various levels of significance are related to each other—how, for instance, in the case of Marxist criticism, the fundamental level of the means of production is to be thought of at the less foundational levels of culture, ideology, law, and politics. The relationships between these various substructures and superstructures, both on a vertical and a horizontal axis, is called "mediation." Marxism sees mediation as a way of overcoming the fragmentation of culture in bourgeois society by discovering the whole present in the superficially different parts. Althusser criticizes as too facile the usual Marxist form of mediation by means of "expressive causality" (2 above), arguing for a truly dialectical relation in which both the difference and the sameness in homology is taken seriously and easy immediacies avoided.

The whole that lies beneath and within the parts is a master code comparable to the middle-Platonic master code in terms of which the semantics of the biblical text were recast by patristic allegorical exegesis. The ascent of the soul to the good, and the struggle between the virtues and the vices, was the content of that master code. The threefold interpretive framework within which Jameson works is analogous to this allegorical master code in that it too demands a philosophy—a philosophy of history—as the matrix of meaning. In the Middle Ages the Christian philosophy of history, expressed definitively by Augustine in the *City of God,* replaced the middle-Platonist content of the allegorical code with "sacred history" and produced the fourfold meaning of Scripture. The literal level concerns the historical experience of the people of Israel, the allegorical level the reduction of that history to the history of one individual—namely Christ, the tropological level provides the opportunity for readers to insert themselves in the text—by asking for the moral implication, and the anagogical level returns the interpretation to history, to the destiny of the whole human race in the eschatological vision of the fulfillment of the creation. This medieval scheme of interpretation is, therefore, like Marxist interpretation in that it is a hermeneutic governed by a philosophy of history.

---

[41] Ibid., 21.

Jameson, as we have seen, has three stages to his hermeneutic, three semantic horizons, in which to place the text. Within the innermost horizon, the object of interpretation is the literary text itself, understood as a symbolic act, intended to resolve contradictions in the next horizon. This next horizon is the horizon of society containing the "great collective and class discourses of which a text is little more than an individual parole or utterance."[42] The object of interpretation here is no longer the text but the "ideologeme"— "that is, the smallest intelligible unit of the essentially antagonistic collective discourse of social classes."[43] The third and widest horizon is that of human history as a whole. Within this context the texts and ideologemes of the two narrower horizons must be read in terms of "the ideology of form, that is, the symbolic messages transmitted to us by the co-existence of various signs systems which are themselves traces or anticipations of modes of production."[44] This final horizon is not "some common-sense external reality . . . but rather must itself always be (re)constructed after the fact."[45] It has the nature of a subtext for the narrower horizons, within which it is being rewritten and restructured.

Literature, therefore, maintains its contact with the real, with the raw material of history, actively, by drawing that material into its own enterprise, not passively, by simply allowing reality to persist inertly in its own being. The real is an "intrinsic and immanent subtext of language."[46]

The Girardian structure of sacred violence is comparable to Jameson's schema. The Sacred corresponds to Jameson's largest frame; it generates the other two frames and is for them a subtext that has to be reconstructed after the fact. It differs from Jameson's frame in not being the result of the means of production in society, but of the more foundational climax of mimetic violence. It lies at the point of hominization rather than at the subsequent point of organization for production. Jameson's second frame corresponds to the emergence of prohibition, ritual, and myth through the double transference (producing not ideologemes but mythologemes), and his smallest frame corresponds to the thematic level of the text on which the mechanisms might be revealed or concealed.

Thus we have two modes of interpretation with which the Girardian hermeneutic is formally comparable. Neither of the three has been unaffected by the epistemological collapse of postmodernism, but they all, nevertheless, like Girard's sacred violence, maintain a certain confidence in representation and referentiality.

---

[42] Ibid., 76.
[43] Ibid.
[44] Ibid.
[45] Ibid., 81.
[46] Ibid.

Sacred Violence as a Theory and
Method of Interpretation

I call the theory sacred violence; it can be schematized by semantic horizons or levels. Girard distinguishes two levels of meaning in a text, the generative and the thematic. The founding mechanism works at the generative level to structure the semantics of the thematic level, while the thematic level can either reveal or conceal this operation. Myth at the thematic level conceals the mechanism, while gospel reveals it. The terms "myth" and "gospel" are thus defined by Girard in terms of the relation of the text to the founding mechanism, as either concealing or revealing its presence.[47] Girard, like Jameson, sees a text, therefore, as the product of the culture in which it arises, rather than the creation of the solitary genius of its author.

The term "thematic" includes within its range more than just what the folklorist calls themes; it includes, in principle, the logic, style, and genre of the text as well. I shall not, in what follows, analyze these formal aspects of the thematic but, since the theory is essentially about human relations, concentrate on the structures of those relations as they are mediated by the themes and generated by sacred violence. My purpose is to show the generative presence of sacred violence behind the themes of the Pauline text.

Within Jameson's widest horizon, where Marxism demands a philosophy of history, Girard proposes something more modest—namely, a theory and a method. To be sure, the theory is a subtext of the kind that Jameson sees his own macrohorizon to be, a text that has to be composed after the event on the basis of the glimpses of the real that one gets in the interstices of the ideologemes and texts within the other two horizons. In this sense it is derived from the posited nonobservables of scientific realism. Nevertheless, as a theory it remains part of the eschatologically oriented hermeneutic of the New Testament, oriented to the transcendent ground of truth, anti-idolatrous because open to future verification and falsification.

Sacred violence points to a religious mechanism; the surrogate victim, not the means of production, is the fundamental organizing power. The gospel reveals the founding mechanism decisively; the Bible is the critical text. Thus Girard points us to a possible restatement of biblical faith that places it at the center of the struggle for a culture beyond violence. This possibility demands to be taken seriously, for the sake of the Bible and the culture. I intend now to take up the challenge and the promise, by showing on the basis of the Pauline texts how the Bible, while still a text in travail between myth and gospel, nevertheless reveals the founding mechanism with extraordinary frankness and

---

[47] This is not an exhaustive description of gospel, however, which includes, along with this negative and disclosive function, the positive and revelatory function of modeling agape love and calling forth faith in response to grace.

so speaks a clear word of criticism and hope to our time of limitless violence. I call this application of the theory of sacred violence a hermeneutic of the Cross.

The Interpretation of Paul

For Paul, Judaism is both the sacrificial structure par excellence and essential for the development of God's plan of salvation. The Jews serve the cause of salvation by rejecting Christ. Paul does not seek to eliminate the Jews, but accepts that they must persist until the eschaton. To accept this negative presence is to accept the negation that deconstructs the idols, especially the idol of Christian certitude. The Jewish rejection of Christ puts the Christian claims in sufficient doubt to prevent them from becoming a metaphysics of presence. It helps to keep faith faith and not knowledge, and preserves the dependency of the creature on the creator.

I intend to begin a rethinking of Christianity from the point of view of the divine determinative negation in the Cross of Christ. The Cross is not a sacrificial mechanism but the deconstruction of sacrifice. Its symbolic significance must be elaborated on the basis of its historical content, not on the basis of an ideology of sacrifice. Its historical content is the shameful death of an innocent young man through an act of violence on the part of the established order. It is a deconstruction rather than a destruction, because it leaves the sacrificial structures in place while exposing them for what they are and thereby enabling us to withdraw credibility and allegiance from them. It is a dialectical overcoming of sacrifice, which supersedes it while leaving it intact. This is the sense of the Pauline freedom from the law and the principalities and powers; they have no more dominion over the Christian, because faith disengages from them by metaphorically and morally dying with Christ.

Life toward death is authentic existence because it is not based on the commonsense public world.[48] "I am not what I am, and I am what I am not"[49] expresses well the eschatological orientation of Christian existence. The Christian exists in the authentic temporality that appropriates the past in faith, the future in hope, and the present in love. When Paul says that he has died with Christ, but he lives, yet not he, Christ lives in him (Gal 2:19), he brings to word the authentic freedom of Christian existence as one that has internalized the violence of the sacrificial structures and moved beyond them in mimetic fellowship with the crucified and in resurrection hope. The mimesis of violence

---

[48] The application of Heideggerian concepts to the interpretation of Paul, well known in the work of Bultmann, has its ground in the now acknowledged influence of Paul on the early Heidegger. See Megill, *Prophets of Extremity,* 373, n. 31.

[49] This is the recurrent theme of J.-P. Sartre's *Being and Nothingness,* by which he means that, although the self is constituted by its past, it is not bound to the past but exists as freely projecting itself into the future. In this sense desire is the essence of existential futurity.

has become a mimesis of faith, hope, and love, the three temporal ecstasies of Christian existence. This existence lives the deconstruction of the icons that replaces the metaphysics of presence with the metaphysics of faith.

Paul experienced a "loss of world" in his conversion.[50] This was more than a mystical experience; Paul does not, as Nietzsche avers, make a neurotic delusion the cornerstone of a new mythic system. Rather he achieved an insight into the mendacity of religious power that is well described as a "renewing of the mind" (Rom 12:2). He saw that religion is the original structure of sacred violence, and therefore that all criticism must begin with the criticism of religion. Paul understood this before Marx, and the prophets of Israel understood it before them both. Paul stands in this prophetic tradition of Israel and mediates its critical rationality to the world.

There is of course a long history of the interpretation of Paul, most of it a methodological hybrid of history and ideology. E. P. Sanders has inaugurated a new era in the historical study of Paul, exposing the bad faith of the hybridizers and grasping the nettle of Paul's theology.[51] While we differ from him on essential points of interpretation (I do not, for instance, consider Paul's Christian position to be a pattern of religiosity, and I make more of the element of rejection in Paul's break with Judaism), I believe he is essentially correct in seeing Paul's Christian experience as a transfer from one community and frame of reference to another. Paul does move out of Judaism definitively and deliberately, he does describe the experience of conversion by means of "transfer terms," and he does find the source of his new understanding of self and world in the life of the Christian community, which he calls "the Spirit."

One of the perennial problems is to determine the "center" of Paul's theology. Questioners usually assume that they can discover by disinterested investigation what the apostle himself considered of fundamental importance and found an interpretation on that. The fact that there has been no agreed answer to the question after many attempts should have warned us long ago of the inescapable hermeneutical circle. Those who deny the circle are condemned to circle endlessly, *impii semper in circulis ambulandi!*

The preunderstanding we bring to the text is well founded on the evidence not only of the texts it interprets but also on other evidence from the human sciences. Furthermore, there is good recent precedent for this procedure in the attempt by Gerd Theissen to interpret Paul by means of psychological templates. He identifies his application of a threefold psychological template made up of learning theory, psychodynamics, and cognitive psychology as a "hermeneutically oriented psychology in the tradition of Dilthey's '*Ideen.*' "[52] My

---

[50] J. L. Martyn makes this point with great effectiveness in several of his recent articles: "Apocalyptic Antinomies in Paul's Letter to the Galatians," and "Paul and his Jewish-Christian Interpreters."

[51] E. P. Sanders, *Paul and Palestinian Judaism.*

[52] Gerd Theissen, *Psychological Aspects of Pauline Theology,* 2.

template of sacred violence is single and therefore commits me to a more risky course than Theissen's, but by the same token it produces a more trenchant, less tentative result.

The signs traced by desire, violence, sacrifice, and mythology, and the institutions of religion, state, and judiciary that they construct, delineate the common horizon of text and interpreter. The text reveals the founding mechanism that generates these things and attempts to conceal its own working. It questions us as we question it, in a conversation of mutual incrimination and comfort. We are disturbed by its attack on the Jews, it is disturbed by our hypocritical denial of any ill will against anybody. We find its belief in the imminent end of the world ludicrous, it finds our assurance that the present world will endure naive. We find its hope for the universal community unrealistic, it finds our contentment with imperfection lazy. And always it holds before our reluctant eyes the Cross of that young man, while we bow to the gilded crucifix and cover our conscience with the hood of the academic "method."

I wish now to allow the Cross to search us and our times as we search it and its texts. The hermeneutical circle that holds us to the Cross has become a conspiracy of silence, and the historical method a conjuration of the critically immune. I wish to break the silence and to renounce immunity, to allow ourselves and our times to be prosecuted by the victim rather than pacified by the inquisitor.

3

Sacred Violence and the Cross

The Death of Christ as an Epiphany of Violence

... Thou dost stone my heart
And makest me call what I intend to do,
A murder, which I thought a sacrifice.
Othello, Act 5, Scene 2

The death of Christ was for Paul an epiphany of sacred violence. As a result of the experience we call his conversion, he realized that his kind of religious observance was a service of the primitive Sacred within a system of sacred violence. This understanding emerged from within Paul's own experience and should therefore not be generalized to all the Judaism of that time. Furthermore, although he often speaks as if the experience of violence through the Law invalidates it altogether, he nevertheless affirms the basic intention of the Law, which he understands as the prohibition of mimetic rivalry and love to God and the neighbor. Therefore, his controversy with Judaism is a hermeneutical controversy about the proper interpretation of the Law, and Paul's main principle of interpretation is the Cross of Christ.

Although the crucifixion was actually carried out by the Romans, Paul saw it as the work of the Mosaic Law in its role as an instrument of the primitive Sacred operating through the sacrificial system. Therefore, we need not enter deeply into the historical question of who was responsible for the death of Jesus, the Romans or the Jews, because we are concerned with Paul's perceptions of that history and not the perceptions of modern historiography.

Jews and Romans and the
Death of Jesus

Some recent scholarship has accused Paul of misunderstanding and even deliberately misrepresenting Judaism,[1] making him a charlatan who launched an
unprincipled attack on a religion he hated. This accusation is part of a larger
trend that sees the New Testament on the whole to be an anti-Jewish docu-
ment that maliciously makes the Jews responsible for the death of Jesus when
in fact the Romans were.

The arguments that would make the Romans alone responsible for the death
of Christ and view the Gospel accounts of the involvement of the Jews as the
invention of anti-Jewish malice,[2] seem to be for the most part ideological
distortions. It is intrinsically improbable that the Jewish establishment had
nothing to do with the death, since there is evidence from non-Gospel sources
like Josephus for Jewish collaboration with the Roman power, and for zealous
Jewish persecution of those who did not observe the Mosaic Law according to
the interpretation they favored. Finally, and for our purpose most importantly,
there is the firsthand evidence of the Jew Saul of Tarsus that the followers
of Jesus were persecuted in the same way as their master. There is, therefore,
ample evidence for religious violence on the part of the Judaism of that time,
which one cannot avoid, except by the desperate expedient of condemning the
priestly establishment of Jerusalem as anti-Jewish, denying that the zealous
element was truly Jewish, and discrediting Paul's experience altogether.

Maccoby has recently tried to do precisely this with remarkable consistency
and ingenuity, arguing that Paul was an adventurer who found employment
in the private army that the collaborator high priest maintained to terrorize
his nationalist enemies.[3] The high priest was for the most part an ignorant
thug and the employer of ignorant thugs, eager especially to eradicate the
true, humane, and enlightened Pharisaic Jews. Paul, originally a high priestly
enforcer and not a learned Pharisee, concocted his Pharisaic background to
further his second career as a religious charlatan. Neither he nor the high
priest knew anything about true Judaism.

The texts do not support this radical reconstruction, but this much must
be said for Maccoby: he has the courage of his concoctions. He sees that once
embarked on the argument that the New Testament is anti-Jewish, one cannot
stop short of the claim that Paul is thoroughly disingenuous and that his case
against Judaism is a fraud. This refreshingly candid, if utterly preposterous,
argument is better than much current Christian scholarship that fails to take
seriously Paul's attack on Judaism, and Judaism's attack on Paul. This much

---

[1] H. Räisänen, *Paul and the Law.*

[2] Cf. Burton Mack, *A Myth of Innocence.*

[3] Hyam Maccoby, *The Mythmaker.*

is clear from an attack like Maccoby's: there was a mighty collision between Judaism and Pauline Christianity. That collision, I shall argue, takes place at the point of the Cross, which is rightly interpreted by Paul as an epiphany of the violence of the primitive Sacred in Judaism.

In order to maintain this, one need not hold that all Judaism at that time was violent in this way, nor that it was without its own antidotes to sacred violence, but only that the Cross and the experience of Paul are authentic disclosures of the sacred violence that was indeed present, and thus enable us to see the working of the mechanism of the Sacred in this particular religious system.

The Cross as a Metonymy of the Gospel

Although he can speak of the death of Christ without referring to the Cross (e.g., Rom 5:6ff.; 6:3ff.), Paul's characteristic references make the Cross a symbol of the whole gospel. It is a symbol of the saving power of the death of Christ, a metonymy of the gospel. The metonymy presents the gospel under two aspects: as given by God and as received by us.

As given by God, the gospel is the benefits of the work of Christ, and the Cross is a summary symbol of these benefits.[4] The phrase "Cross of Christ"(σταυρὸς χριστοῦ) describes the power of the gospel that can be drained away if it is proclaimed as a human wisdom (1 Cor 1:17). This power opposes those who base their conduct on the principles of greed and rivalry (Phil 3:18), and who boast in the privilege of Jewish exclusiveness (Gal 6:12, 14). We may also include in this metonymic category the texts that identify Jesus as "the crucified" (1 Cor 1:23; 2:2; Gal 3:1), as well as some of the texts that use the verb σταυροῦν. The fact that Christ was crucified for us is the basis of the Christian community (1 Cor 1:13). The fact that the powers crucified him exposed their reign of violence (1 Cor 2:8). Philippians 2:8 is especially noteworthy because it interprets the Cross as the symbol of the non-acquisitiveness of Christ, his willingness to give up even the divine equality rather than to grasp it possessively. Paul recommends this nonacquisitiveness as the moral pattern for life in the community (cf. 2 Cor 13:4; Gal 5:24). Thus the Cross stands for the power of the gospel that comes from beyond the structures of the Sacred formed by acquisitive and conflictual mimesis.

To receive the gospel is to be "crucified with Christ" (Χριστῷ συνεσταύρωμαι—Gal 2:19; Rom 6:6), that is, to identify mimetically with the crucified. This suggests that Paul's conversion was an experience in which the fact of the crucifixion was of determinative importance. He understood the

---

[4] Cf. H. Weder, *Das Kreuz Jesu bei Paulus.*

sacred violence of Judaism suddenly in the experience that we, not inappropriately, call his conversion. This understanding deepened over time as he was persecuted by the Judaizers, but it was essentially complete at its inception.[5]

The references to the conversion emphasize the divine intervention, as if to say that an enemy of the gospel such as Paul could not have been changed by anything less. This intervention took the form of a vision (1 Cor 9:1; 15:8; Gal 1:15; 2 Cor 4:6), and there can be no doubt that Paul was a visionary. The accounts of the Damascus road incident in Acts (9:1-19; 22:6-16; 26:12-18), which record the communal memory of that event, also make the vision central to the action. Paul does not, however, make such an extraordinary experience the necessary cause of faith in Christ.

Vision is an extraordinary experience and the validity of the gospel does not depend on it. The validity of the gospel rests rather on the more general basis of its power to illumine the human condition and to convince the mind and will (Rom 12:1-3). It is the re-creation of the insight of prelapsarian Adam (2 Cor 4:6), the renewal of the reprobate mind "to discern the will of God, the good, the pleasing, and the perfect" (Rom 12:3; Phil 1:10; cf. Rom 1:28; 2:18; 14:22). Under normal circumstances one comes to faith as a result of the witness of scripture (Gal 3:6; 2 Cor 3:7; Rom 4), the testimony of preaching (Rom 10:14), rational insight (Rom 6:3,9; 7:1; 8:28) and experience (Gal 3:1-6).[6]

The Pauline gospel, therefore, is not the offer of the possibility of supernatural experiences, but the offer of the possibility of a renewal of the mind that enables one to see the truly important things. This renewal of the mind, I would argue, takes the form of an insight into the meaning of the Cross as the epiphany of sacred violence. For Paul this insight is summarized in Galatians 2:19, which we must now consider at some length.

"Through the law I died to the law so that I might live for God" (ἐγὼ γὰρ διὰ νόμου νόμῳ ἀπέθανον ἵνα θεῷ ζήσω) (Gal 2:19, cf. Rom 6:10-11; 7:4)

Although he does not generalize the visionary experience Paul does generalize the element of self-discovery expressed in the Lukan question from heaven, "Saul, Saul, why do you persecute me?" (Acts 9:4; 22:7; 26:14; cf. Gal 1:13, 23; 1 Cor 15:9). As a result of the vision Paul identified his persecuting violence as the work of the Mosaic Law in his life. The Law had created a way of life founded on sacred violence and the crucifixion of Christ is the logical outcome of such a way of life. Once Paul realized this he could only "die to the Law

---

[5] Against H. Räisänen, "Paul's Conversion and the Development of his View of the Law," 404–19.

[6] C. Dietzfelbinger, *Die Berufung des Paulus als Ursprung seiner Theologie,* 54.

in order that he might live for God."[7] He implies, therefore, that life devoted to the Law is not a life devoted to God.

It is significant that Paul says that it was the Law itself that caused his death to the Law. He does not say that it was the vision of Christ alone, but something that the vision revealed in the Law itself that caused his defection from it. This puts in question the interpretation that says that it was for positive rather than negative reasons that Paul left Judaism.[8] The positive aspect of the experience revealed the negative element in the Law, and so the two moments are fused together as two sides of the same coin.

In order to understand the force of this brief reference to his conversion, and how the negative and positive moments are fused in his experience, we must read it as part of a climax to the autobiographical account that begins at Galatians 1:11 and extends to 2:21, which Paul gives to establish his authority vis-à-vis Peter. The bedrock of that authority is a revelation of Christ (δι' ἀποκαλύψεως ᾽Ιησοῦ Χριστοῦ—Gal 1:12) that occurred to him amid an active persecution of the church. He had intended not merely to harass the church, but also to destroy it, in fulfillment of his Jewish "zeal" (Gal 1:13-14; 1 Cor 15:9). In the midst of this, God, who had chosen him from the womb, revealed his Son to him and commissioned him apostle to the gentiles (Gal 1:15-17). His commission was corroborated by the Jerusalem "pillars," Peter, James, and John (Gal 2:1-10). Paul embarked on a mission to invite gentiles into full fellowship with the God of Israel through faith in Jesus alone and without observance of the ritual laws.

The most revealing indications we have of what it was in the Law that disenchanted him come from the debate with Peter and the Judaizers in Antioch,[9] an account of which immediately precedes this statement (Gal 2:19). Paul accused Peter of making Christ the agent of sin by withdrawing from table fellowship with gentiles under pressure from Jewish Christian representatives of James and the Jerusalem church (Gal 2:14-21). He argues that he and Peter had been living as gentiles, ignoring the ritual laws of circumcision, Sabbath, and kashruth, because they believed that one is justified not by living in the Jewish way (= "works of Law") but by faith in the death and resurrection of Christ. To return to the Jewish way is tantamount to saying that Christ caused them to sin (Gal 2:17), because it was through faith in him that they had chosen to ignore the ritual laws in the first place. Paul refused to return because that would be to build up the wall of partition[10] that had been broken

---

[7] Dietzfelbinger (*Berufung,* 96) has essentially the same view of the impact of conversion, but he does not explain the nature of the "service of the curse" as the service of violence.

[8] E. P. Sanders, *Paul and Palestinian Judaism.*

[9] R. Hamerton-Kelly, "Sacred Violence and 'Works of Law.' "

[10] F. Hahn ("Das Gesetzesverständnis im Römer- und Galaterbrief ") points out that in Gal 2:18 Paul uses terminology reminiscent of the sayings of Jesus against the temple, specifically the terms καταλύω and οἰκοδομέω (cf. Mark 13:2; 14:58; 15:29; Matt 26:61; 27:40; Acts 6:14; John

down in his conversion. This experience of Jewish exclusiveness in Antioch challenged his commission as Apostle to the gentiles and caused him to invoke his conversion as a justification for it.

This account enables us to reconstruct Paul's reinterpretation of the Law in the light of the Cross. Through a double realization that the Law had been responsible for the death of Christ, and that the sharp distinction between Jews and gentiles expressed the same violence as had killed Christ, Paul had identified the Law and its community as a system of sacred violence and had left it to join the church. The shock of the double realization accounts for the vehemence with which he repudiates the Jewish way of life as "loss" (ζημία) and "garbage" (σκύβαλα) (Phil 3:7-8).[11] The revelation of Christ in the midst of his zealous fulfillment of the Law caused him to see what the Law really is and at that moment he died to its claims.

The compressed nature of his statements here might mislead if it is taken to mean that he no longer recognized any claim from the Law. He continues to acknowledge its basic intention to command love of God and the neighbor,[12] and so his death to the Law is, strictly speaking, a death to its ritually excluding aspects that undergird Jewish separatism, signified by his leaving the Jewish community.

"I have been crucified with Christ" (Χριστῷ συνεσταύρωμαι) (Gal 2:19)

The precise nature of Paul's identification with Christ remains unknown despite a long literature on the subject.[13] Practically it meant leaving the Jewish community and joining the church, a transfer that he describes as an identification with Christ in his death. In Romans 7:4 one dies to the Law "through (διά) the body of Christ," by membership in the church, which is metaphorically his body. To die with Christ is to move from one community to another, and since this is to leave the persecutors and identify with the victim, it can be called co-crucifixion. The discovery of the violence in the Law was the same as the discovery of the suffering of Christ in his afflicted community ("Saul, Saul why do you persecute me?"—Acts 9:4). To exclude the gentiles was to afflict the body of Christ.

2:19). The temple was the only place where there was an explicit system of exclusion in operation, and Josephus brings the "balustrade" (ὁ δρύφακτος), upon which the warning excluding gentiles was inscribed in Greek and Latin, into specific association with the zealot faction of John of Gischala (BJ 6.124–26; cf. 5.193–96) (cf. Eph 2:11-22).

[11] Dietzfelbinger, *Berufung,* 97.

[12] R. W. Thompson ("How is the Law Fulfilled in Us?") referring to Rom 8:4, 13:8-10, and Gal 5:13-16, argues that δικαίωμα refers primarily to the love of neighbor as the "just requirement" of the Law. Cf. P. Stuhlmacher, *Versöhnung, Gesetz, und Gerechtigkeit,* 188, n. 46.

[13] R. C. Tannehill, *Dying and Rising with Christ,* summarizes the possibilities.

The transfer from one community to another signals a change in the function of desire, because those who have entered the realm of Christ have "crucified the flesh with its passions and desires" (Gal 5:24). This warrants an interpretation in terms of mimetic theory. To leave the community of sacred violence is to refuse the unanimity of conflictual mimesis. As soon as one dissents, one becomes a victim oneself. Such dissent is tantamount to identifying with the victim, because the group of conflictual mimesis needs unanimity to function and can treat dissenters only as victims. Thus Paul is transformed from persecutor to persecuted (Gal 5:11), he is crucified with Christ.

Mimetic theory therefore provides a better framework for understanding "co-crucifixion" than vaguer terms like "mysticism" or "corporate personality." Paul mimed the renunciation of desire by Christ the victim and became the mimetic double not of the executioner but of the victim. Co-crucifixion, therefore, is the realization of the good mimesis that was forfeited in the original double transference. By mimetic identification with the victim, Paul broke free of the system of sacred violence and opened himself to the possibility of love in relationship with true transcendence, within the new community of non-acquisitive and nonconflictual agape love. This mimesis of Christ became the foundation of his understanding of Christian existence as structured by faith, hope, and love. The key to the structure of the Christian subject is the mimesis of the crucified Christ,[14] within the community of such nonacquisitive mimesis.

This mimesis is the presupposition of all that Paul writes about the nature of Christian existence as a living out of the nonviolent life of the divine victim in the world of sacred violence. The result of having died with Christ is: "I no longer live, but Christ lives in me, and the life I now live in the flesh, I live by faith in the son of God who loved me and gave himself for me" (Gal 2:20). To live by faith means to let the will of Christ replace one's own will, to be his slave, as Paul repeatedly says (Rom 1:1; Phil 1:1; 1 Cor 7:22), or, in mimetic terms, to let him be the mediator of nonacquisitive desire. Given that we are the slaves of desire in any case, the true mimesis is to let one's desire be shaped by the nonacquisitive divine desire as seen in the Cross, and thus be liberated from the realm of mimetic rivalry and sacred violence. This, in turn, takes the form of a new inclusive quality of communal life, free of scapegoating.

In the Sacred, mimesis takes place before the point of the surrogate victim is reached, whereas here mimesis is the mimesis of the surrogate victim himself. This entails a redefinition of the meaning of sacrificial terms, which in this case can be seen in the way Paul uses the idea of sacrificial substitution to support the understanding of community. In 2 Corinthians 5:14 he writes that if once we conclude that one has died as the representative of all, it follows that all have died. A normally sacrificial reading of this statement would be that once we

---

[14] R. G. Hamerton-Kelly, "A Girardian Reading of Paul."

conclude that one has died for all, then it follows that all no longer need to die; but in Paul's interpretation it means that all have died in the sense that all are now victims, and if all are victims, then none is a victim. Thus Paul describes a free mimesis of the victim (cf. 2 Cor 5:21, which must be interpreted in the same terms) rather than the automatic mechanism of sacrificial substitution, which separates the group from the victim.

The free mimesis takes the form of mutual representation. In terms of the Sacred, the many can represent the one and the one represent the many, precisely because of the fundamental structure of representation as it arose out of the surrogate victim and the double transference. All tropes in which the one stands for the many or vice versa (synecdoche/metonymy) or the one for the other (metaphor) are sacrificial. So there is no need to introduce speculations about mysticism (psychological explanations), or parallels from the history of religion (that merely extend the range of the *explicandum*) to explain the sense in which the Christian and Christ are identified. It takes place through a reconstitution of honest representation by a decoding of the double transference through mimesis of the nonacquisitive desire of the victim.

To mime the victim is to see the truth about oneself in the mirror of the victim, decoding the transference so that the representation appears as the representation of one's own mimetic rivalry and surrogate victimage. In this sense one can say that once we conclude that one has died representing all, then it follows that all have died, because they see in his death the effects of their mimetic rivalry and can therefore freely renounce it by choosing to mime the nonacquisitive desire of the victim, and thus "crucify the flesh with its passions and desires" (Gal 5:24). The Christian subject is, therefore, constituted mimetically within the community of the crucified, as Christ represents the community and the community represents Christ. They are reciprocally both synecdoche and metaphor of each other.

That is why the rite of entry into the community is a rite of identification with the crucified. Co-crucifixion (Rom 6:6) is part of an exposition of baptismal theology in terms of which baptism is an identification with Christ's death (σύμφυτοι γεγόναμεν τῷ ὁμοιώματι τοῦ θανατοῦ αὐτοῦ—Rom 6:5), burial (συνετάφημεν—vs. 4), and resurrection (συζήσομεν αὐτῷ—vs. 8). The passage from the world to the church mimes the passage from the present age of sacred violence to the eschatological future of nonacquisitive love. The ancient Christian rite of baptism may have involved a drama of descent into and ascent from the water that mimed death and resurrection, as well as the exchange of old clothes for new.[15] In any case, it is significant for my thesis that the rite of initiation should be understood as a mimetic identification with the death of Christ. This is consonant with Paul's actual experience of conversion as an experience of the significance of the Cross.

---

[15] *Didache* 7; cf. Gal 3:27; Rom 13:14.

The Law is therefore the instrument of Paul's metaphorical death as it was the cause of Christ's actual death. This metaphor can only mean that the interpretation of the Mosaic Law that led to such action ceased to have any positive significance for Paul. More than that it meant that status claims based on this-worldly values also became insignificant (Gal 6:14). Most prominent among such claims was the boasting in Jewish privilege that he had previously indulged (Rom 2:17-29). The Law in this sense was a marker of this-worldly value and an instrument of the prestige of the order of the Sacred.

The evidence of Galatians, therefore, is that the references to the Cross belong to the situation of zealous Jewish persecution for the sake of strict observance of the ritual requirements of the Law. Paul brings the crucifixion out of the past and applies it metaphorically to the present because the crucifixion of Christ and the expulsion of the gentiles are formally the same acts of sacred violence.

The "Scandal of the Cross" (Gal 5:11; cf. 1 Cor 1:23), the "Curse of the Law" (Gal 3:13), and the Nature of Jewish Zeal[16]

The "word of the Cross" (ὁ λόγος τοῦ σταυροῦ—1 Cor 1:18) and the "scandal of the Cross" (τὸ σκάνδαλον τοῦ σταυροῦ—1 Cor 1:23; Gal 5:11) are probably Pauline coinages from his days as a persecutor. This is how he once summarized to himself the threat that he sought to eradicate, but now he uses the phrases to summarize the Gospel he holds dear. The statement in Galatians 2:19 suggests that he would have had the transgression of the ritual boundary markers in mind. The Law that he was enforcing was a wall of separation between Jew and Gentile. The Christians whom he persecuted had removed the wall. That fact constituted the scandal for Saul the Pharisee.

The scandal of the Cross, from the point of view of these ritual rules, is that Christians do not observe circumcision, kosher, or Sabbath (Gal 5:11). Scandal, we have seen, has the sense of a hindrance that one needs to keep desire alive. The scandal is the model/obstacle or the victim that desire cannot live with and cannot live without. Those who persecuted the transgressors of the ritual laws (Gal 6:13) needed the transgressors as victims to evoke their own conflictual mimesis and thus unify the group against the centrifugal force of acquisitive mimesis. The scandal of the Cross is, therefore, precisely the lowering of the ritual barriers around the group, the admission of scapegoats, which the zealous Jews hated and loved. The Cross is a scandal because it stands for the inclusion of those that the Law excludes, and gives zealous desire the

---

[16] R. Hamerton-Kelly, "Sacred Violence and the 'Curse of the Law.'"

motivation it needs to engage the surrogate victim mechanism on behalf of the order of good violence, and thus rally people to unity.

The scandal of the Cross for a zealous Jew could also have been that the Christians identified one who had been cursed by the Law in accordance with Deuteronomy 21:23[17] as Messiah (Gal 3:13). It is, however, unlikely that a belief so absurd to Jews would by itself warrant persecution. To be sure, the claim that the Torah had cursed the Messiah would be scandalous to a Jew, but as long as it remained the opinion of a marginal group, it is unlikely to have attracted enough attention to be persecuted. If, however, the Christians drew the corollary that the curse of the Torah was its exclusionary regulations, and that these expressed the same violence as had crucified Christ, they would conscientiously have ignored them. Thus they would have attracted the attention of the zealots for the Law.

These zealots are the ones whom Paul specifically opposes; they are the chief representatives of the sacred violence in the Judaism of Paul's experience. It would take us too far afield to enter into a full-scale discussion of the identity and nature of Paul's opponents in general,[18] and in any case that is not necessary, because we are only concerned to establish that the kind of zeal that Saul the Pharisee displayed was not idiosyncratic but representative of a section of Judaism. In the person of Paul and in his texts we have evidence of the existence of this zeal, and it remains for us simply to describe it more fully on the basis of those texts.

The immediate background to Galatians 3:13 is the controversy between Peter and Paul concerning exclusion and inclusion, and the wider background is the phenomenon of "zeal for the Law." Paul begins this stage of the argument with "Jesus Christ portrayed as crucified before your eyes" (Gal 3:1),[19] which stands in contrast to "works of Law." The Cross, therefore, opposes zeal for the Law. Paul allows that there is a good zeal (Gal 4:17-18; cf. Sir 51:18), but it is the paradoxical zeal of the Cross (Gal 6:12-14). The zeal of the Law

---

[17] "Paul must have judged the Christian proclamation of the crucified Jesus as Messiah to be a blasphemy against God. . . . So Paul, the 'zealot' for God's honor, was compelled to persecute the Christians. Deut 21:23 must have been a catch-phrase of Paul when he went about persecuting the Christians" (S. Kim, *The Origin of Paul's Gospel,* 47).

[18] On the identity of the opponents, see the recent summary by V. P. Furnish, *II Corinthians,* 48–54. Furnish concludes that they were Hellenistic Jews who did not Judaize, in the sense of trying to impose Jewish ritual observance on the Corinthians, but merely downgraded Paul because he was deficient in religious experiences of an ecstatic kind and failed to measure up to certain other Hellenistic religious standards. I prefer C. K. Barrett's identification of them as Judaizers. He writes: "A main theme of 2 Cor XI is that Paul is as good a Jew as any of his opponents; they must have been Jews and Jews who insisted on their Jewishness" (*A Commentary on the Second Epistle to the Corinthians,* 30). Cf. C. Mearns, "The Identity of Paul's Opponents at Philippi." G. Baumbach, "Die Frage nach den Irrlehren in Philippi," 252–66, gives a tabular presentation of the current theories concerning Paul's opponents.

[19] This is a summary of the Pauline kerygma; 1 Cor 1:23, 2:2; cf. 1 Cor 1:13, 17, 18; 2:8; 2 Cor 13:4; Gal 5:11, 24; 6:12, 14, 17; Phil 2:8, 3:18. (H. D. Betz, *Galatians,* 132).

excludes; the zeal of the Cross includes all those who through Christ, the "seed of Abraham," constitute the true "Israel of God" (Gal 6:16). Paul understands the zeal of the Law very well from his former life (Phil 3:6, Gal 1:13-14; cf. Acts 22:3; Rom 10:2).

The word "zeal" was probably a favorite of his opponents, since it occurs chiefly in the Galatian (Gal 4:17-18) and Corinthian correspondence (1 Cor 3:3; 12:31; 13:4; 2 Cor 7:7,11; 9:2; 11:2; 12:20; cf. Gal 5:20)[20] where the opponents are most in evidence. The cry "*I* am zealous for you with the zeal of God!" (2 Cor 11:2) makes good sense as a slogan of the opponents used by Paul to insist that he, not they, have the true divine zeal.[21]

On the assumption that "zeal" was the central term in the debate with the Judaizing opponents, Galatians must be placed in the context of the larger struggle among the Jews of the late second temple period over what constituted a proper zeal for God.[22] The extracanonical evidence for the nature and extent of the "zealot"[23] movement is well known. Zeal included both nonphysical coercion and the resort to force.[24] Luke certainly knew of it: Acts 23:12-22 shows Paul the target of violent activism; Acts 5:34-39 shows the Christian movement compared by Pharisaism, in the person of Gamaliel, to the "zealot" movements; and Acts 21:20 tells us that there are thousands of Jewish Christians "zealous for the Law, and they have been told about you [Paul] that you

---

[20] In Romans it occurs only in the reference to ignorant zeal in 10:2, and in a list of vices (13:13) that is probably taken over from tradition.

[21] This zeal seems to characterize his opponents in Corinth as well as in Galatia. 2 Cor 11:2 is strongly reminiscent of Gal 1:6-10 with its insistence that there is no other gospel. It seems that when he thinks of "another gospel" he also thinks of "zeal"; the two ideas are linked in his mind.

[22] Robert Jewett ("The Agitators and the Galatian Congregation") suggested that "Jewish Christians in Judea were stimulated by Zealotic pressure into a nomistic campaign among their fellow Christians in the late forties and early fifties. Their goal was to avert suspicion that they were in communion with lawless Gentiles" (205). The strategy of the Judaizing missionaries was not to introduce the gentile converts to the whole Torah but rather to secure prompt observance of the law of circumcision and observance of the festivals, so that they, the Judaizers, might not suffer persecution for the sake of the Cross of Christ (6:12). Marcus Borg ("A New Context for Romans 13") places Rom 12:14—13:7 in the context of the "zealot" movement, and gives evidence for zealot activities in Rome. Cf. K. Haacker, "Paulus und das Judentum im Galaterbrief." (I owe the last reference to W. D. Davies).

[23] I put "zealot" in quotation marks to show that I am aware of the inappropriateness, strictly speaking, of lumping together all the activist resistance movements of the pre-70 C.E. period by this name. Nevertheless, it is the general term used in scholarship.

[24] David M. Rhoads (*Israel in Revolution, 6–74 C.E.*, 82–87) warns against assuming that "zealot" automatically means "revolutionary." There were at least four types of zeal in the fifties and sixties of the common era. Zeal was not an exclusive characteristic of any one group; it is widely attested in the literature, and directed against a variety of activities, like intercourse with foreign women, idolatry, the presence of the uncircumcised in the land, defilement of the sanctuary, profanation of the divine name, and offences against the legal traditions (86). R. Horsley (*Jesus and the Spiral of Violence*, 121–29) argues that zealotry was not widespread in the second temple period. Such as it was, it "focused on the internal affairs of the Jewish community . . . obsessed with sin and sinners. . . . Saul the Pharisee, intensely zealous like Phineas, 'burning' with zeal, persecuted fellow Jews for breaking the Law" (128). Cf. J. L. Martyn, "A Law-Observant Mission to Gentiles."

teach all the Jews who are among the gentiles to forsake Moses, telling them not to circumcise their children or to observe the customs"[25] (cf. Acts 17:5, 13:45, cf. 5:17; and 1 Thess 2:14-16). It is probable, therefore, that those "certain people from James" who intimidated Peter and Barnabas and all the Jews into withdrawing from table fellowship with gentiles were Jewish Christian "zealots"[26] in this sense.

In Galatians 3:6-14 Paul interprets the death of Christ against the background of a midrash on Numbers 25:1-13,[27] in which Abraham and Phineas are linked by means of Psalm 106 and Genesis 15:6. Phineas is the archetypal zealot (Num 25:11)[28] who killed an Israelite man and a Midianite woman in the act of love, hanged the guilty chiefs, slaughtered the other race mixers, and stopped the plague.[29] Thus he won a "covenant of peace and of an everlasting priesthood" (Num 25:12-13; Sir 45:23; 1 Macc 2:54). The prominence of this story in the time of Paul is well established.[30]

In Psalm 106:30-31 Phineas's deed "has been reckoned to him as righteousness / from generation to generation for ever."[31] This recalls Galatians 3:6, "Thus Abraham 'believed God and it was reckoned to him as righteousness,'" which is, in turn, based on Genesis 15:6. By means of the phrase "reckoned to him as righteousness" the midrash interprets Abraham in terms of Phineas, and thus interprets faith to be zealous action. There is precedent for this in 1 Maccabees 2:52, "Was not Abraham found faithful when tested, and it was reckoned to him as righteousness?,"[32] where faith means perseverance

---

[25] Cf. 1 Macc 2:45 where we are told that Mattathias and his friends forcibly circumcised the uncircumcised boys they found within the borders of Israel.

[26] Whether they insisted on observance of all the Law or just of the boundary markers is not clear because of Gal 5:3, where Paul seems to be informing his readers of something they did not know—namely, that to accept circumcision is in principle to accept the obligation to the whole Law. We have evidence of Jewish missionaries reducing the demands on proselytes (P. Vielhauer, "Gesetzesdienst und Stoicheiadienst im Galaterbrief," *Rechtfertigung: Festschrift für Ernst Käsemann zum 70. Geburtstag*), and so it is not impossible that the Judaizers absolutely insisted only on the external signs of membership, while being less adamant about less obvious observances.

[27] T. Callan ("Pauline Midrash") refers to N. A. Dahl's demonstration that the compressed and elliptical style of Gal 3:1—4:7 is due to allusions to midrashim that Paul and his opponents all knew. Callan interprets vs. 19b against the background of the golden calf episode in Exod 32 on the basis of the phrase "by the hand of" in Exod 34:29.

[28] 1 Macc. 2:24, 27, 54.

[29] On a Girardian reading, the plague is a sign of violence erasing differences, and the killing and hanging of the transgressors represents the sacrificial violence that restores order.

[30] M. Hengel, *Die Zeloten*.

[31] Ps 106 was well known to Paul. Among the 28 psalms he quotes or alludes to in the genuine letters, only 4 are referred to more than once (94 x 3; 106 x 2; 116 x 2; 142 x 2). Ps 106 is, therefore, one of the few psalms to which Paul returns. Vs. 20 is alluded to in Rom 1:23 and vs. 37 in 1 Cor 10:20 (according to the Nestle text). Both of these passages are indictments of idolatry, possibly drawn from existing Hellenistic Jewish midrashim. The Phineas psalm is an appropriate weapon against idolatry. 4 Macc 18:12 shows that Phineas was honored among the diaspora Jews. For the phrase "it was reckoned to him as righteousness," see Gen 15:6, 1 Macc 2:52, Rom 4:3.

[32] Cf. John 8:33, where the Jewish Christians link descent from Abraham with freedom. This suggests that a "zealotic" interpretation of Abraham was current in the Johannine church.

under trial and not humble trust in God. The opponents connect Abraham and Phineas by means of Psalm 106.

Paul, however, disconnects them by interpreting Genesis 15:6 in the light of the death of Christ, and thus proposes an alternative understanding of faith as trust in God's promises (nonacquisitive mimesis) rather than resolute action in defense of God's people (acquisitive and conflictual mimesis). By citing Deuteronomy 21:23 in a "zealot" context, Paul connects the death of Christ to the tradition of sacred violence,[33] and opposes an interpretation of Abraham in terms of the death of Christ to the opponents' interpretation of Abraham in terms of Phineas. Thus he redefines the meaning of "reckoning as righteousness" (Gen 15:6; Ps 106:31-32) and "hanging on a tree" (Deut 21:22-23) or "hanging in the sun before the Lord" (Num 25:4). True faith is mimesis of the nonacquisitive divine desire as shown by Abraham, not of acquisitive and conflictual desire as shown by Phineas,[34] which results in the scapegoating structures of sacred violence that crucified Christ and are excluding the gentiles. In this regard Abraham is a type of Jesus, who bore rather than inflicted the curse of sacred violence. The hero of the story is not the xenophobic killer but the victim, not Phineas but patient Abraham, who is the type of his "seed," Jesus (Gal 3:16), who was hanged on a tree. Thus Paul reverses the valences of the paradigmatic zealot story and shows up the lie of sacred violence, which deals with violence by means of violence, purchasing order by means of victims.

There are two communities in mind in Galatians 3:1-14, corresponding to the two interpretations of Abraham, one "of works of Law" (or "in Law") and one "of faith" (or "in Christ"). Each proclaims the other to be under a curse (Gal 3:10, 13). The zealot Jewish Christians argue that every one of the laws

---

[33] Deut 21:23 is the legal formulation of a custom that comes from the ideology of the holy war and, more remotely, is rooted in the surrogate victim mechanism. Cf. the accounts of the hanging of the kings in Josh 8:24-29 and 10:22-27 and their burial under piles of stones. Of these piles it is said that they exist "to this day"(8:29; 10:27) showing that they were there in the time of the writer as sacred places in Ai and Makkedah, respectively, that played a role in the social organization of those communities. The association with the pyramids is obvious, as with the Girardian themes of the sacred kings who live and die as sacrificial victims, the power of whose deaths to found the community is signified by these monuments. On the holy war, see N. Gottwald, *The Tribes of Yahweh,* 543–44. Deut 21:23 and Num 25:1-5 are linked in the Palestinian Targum. A. T. Hanson (*Studies in Paul's Technique and Theology,* 6) quotes the Targum as follows: "And the people of the house of Israel joined themselves to Baal Peor, like the nail in the wood, which is not separated but by breaking up the wood. And the anger of the Lord was kindled against Israel. And the Lord said to Moshe, 'Take all the chiefs of the people, and appoint them for judges, and let them give judgment to put to death the people who have gone astray after Peor, and hang them before the word of the Lord upon the wood over against the morning sun, and at the departure of the sun take them down and bury them, and turn away the strong anger of the Lord against Israel.' " The mention of the wood on which they are hanged and the command to take them down at sunset links the incident with Deut 21:23. Cf. Col 2:14-15. It is, therefore, possible that Num 25:1-5 was in the mind of Paul and the Pauline school. Cf. F. F. Bruce, "The Curse of the Law," 35, n. 12.

[34] Compare Rom 4:16, "He is the father of us all" with 1 Macc 2:54, "Phineas our father, because he was deeply zealous, received the covenant of everlasting priesthood."

is inviolate, especially the boundary markers, and quote Deuteronomy 27:26 to support the point that the Pauline Christians are cursed because they do not observe all the Law, and Leviticus 18:5 to underline the fact that it is the doers, not the hearers, who are justified. The Pauline Christians argue that since justification has always come by faith (Gal 3:11), it is not necessary to obey every item of the Law, and in this case especially the Laws that exclude the gentiles. Those who insist on such observance are under the curse of sacred violence. Paul accepts the principle that deeds not words are what count (Rom 2:17-29), but understands the deeds of the Law to be the works of love to the neighbor (Gal 5:14; Rom 13:8-10), and not the observance of the ritual markers.

Thus, for Paul the curse of sacred violence takes the form of Jewish religious existence without this mutual love, expressed especially in the xenophobia of zealotism, and revealed in the Cross. In order to reveal this and to prevent us from entering into it by becoming obedient to the Mosaic Law, Christ entered into the sphere of that violence by allowing himself to be cursed— that is, driven out and killed. In this way he revealed the real nature of life based on the Mosaic interpretation of the Law and made it clearly unnecessary and undesirable for the gentiles, or any Jew, ever to adopt that way of life again.

Accordingly, from this perspective it makes perfect sense that the Law, as the instrument of sacred violence, was given only to contain trespasses for the time being (Gal 3:19)[35]; and not directly by God but through angels,[36] because God is not a God of violence. Nevertheless, it served the negative purpose of holding bad violence in check by good violence, holding society together until the truth could be made known. As a product of the surrogate victim and the double transference, it was an advance on the primordial chaos of unconstrained mimetic rivalry. "We were confined under Law, kept under constraint until faith should be revealed. So the Law was our custodian until Christ came" (Gal 3:23-24). This is a marvelously apt description of the interim role of the surrogate victim mechanism, and an indication of Paul's conservatism. He realizes that the order of the Sacred is necessary for most of the world. It becomes intolerable only in a situation like the one he faced in Galatia where sacred violence has been exposed, an alternative given, and people nevertheless argue for the superiority of the old to the new.

As soon as the Law is superseded by the "revelation of faith" (Gal 3:23), distinctions based on the order of the Sacred should disappear. "There is neither Jew nor Greek, there is neither slave nor free, there is neither male nor female" (Gal 3:28). Such people have attained majority and are no longer

---

[35] D. J. Lull ("The Law was our Pedagogue") shows convincingly that this is the point of the argument.

[36] See T. Callan, "Pauline Midrash."

under tutelage to the "elemental spirits of the universe"—the monsters and myths spawned by mimetic rivalry and channeled in the sacrificial system (Gal 4:3, 8-11).

In this passage Law must be taken as a compressed reference to the violent interpretation of the Law that excludes the gentiles and crucified Christ, because Paul does not believe that all the Law is violent. The basic intention, expressed in the commandment to love God and neighbor, remains valid. The representatives of sacred violence are, therefore, in Paul's experience, the zealous Jews and Jewish Christians who interpret the Torah in such a way as to exclude from the community of the true Israel gentiles who do not observe the ritual laws that mark off Jewish existence. This interpretation misses the central thrust of the Law as the command to love God and the neighbor, and creates a structure of sacred violence. The Cross of Christ discloses this state of affairs definitively. Therefore, to insist on such ritual observance is to betray the crucified.

The Cross and the Category of Sacrifice

Galatians 3:13 says that "Christ purchased our freedom from the curse of the Law, becoming a curse on our behalf " (Χριστὸς ἡμᾶς ἐξηγόρασεν ἐκ τῆς κατάρας τοῦ νόμου γενόμενος ὑπὲρ ἡμῶν κατάρα). The Cross is the basis of the new community because it is the sign that Christ has "purchased" us (ἐξαγοράζειν, 1 Cor 6:20; 7:23; cf. 8:11-13). The basis of the metaphor is not sacrifice, but ransom; one takes the place of the many, and the many are transferred from one realm to another.

The subsequent discussion in terms of the metaphor of the transition from slavery to sonship is therefore appropriate (Gal 3:21—6:10). Before the advent of faith we were under the tutelage of a guardian, but the Spirit bestows upon us sonship and the right to call God Abba. We are the children of the free Sarah, and not of the slave Hagar, and "it is for freedom that Christ has set us free" (Gal 5:1). The exercise of this freedom should be inspired by love and take the form of the fruits of the Spirit, which may be summed up in the general maxim, "Bear one another's burdens and so fulfil the Law of Christ" (Gal 6:2). On the Cross Christ paid the price of our freedom and ransomed us from the realm of the curse; therefore we can live as free children of God, in mutual love and service.

The precise nature of this redemptive purchase can be seen by considering the pattern of action in Galatians 4:1-10. Prior to the coming of Christ we were slaves to the elements of the universe, the powers of this world that did not know the divine plan. Then God sent forth his son "born of a woman, under the Law, in order that he might purchase the freedom of those under the Law, so that we might receive adoption" (Gal 4:4). At the same time God sent forth the Spirit to replace the Law as a guide to conduct and to confirm our status as the children of God.

The imagery behind this passage is the image of the scapegoat that is sent out to redeem, but the direction of the scapegoat's movement is reversed; rather than moving from the sphere of the Sacred, this scapegoat moves into that sphere, and rather than removing sin from that sphere he removes all those who have been imprisoned under the powers of violence there. D. Schwartz[37] calls our attention to two allusions in the text that recall the scapegoat. Galatians 3:13, he says, should be interpreted in terms of 4:4-5, which presents the incarnation in terms of the scapegoat tradition. Ἐξαποστέλλω in Galatians 4:4, which is used only here in Paul and, for symmetry, in Galatians 4:6, is the LXX translation for שלח in the MT. There are two cases where שלח has the sense of "the sending forth of *x* redeems *y*." They are Leviticus 14, where in order to remove certain impurities a priest must send forth a live bird after transferring the impurity to it, and in Leviticus 16, where in the day of atonement ceremony the priest puts the goat under a curse by transferring to it the sins of the people, and sends it out into the wilderness.

It is possible, therefore, that the word ἐξαπέστειλεν carried the connotation of "scapegoat" for Paul and so it was not necessary for him to explain how the sending out of Christ purchased freedom for us (Gal 4:4-5). There is, however, a critical difference between this scapegoat and the usual one; normally the scapegoat is sent out from the sacred precinct, whereas Christ was sent into it, "born under the Law." Therefore Paul is inverting the scapegoat ritual, as part of the disclosure of sacred violence; he is telling us that scapegoating is itself a fantasy of religious violence and that chaos reigns in the sacred precinct as much as in the wilderness.

Schwartz also calls attention to Romans 8:32, which confirms that Paul sets the death of Christ in the context of the accounts of "hangings" in the Old Testament, as well as the inversion of the scapegoat idea. One should read Romans 8:32 not in terms of the Akedah (Gen 22), as is usually done, but rather in terms of the hanging of the sons of Saul in 2 Samuel 21:1-14. The objections to an interpretation in terms of the Akedah are that Isaac is not said to be "given," that he did not die, and that had he died, his death would have been on an altar and not on a cross. Furthermore, his death would not have been "for" anyone, while Paul emphasizes that Christ's death was "for us all."

In 2 Samuel 21:1-14 a famine is sent by God because of the unavenged blood of the Gibeonites. The Gibeonites would take no ransom of silver and gold, but demanded the death of seven sons of Saul. David spared Mephibosheth, son of Jonathan, the most prominent representative of the line, despite the fact that one might have expected that the more prominent the victim, the more efficacious would be the atonement. Seven other sons were given to the

---

[37] D. Schwartz, "Two Pauline Allusions."

Gibeonites to hang, and after their corpses and those of Saul and Jonathan were properly buried, "God heeded supplications for the land" (2 Sam 21:14). The parallels with Romans 8:32 are that David "spared" (ἐφείσατο) Mephibosheth, he "gave" (παρέδωκεν) the seven sons to the Gibeonites, and they, in turn, were hanged or crucified. Paul is arguing *qal wahomer,* from the lesser case to the greater; David spared someone else's son, God did not spare "his own" son.

Thus we again have an inversion of sacrifice. In 2 Samuel 21 the recipients of the ransom of the seven sons were the Gibeonites, not God. In terms of the analogy, therefore, in Romans 8:32 the son is given to human beings, not to God. It is not God's justice but human justice, in the form of vengeance, that demands victims.

This Pauline midrash on 2 Samuel 21:1-14, in which God gives God's own son to stop the cycle of vengeance and does not demand anything in return, but rather because of this, "cannot fail to give us everything" (Rom 8:32b), is intended to show that God does not need to be appeased like the Gibeonites. Thus we have another inversion of sacrificial violence; we are told that God does not take vengeance, but rather suffers it.

The curse constitutes a realm that in the context of Galatians 3 can only be the exclusionist interpretation of the Law. The metaphor in play is not explicitly sacrifice but imprisonment and ransom; Christ purchases our freedom from imprisonment in the realm of the curse by substituting himself for us (cf. Gal 4:4-5; Rom 8:3). By his violent fate there he reveals the curse to be sacrificial violence, and this, along with the element of substitution, shows that the image of imprisonment is a subset of an overarching sacrificial metaphor that is being inverted. By entering that realm on our behalf, Christ unveils the surrogate victim mechanism on which it is founded, and by substituting himself for us frees us from sacred violence. He exposes the myth of the double transference.

The realm of the curse that Christ enters "on our behalf" (or "instead of") (ὑπὲρ ἡμῶν—Gal 3:13; Rom 8:32) is, therefore, a realm of human, not divine, vengeance. The mendacity of the double transference, which identifies human violence as divine, became inescapably evident when the "divine" vengeance fell on Jesus, because it punished the one person who had truly fulfilled God's will of mutual love. This meant that the zealot interpretation of the Law had not merely made a mistake in one particular case, so that the principle of divine vengeance remains intact, but that the whole system of sacred vengeance based on Law was undermined, because the curse is not divine vengeance at all but rather human violence dissembled through the Sacred into the vengeance of the god.

One must conclude, therefore, that for Paul the primary saving effect of the Cross is as a disclosure of religious violence, not as a sacrificial transaction that appeases the divine wrath. When we see the effect of religious exclusiveness in the Cross we can withdraw credibility from the religious system (Gal 6:14) and receive "the blessing of Abraham in Christ Jesus" (Gal 3:14). Negatively, it reveals that the Jews who live ἐξ ἔργων νόμου are caught in the coils of sacrificial violence, slaves to the system of vengeance and exclusion that operates through the temple cult and Jewish privilege, and spawns the zealot spirit. Christ experienced the exclusionary power of that system and thus revealed the violence that drives it.

Clearly we are on the way to a radical reorientation of the understanding of the relationship between the death of Christ and the sacrificial categories of Judaism, which entails a restatement of the sense in which Christ's death can be called a sacrifice. The major new element is that Paul inverts the traditional understanding of sacrifice so that God is the offerer, not the receiver, and the scapegoat goes into the sacred precinct rather than out of it. Christ is a divine offering to humankind, not a human offering to God.

These features can be seen in Paul's adaptation of the Jewish Christian idea of Christ's death as a sacrifice in Romans 3:21-26.[38] The first point to note is that the initiator of the offering is God. In the normal order of sacrifice, humans give and the god receives; here the god gives and humans receive. We must insist on the fact that the recipients are human, otherwise we fall into the absurdity of God's giving a propitiatory[39] gift to God. The usual explanation of this passage is that human sin deserved divine punishment, but in mercy God substituted a propitiatory offering to bear the divine wrath instead of humanity. The second point to note is that not only the order of giver and receiver is reversed but also the spatial order. Normally the offerer goes from profane to sacred space to make the offering; here the offerer comes out of sacred space into profane, publicly to set forth (προέθετο) the propitiation (ἱλαστήριον) there. These inversions of the normal order of sacrifice mean that it is not God who needs to be propitiated, but humanity, and not in the recesses of the Sacred, but in the full light of day.

---

[38] On Rom 3:24-26 see T. W. Manson ("ἱλαστήριον") who showed that the atonement ritual is in mind. (We cannot, however, agree with his interpretation of ἱλαστήριον as the mercy seat.) P. Stuhlmacher, "Zur neueren Exegese von Rom 3,24-26," *Versöhnung, Gesetz, und Gerechtigkeit,* 117–207; M. Theobald, "Das Gottesbild des Paulus nach Rom 3,21-31"; B. Meyer, "The Pre-Pauline Formula"; J. Piper, "The Demonstration of the Righteousness of God"; H. Hübner, "Sühne und Versöhnung." The antisacrificial adaptation of the atonement ideas may have been the work of Jewish Christianity if Pseudo-Clementine can be taken to indicate the Jewish Christian attitude. Cf. H III 26.3 (Hennecke-Schneemelcher, *New Testament Apocrypha 2,* 116): "[The true prophet] hates sacrifices, bloodshed and sprinklings, he loves pious, pure and holy men, he puts out the altar fire." See also H II 16.7 and H II 44.1 (Hennecke-Schneemelcher, 120–21). Paul probably inherited the general tendency to redefine sacrifice from Jewish Christianity but responded to it more radically. While they were content to argue as in the Epistle to the Hebrews that Christ's death is the perfect sacrifice that renders the system passé, he argues that Christ's death shows the system always to have been a grotesque error that in fact caused the death of Christ.

[39] We accept the common meaning of ἱλαστήριον as "propitiation" rather than "mercy seat" for reasons set out by L. Morris, *The Apostolic Preaching of the Cross,* 125–85. A propitiation is a gift given to appease the wrath of someone. In the Girardian scheme it is the proposed substitute target of vengeance.

The element of substitution, which is part of the traditional interpretation of these verses, might be explained in the terms I am proposing by a reconsideration of the concept of "the wrath." Below I have argued that for Paul wrath is not the active divine vengeance but the effects of sacred violence in the human world. The wrath that falls on Christ instead of on humanity is, therefore, human vengeance dissembled through the Sacred and borne with absolute vulnerability, with the result that Christ stands out as the one complete victim and target of the wrath. All the rest of us pull back more or less into the defensive structures of the Sacred and protect ourselves against bad violence by means of good. He alone eschews all aid from sacred violence and thus bears the wrath for us, to disclose and thus disarm it.

This means that substitution has become representation; Christ the perfect victim does not bear the wrath instead of us in the sense that we therefore need not bear it; rather as perfect representative he represents our wrath to us, in the sense of mirroring the decoded double transference. To bear it in our place would be to continue to hide our violence from us and thus perpetuate the deception of the double transference. To represent our wrath to us is to give us the opportunity to take responsibility for it, and make the proper changes from acquisitive and conflictual to nonacquisitive and consensual mimesis. We have seen how the victim is the synecdoche/metonymy and the metaphor of the group. In this sense Christ is a substitute for the human race; he is the one who stands for, in the sense of represents, the many(metonymy/synecdoche), and the one who stands for the other (metaphor). To decode the double transference all we need to do is decode the metonymies and metaphors of the Cross.

The Cross and the Plan of Salvation

We have seen that the negative insight into the violence of this zealot way of life was accompanied by the positive identification of Jesus as the Christ. The disclosure of the risen Christ and the discovery of the violence of the Law are two sides of the same coin. Paul "saw" the risen Lord (1 Cor 9:1; 15:8) at the same time as he saw the significance of the Cross. This experience was for him, in the language of apocalyptic, "the unveiling of a mystery" (1 Cor 2:6-16), an insight into the divine plan of salvation to bring to light the victim at the foundation of the world.

The Mystery of Salvation

"Mystery" (μυστήριον) is a technical term in apocalyptic discourse for the plan of salvation kept secret by God and revealed to chosen seers. Paul uses the term to refer to the whole gospel (Rom 16:25-26; cf. 1 Cor 4:1); the plan for the final salvation of Israel (Rom 11:25); the events of the end of time (1 Cor 15:51); and private insights into the purpose of God (1 Cor 13:2;

14:2). It has the same meaning as the term "revelation" (ἀποκάλυψις), which in either its nominal or verbal form describes the whole gospel (Rom 1:17; 16:25; 1 Cor 1:7; Gal 3:23), the eschatological judgment or blessing (Rom 1:18; 2:5; 8:19; 1 Cor 3:13; 2 Thess 2:3, 6, 8), and private revelations (Gal 1:12; 2:2; 1 Cor 14:6, 26, 30; 2 Cor 12:1, 7). Therefore, although Paul does not use the word, the content of his conversion in Galatians 1:16 is a mystery in this sense, because it is the result of a revelation that enabled him to understand the plan of salvation. Thus we are justified in looking to the classic passage on the content of the mystery in 1 Corinthians 2:6-16, for help in understanding the content of his conversion experience.

The essence of the mystery is the crucifixion of Christ, for if the powers of this age had known it, "they would not have crucified the lord of glory" (1 Cor 2:7-8). This is exactly what Paul discovered from the revelation that he received in his conversion—namely, that the crucifixion is the crux of God's plan for unmasking and overthrowing the powers of this world, understood through the Cross as the structures of the Sacred. In his circumstances he was ideally placed to see that the sacred powers of this world worked through religious institutions. His own zeal and the Law he served had murdered an innocent man. Having drawn that conclusion he went over to the side of the victim. Instead of continuing the crucifixion he joined the crucified. The revelation of the significance of the Cross uncovered the sacred violence in the institutions of this world.

The Tradition of the Persecuted Prophets

At this point Paul was able to connect the crucifixion, his own persecution of the Christians, and the scapegoating of the gentiles with the tradition of the persecution of the prophets. He presents his conversion in Galatians 1:15–16 in terms that are reminiscent of the prophetic "call" stories in the Old Testament, especially the call of Jeremiah, who was also "set apart from his mother's womb" (Jer 1:1-8). We have seen how in Paul's text the "revelations" (Gal 1:12; 2:2; 1 Cor 14:6, 26, 30; 2 Cor 12:1, 7) also refer to private prophetic visions and insights. This is enough evidence to suggest that he consciously identified himself as part of the prophetic tradition in its latter day apocalyptic manifestation, and drew on the tradition of the persecution of the prophets to locate himself vis-à-vis Israel. For that reason the much disputed passage in 1 Thessalonians 2:14-16 is absolutely genuine and expresses the heart of the Pauline sensibility; "the Jews, who killed the Lord Jesus and the prophets, and drove us out."[40] For Paul the Jews, not the Romans, killed the Lord Jesus, and

---

[40] K. Donfried, "Paul and Judaism"; W. D. Davies, "Paul and the People of Israel." A recent argument for interpolation that reports the literature to that time is D. Schmidt, "1 Thess 2:13-16: Linguistic Evidence for Interpolation." Donfried (250–53) relates the discussion of 1 Thess 2:16 to the occurrence of the term "wrath" in Romans.

drove the Pauline Christians out, and in doing so they were carrying on the tradition of the persecution of the prophets.[41] This is what Paul had in mind as he responded to Peter and the Jewish Christian zealots in Antioch.

There is a paradox in the idea of Israel's persecution of the prophets, which Paul brings out in the discussion of the role of Israel in the plan of salvation (Rom 9–11). It is that the persecutors as well as the persecuted perform an essential task for that plan. By persecution God creates the prophetic remnant and so both roles are needed. I shall return to this theme below.

The Community of the Cross

"Surely Paul was not crucified for you?" (1 Cor 1:13), is how the Apostle expresses the fact that the Cross is the foundation of the Christian community. Living together on that basis should prevent schism, because allegiance to the one who provides the foundation takes precedence over allegiance to other group leaders. Christ's death alone is the founding event and, therefore, his person alone is the commanding pole of loyalty (1 Cor 3:11; 8:5-6). This is the nub of Paul's argument against the sectarianism in the Corinthian church.

Having used the Cross to make a very polemical point against the Judaizers in Galatia, Paul appears to be inconsistent when he uses it in Corinth to preach reconciliation and cooperation. This is only a superficial contradiction, however, because of the differences in the two situations. The force of the two arguments is the same although the form is different, because they are both directed against the formation of sects on the basis of external criteria.

In the Galatian case the criteria are Jewish and ritual; in Corinth they are, in addition, gentile and social. The four parties—of Paul, Apollos, Cephas, and Christ—probably represent both the positions known from the Galatian debate (Paul and Cephas), and a ritual-free Hellenistic mysticism that emphasized eloquence and insight (Apollos). The Christ party probably included all the others, but on the basis of the misunderstanding of Christ as a Hellenistic hero. To correct all these misunderstandings, Paul makes the Cross the basis of Christian life. On that basis there can be no heroizing of leaders, not even of Christ.

The "word of the Cross" (1 Cor 1:18-25) saves those who will listen and identifies the forces that oppose it as foolishness (1 Cor 1:22-23). These are Jewish ritualism[42] and Greek rhetoric (σοφία λόγου—1 Cor 1:17-18; cf. 1 Cor 2:4), probably represented by the Cephas and the Apollos parties, respectively. They do not save but rather exacerbate our bondage to the sacred order by their

---

[41] O. H. Steck, *Israel und das gewaltsame Geschick der Propheten.*

[42] The "signs" sought by Jews (1 Cor 1:22) are the marks of ritual observance, like circumcision and observance of Sabbath and kashrut, and not miracles.

pretensions. Christ crucified is the divine contrast to the signs and wisdom of sacrificial violence, the uncovering of the surrogate victim mechanism that they sought to hide.

The "word of the Cross" is the opposite of rhetoric. It is essentially a description of an act of violence, the portrayal of the crucified in vivid terms (Gal 3:1). Paul deliberately avoids rhetorical method because it may convince his hearers by violent means (1 Cor 2:4). To be sure, the disavowal of rhetoric might itself be a rhetorical trick, but this is not the case here. He has been accused of being less than eloquent by comparison with other preachers whom the Corinthians have heard, perhaps Apollos, and here he is defending his procedure (2 Cor 10:10). Either he is hopelessly disingenuous or he really does believe that there is an inherent incommensurateness between rhetorical aesthetics and the ugliness of the Cross, an incommensurateness that reflects the deeper disjunction between the Sacred and the Spirit.

The word of the Cross is, therefore, the kind of blunt and honest talk about the violence that religion and philosophy cover over with ritual, myth, and rhetoric, even and especially the myth and rhetoric of nonviolent rationality. The word of the Cross reveals the founding mechanism. One should not, therefore, interpret it in such a way as to obscure this literal reference to brute violence dissembled to justice through the praetorium and temple. It is the disclosure of the lie in Horace's fatal couplet, *Dulce et decorum est, Pro patria mori,* in Caiaphas's heavy public burden, which he so nobly bears when he sends just one more young man to his death for the sake of the people (John 11:49-50). The word of the Cross cries, "Fraud!" to all this death-obsessed humbuggery.

In literary terms the divine power of the Cross would be called ironic; it works through its apparent opposite; life appears as death, light as darkness, strength as weakness, and something as nothing (1 Cor 1:26-31). Christians intend the world ironically, possessing it "as if they did not" (1 Cor 3:21; cf. 1 Cor 7:29-31). But irony is a violent genre expressing the clash of the violence that constructs the idols with the violence that destroys them,[43] while the view from the Cross interdicts the idols, leaving them in place while deconstructing their power. This irony is, therefore, to be qualified as a gracious rather than a violent irony, and it can be seen only by those who are already in principle and by faith free from the domination of sacred violence. This irony describes the point of view of those who, freed from the principalities, continue to live within their realm. Knowing the truth through the Cross, that the "emperor has no clothes on," they withhold cooperation from the superstition and self-deception of the Sacred. Since sacred power depends on the conspiracy of all to maintain it, those who withhold consent from the conspiracy are dangerous

---

[43] This is a reference to Horkheimer and Adorno's analysis of a certain kind of "enlightened" reason as a "myth of enlightenment." See Appendix II.

and their gracious irony threatens the foundations. They are the "nothings" that God uses to bring the "somethings" to nothing (1 Cor 1:28).

For this reason the apostle comes before them as a "nothing" in "fear and trembling" to bring the message of the Cross (1 Cor 2:1-16). The true wisdom of the gospel is the divine purpose, firm since before the creation, contained in a mystery, and revealed to those who understand the word of the Cross. This present world of the Sacred is passing away, and its rulers have simply hastened that passing by their crucifixion of Christ. Had they understood the divine purpose they would never have cooperated with it in the crucifixion. That murder of God's son sealed their doom because it revealed with vivid clarity the origin of this world in sacred violence. On the Cross these stupid powers displayed for all to see the one secret that they had to keep if they were to retain their power, the secret of founding violence. This knowledge is the saving wisdom given by the Spirit, in the form of an understanding of the foolishness of the preaching of the Cross (1 Cor 1:18). To know the wisdom of this foolishness is to have "the mind of Christ" (1 Cor 2:16), and that is to see the violent world from the point of view of the new possibility of nonviolence.

Paul addresses this argument to the problem of schism in the church. It is characteristic of our sources that we do not have theoretical discussions of the Cross but rather practical applications. So far the Cross has been invoked to argue that if the Corinthians really understood the foolish wisdom of the Cross and were imitators of the crucified (1 Cor 4:16; 11:1), they would not engage in partisan rivalries. To imitate the crucified is to renounce mimetic violence and embrace the other in self-giving love (1 Cor 13).

At this point we should ask whether in his doctrine of the church Paul succeeds in escaping from the partisan politics of this world or whether he merely founds another "sect of the Cross." The first sign that he has succeeded is the retreat of ritual categories before the advance of moral categories as qualifications for membership. Nowhere can we see more clearly the essentially practical nature of the Pauline Epistles than in the way he expounds the moral significance of the Cross for the life of the community (cf. Gal 5:24; Phil 2:1-11). As the basis of the new community the Cross provides the standards for membership, and, apart from the founding requirement of faith, they are all moral rather than ritual standards.

Baptism, the rite of entry, is a metaphor for dying with Christ (Rom 6:3; cf. Gal 3:27). However, when baptism threatens to become the talismanic sign of a new sect, he disclaims its importance (1 Cor 1:17) in favor of the preaching of the Cross. Baptism is acceptable as long as its proper metaphorical meaning is maintained. It symbolizes the dying with Christ to all status claims based on the hierarchies of this world.

The eucharist (1 Cor 11:17-34) is an essential ritual of membership chiefly because it proclaims the death of the Lord until he comes, and thus reminds us of our solidarity in the divine humiliation (1 Cor 11:26). Paul invokes it as the symbolic basis for an exhortation to collegiality in the faction-ridden church. In this process he recalls elements from the sacrificial customs of Jewry, especially the solidarity of those who eat the sacrificial victim together (1 Cor 10:14). In using this imagery Paul does not intend to identify Christ's death as a sacrifice in the old sense of the term, rather he uses the sacrificial imagery to preach unity.

In dealing with moral problems in the community, Paul invokes moral rather than ritual principles of judgment, but in the matter of inclusion and exclusion, not even the moral principles count. Paul does not exclude even the man guilty of incest (1 Cor 5) from the community irrevocably, but only for a period of repentance with a view to his return. In 1 Corinthians 3:10-17 he argues that even if all one's spiritual labor in this world fails the test, one will still not be excluded. Adapting the central ritual item, the temple, for use as a moral metaphor, Paul argues that the foundation of the temple/church is Christ crucified, as Paul presented him in the preaching of the Cross (1 Cor 3:10-11). Building the community is like building the temple, and the quality of each one's construction will be tested by the eschatological fire. On that day, one might lose all the fruit of one's labor, but still escape with one's soul (1 Cor 3:15). Thus one's membership in the church is not dependent on one's achievements, but entirely on God's grace. Not even the failure or success of one's spiritual labor is an index for inclusion or exclusion.

Only apostasy from faith in Christ can exclude one ultimately from the community of the new creation (1 Cor 16:22). Therefore, the Pauline community is not entirely amorphous, and the question arises whether the demand for faith in Christ does not constitute a formal rather than a moral qualification for membership that is functionally the equivalent of ritual. The first thing to note is that faith in Christ can express itself in conflicting forms of observance, like celibacy or marriage (1 Cor 7), accepting support from the congregation or supporting one's own ministry (1 Cor 9), eating meat sacrificed to idols or abstaining from such meat (whether for the sake of one's own tender conscience or out of respect for the tender conscience of another) (1 Cor 8). This conflicting variety of the forms of Christian life is different from the uniformity of legal observance, and suggests that Christian faith is not the formal counterpart of ritual law.

I shall return to the question of the nature of the faith that constitutes the Christian community in the discussion of the triad of faith, hope, and love. Here I might anticipate that discussion and say that faith as the mimetic identification with the crucified is constitutionally different from an excluding force. It suffers rather than inflicts violence, it is generous rather than acquisitive, and consensual rather than conflictual. Its paradigm is the victim seen for what he is and not transformed into the god by the double transference. Faith resists Jesuolatry by insisting that the crucified not be used as the talisman of a new sect but rather seen as the revelation of sacred violence and the challenge to nonacquisitive love of God and neighbor.

In this sense the church of Paul based on the Cross is not a power among the powers of this world; it is rather an outbreak in time and before its time of the extratemporal new creation (2 Cor 5:17; cf. Gal 6:15). It is, therefore, in principle boundless; one can as much define the limits of the new creation as one can those of the old. Potentially all existing things are included in the church; it is an eschatological thing, metaphorically, metonymically, and mystically the body of the risen Christ. All things tend to their fulfillment in the church. That is why it is the community of the Cross, the living witness to the violence of the existing order, and the pledge of the new nonviolent creation.

In Paul's view, therefore, the Cross reveals the realm of sacred violence whose characteristic expressions are exclusiveness and scapegoating. It grounds the insight that the principalities and powers of this world are structures of sacred violence and founds the new community of freedom and mutual acceptance. As the foundation of the new community it witnesses to the grace of God, and as the revelation of sacred violence it discloses the sin of humanity.

4

Sacred Violence
and Original Sin

Adam's Transgression as the
Deformation of Desire

> Let us now consider Adam and also remember that every subsequent
> individual begins in the very same way, but within the quantitative
> difference that is the consequence of the relationship of generation
> and the historical relationship.
>
> Kierkegaard, *The Concept of Anxiety*, 90

Sin is a theological category posited, in Kierkegaard's terms, along with faith.
Like faith it is a form of desire, a configuration of the mimetic triangle, something desire does to deform itself to rivalry. Adam symbolizes this deformation.
He was the first to turn desire to acquisitive and conflictual mimesis, and commit the double transference, and everyone repeats his crime mimetically. The
deformation and the double transference produce the primitive Sacred, and all
religion is more or less a structure of sacred violence. Anxiety is the subjective
state that corresponds to the structure of the Sacred. It is the subliminal awareness of our vulnerability to violence and of the sacrificial delusion. The way
out of anxiety begins with the understanding of sin as sacred violence.

Sin is an activity, an attitude, and a state of affairs. As an activity it is mimetic
rivalry with God (φθόνος),[1] as an attitude it is concupiscence (ἐπιθυμία), and
as a state of affairs it is the system of sacred violence (ἁμαρτία). Sin begins in
the mystery of free human desire, and takes shape in the deformation of that
desire. From Paul's pen desire is usually wrongful desire, in the sense of desire
deformed to rivalry, and especially to rivalry with God.

---

[1] Cf. T. Sim 3:2 "Envy rules over the whole human disposition." Cf. Wisd 2:24 "Through
the envy of the devil death came into the world, and they that belong to his realm experience it."

Bultmann expresses this understanding as follows, "the ultimate sin reveals itself to be the false assumption of receiving life not as a gift of the Creator but procuring it by one's own power, of living from one's self rather than from God."[2] To sin is to deform desire to acquisitive and conflictual mimesis, to "procure" being through rivalry with God rather than to receive it as a gift from God, and thus to set desire on its way through the double transference to sacred violence.

Sin and Desire

It is not unusual among religious thinkers to locate the human problem in the field of desire. The Buddha is only the best known and most radical of many teachers who located it there. Rabbinic Judaism regarded the moral struggle to be between the evil impulse and the good. Although the former had the advantage of being active from birth, the latter, which came alive at the age of discretion, rapidly made up any lost influence and could control the evil impulse if nourished daily from the Torah.[3] Philo provides a good example of the importance of the problem of desire in the milieu of the Hellenistic religio-philosophic situation in which it took the form of the problem of the conflict between the mind and the passions. For Philo the Scriptures were an allegory of the struggle of the rational/spiritual mind to gain control over the irrational/material body and eventually to escape from it altogether in an ascent to the divine, which could be anticipated here and now by mystical experience. The moral life was a struggle for mastery and against enslavement by wrong desire. Particularly, therefore, in the use of the master/slave metaphor (Rom 6) Paul stands in the mainstream of Hellenistic moral thinking.[4]

Paul is somewhat more idiosyncratic, however, in his claim that the prohibitions intended to curb desire actually provoke it (Rom 7:7),[5] but not entirely so. It could be argued that this was the basic insight of the Buddha as well; the struggle with desire only enhances its power, therefore one must drop back a stage and attack the roots by withdrawing cooperation from all desire,

---

[2] R. Bultmann, *Theology of the New Testament 1*, 232.

[3] W. D. Davies, *Paul and Rabbinic Judaism*, 30. Davies interprets Rom 1:18ff. by means of the rabbinic categories of the *yetzer ha-ra* and the *yetzer ha-tob*, which is quite appropriate if one understands "yetzer" to signify desire as such. R. Yannai (C.E. 200) said: "He who hearkened to his evil impulse is as if he practised idolatry: for it is said, 'There shall no strange God be within thee: Thou shalt not worship any God" (J. Ned. 9.41.b). Here idolatry is identified with every obedience to the *yetzer ha-ra*. The *yetzer* is, therefore, desire as such seen from two possible points of view; when it deviates to mimesis it is the *yetzer ha-ra* and when it maintains its proper orientation to God it is the *yetzer ha-tob*.

[4] G. Röhser, *Metaphorik und Personifikation der Sünde*, 106–7.

[5] Cf. G. Bataille, *Erotism*.

whether good or bad. Paul is, however, quite idiosyncratic vis-à-vis his ancestral Judaism, which had a remarkably robust confidence in the power of the rational will reinforced by divine grace to guide desire to the proper goal. Protestant theology on the whole sees Paul as condemning this confidence as itself the essence of wrong desire—to be God to oneself—because it flows from an unwarranted independence of the creature over against the creator.

The keynote of Paul's doctrine of sin is struck in Romans 7:7: "What therefore shall we say? That the Law is sin? Not at all! But I would not have known sin excepting through the Law, I would not have known [wrong] desire (ἐπιθυμία) had the Law not said, 'Thou shalt not desire (ουκ ἐπιθυμήσεις).' "[6] Thus sin is identified as a problem of desire, and the prohibition is identified as an intrinsic part of this problem. Sin is the general term for the whole dynamic by which desire uses the Law to provoke and exacerbate concupiscence. This insight comes from an extended meditation on the account of the fall in Genesis 2–3; Adam is the éminence grise behind sin, and Paul shapes his whole theology of sin and redemption around the figures of Adam and Christ (1 Cor 15:22). His reading of the Adam story, like the interpretation of the Abraham figure in Galatians 3, is another example of the interpretation of the Torah in the light of the Cross.

Adam and the Deformation of Desire

Romans 5:12, that sin and death entered the world through Adam's transgression, is the general rubric over our discussion, and Romans 1:18—3:20, 5:12-21, 7:7-13, and 8:18-25 are the lenses through which we shall read Paul's interpretation of the Adam story.[7] The first and last passages are point and counterpoint, expounding the problem and the solution respectively, while 5:12-21, at the center of the argument, reveals its balanced structure, and 7:7-25 begins the presentation of the solution that culminates in 8. I shall discuss each passage in turn.

Paul's explanation takes the form of a meditation on the story of the first sin in Genesis 2:15-17 and 3:1-24. Adam is the symbol for both the individual and the race, and for the fact that "ontogeny recapitulates phylogeny." By means of this figure Paul is able to communicate the nature of sin as something that is both an act of individual irresponsibility and an imprisonment within a system of racial irresponsibility, both the individuality and the universality of sin.

---

[6] J. C. Beker, *The Apostle Paul,* 217–18. For the absolute use of "desire," see 4 Macc 2:6; Vita Adae 19; Philo, *Dec* 10, 42, 150, 173.

[7] For Rom 1, see M. D. Hooker, "Adam in Romans 1"; idem, "A Further Note on Romans 1." C. K. Barrett, *From First Adam to Last.* For Rom 7, see S. Lyonnet, " 'Tu ne convoiteras pas' (Rom vii 7)," and G. Theissen, *Psychological Aspects,* 202–10; P. Perkins, "Pauline Anthropology"; H. Räisänen, "Zum Gebrauch von ἐπιθυμία und ἐπιθυμεῖν bei Paulus."

From his reading of this story, as we are able to reconstruct it primarily out of the text of Romans, we get a clear indication of the role of mimesis in his thought.[8] To be sure, there is no direct reference to imitation in the Genesis story, but the congeries of desire, rivalry, and scapegoating testifies to the presence of sacred violence. The serpent is the symbol of the possibility that desire might degenerate into mimetic rivalry, and the prohibition is the symbol of the divine resistance to that degeneration. Desire, temptation, and the Law are, therefore, the three elements of Paul's understanding of sin.

The contemporaneous Jewish tradition saw deformed desire as sensuality. Taking its cue from the shame that Adam and Eve felt after their transgression (Gen 3:7), it emphasized the erotic rather than the mimetic aspect of desire.[9] According to the Genesis text, however, sexual shame and concupiscence were the results of transgression, not the transgression itself. This misplacing of the emphasis is probably due to the influence of the account of the fall of the "watchers" (Gen 6) who fell primarily because of lust. Their very name suggests voyeurism. According to the sources, however, the watchers seem to have been corrupted before they fell to lusting, suggesting that for these sources too concupiscence is the result of sin, not the act of sin itself.[10] The fact that in this version of the fall too the link between sin and violence is close, because lust leads directly to violence and the giants produced by these illicit unions teach humanity how to eat flesh and how to make weapons and wage war,[11] suggests that it also intuits the priority of mimetic rivalry to concupiscence in the order of sin.

Adam, seen from the point of view of faith in the death of Christ, is, for Paul, the symbol of the human condition. He reads the Adamic tradition in the light of the Cross, and in this reading the violence of the Cross guides him to the signs of violence in the Adam story. The signs of violence disclosed by the Cross are the signs manifested in Paul's own experience of persecution of the Christians, and in the Judaizers scapegoating of the gentiles. They are the marks of mimetic rivalry and sacred violence in Paul's experience of Judaism. He reads the Adam story with this understanding of violence in mind.

In this light sin appears as mimetic rivalry with God. The usual reading of Paul's reading, of which C. K. Barrett's is a good example, comes very close to seeing this, but does not quite. Adam is said to wish to supplant God, to "be as God," in the sense of ruling over his own life, "marked by a will-to-power, an impatience with a position suggesting any kind of inferiority."[12] However, in

---

[8] R. Hamerton-Kelly, "Sacred Violence and Sinful Desire."

[9] *Apoc Mos* 19, 25; *Apoc Abr* 23:6-8; 4 Macc 18:8. G. Theissen, *Psychological Aspects,* 204–5.

[10] The watchers must have transgressed already to be watching women in such a way. They had been distracted prior to the outbreak of sexual desire (Jub 5:2, 9; 7:21; 1 Enoch 6:1-2; 7:1-6; 10:9; 15:8, 11; 16:1).

[11] 1 Enoch 7:4—8:1; 1 Bar 3:26.

[12] C. K. Barrett, *From First Adam to Last,* 16.

the light of Paul's experience of co-crucifixion, "being like God" has a mimetic ring, and the will to power sounds like mimetic rivalry with the divine. Thus the mimetic violence of the Cross highlights not only the disobedience of Adam but also the violent results of that disobedience. It must have been an act of the kind that caused structures of violence like the one that murdered Christ to come into being. The deformation of desire to acquisitive and conflictual mimesis, which sets in motion the mechanism of sacred violence, is, therefore, a plausible preliminary description of Adam's sin on the basis of its perceived results in the death of Christ. We must now test this preliminary description against the text.

Genesis 2:16-17; 3:1-24

We shall first present a Girardian reading of these passages in Genesis, as an example of the way Paul might possibly have understood them. We shall then show how such a reading makes good sense of the passages in Romans that are based on them.

The characters in the story are desire played by Adam and Eve, desire's propensity for acquisitive mimesis, played by the serpent, and the divine warning against acquisitiveness represented by the primal prohibition. The original state was one in which desire accepted the primal prohibition as a proper limit to its acquisitiveness. By prohibiting the one tree, God warned against the principle of acquisitiveness. The Adam story tells how desire, nevertheless, freely corrupted itself by choosing the possibility represented by the serpent to desire acquisitively the prohibited object and thus enter into a relationship of mimetic rivalry with God. This transgression is rivalry because, to corrupted desire, the prohibition represents the desire of God for the prohibited object, and human desire mimes this misperceived divine desire.

The story is a subtle presentation of the progress of this self-corruption of desire. The note of mimetic rivalry sounds right at the beginning when the serpent exaggerates the prohibition by extending it to all the trees (Gen 3:1, cf. 2:16-17). By exaggerating the prohibition, desire intensifies its own mimetic response to the divine desire, because the stronger the prohibition, which is an expression of God's desire for the prohibited objects, the stronger the human desire that mimes God's desire. Thus the serpent's exaggeration of the prohibition symbolizes how desire whips itself up into mimetic rivalry with God. This is the manipulation of the commandment to deceive and kill that Paul refers to in Romans 7:11. Once mimetic rivalry has been joined, all the violence of the Sacred will follow.

We know that Eve has been affected when she, in turn, exaggerates the prohibition even as she corrects the serpent's exaggeration, adding her own prohibition on touching the tree to God's prohibition on eating from it (Gen 3:3). Thus she indicates the aggravation of her feeling of exclusion and her temptation to mimesis. Now she has lodged in her mind the idea generated by her own desire that she is being excluded by the divine desire from something valuable. The prohibition now signifies that God desires the prohibited object and Eve mimes that desire. The woman "saw that the tree was good for food, and that it was a delight to the eyes, and that it was to be desired to make one wise" (3:6—RSV).[13] Only after the serpent had persuaded her by this deception to imitate God's acquisitive desire for the fruit did it become desirable to her; she learned rivalry from mimesis's misrepresentation of the divine desire as envious. The moment of mimetic acquisitiveness has been reached and the train of events leading to the Sacred set in motion. Thus desire transforms God from creator, to whom one should be related in gratitude, into rival, to whom one is related by envy, and it does so by manipulating the prohibition (Rom 7:11). This is the act of sin as envy (φθόνος).

Desire corrupts itself to envy by persuading itself that God is envious first.[14] Envy is defined not by the desire to have something oneself, but by the desire to deprive the other of that thing. Envy thinks that it will walk better if its neighbor breaks a leg. It is the essence of rivalry in its most metaphysical form, where the object has become relatively unimportant by comparison with the rival. Thus desire made God the ultimate model and obstacle, and the prohibition became an instrument of rivalry, the divine obstacle to human fulfillment rather than the divine warning against acquisitive mimesis that defines human identity as distinct from God and points the way to the tree of life (Gen 3:22).

The misrepresentation (= myth-representation) of the divine prohibition causes the original sense of lack. The serpent persuaded Eve that she lacked something, and that God had what she lacked, because God prohibited her from it. The ontological fact upon which this conjured sense of lack is based is the contingency of the creature upon the creator. Desire distorts this into an envious ploy on the part of the divine to best us in the game of acquisitive desire. Out of envy God withholds from us the secret of being, and once we realize this we reach out beyond the prohibition to acquire it.

In fact, there is no envy in the divine, and the prohibition is not an expression of the divine desire for the object but of the divine desire to prevent humanity from acquisitive mimesis and the ensuing course of violence. The prohibition does not symbolize human lack but human completeness and sufficiency in

---

[13] The LXX adjectives καλός, ἀρεστός, and ὡραῖος are more aesthetic than their Hebrew equivalents, emphasizing the surface appearance of the fruit. In any case, although the word ἐπιθυμία is not used, the idea of desire is powerfully present, and the RSV translation fairly reproduces the thrust of both the Hebrew and the Greek.

[14] Cf. Wisd 14:30, "They think evil of God in turning to idols." Cf. 2:24, "By the envy of the devil death entered the world." On the general theme of envy in the divine, see Plato, *Tim* 29e, *Phaedr* 247a, quoted by Philo in *Quod Lib* 13; cf. *Spec Leg* 2.249, *Leg All* 1.61, 3.7, *Abr* 203–4. That the gods need nothing is a commonplace of Greek philosophy; see the evidence cited by H. Conzelmann, *Acts of the Apostles,* 142, in commenting on Acts 17:25. The generosity of the divine was, therefore, a commonplace of Hellenistic philosophic and religious thought.

trusting dependence on the divine solicitude. Had human desire remained in the proper relation of dependency on the creator, the cycle of mimetic rivalry arising out of the false sense of lack would never have started and desire would have been free to desire the other in and for itself, and not as a means to make good its lack.

Desire, however, made the creator into the obstacle that prevents desire from fulfillment, and this had its effect on the relation between human beings. The misrepresentation of the divine desire is the paradigm of the misrepresentation of all desire. Once the principle of lack has been installed in the heart of desire, acquisitive and conflictual mimesis follow. Everyone now becomes model and obstacle, and the game of mimetic rivalry among humans is underway. Human being is unwilling to accept its ontological contingency and turns it into a lack of being that can in principle be supplied. It does this predictably by means of the strategies of desire. It whips up mimetic rivalry by pretending that the desire of the power behind the universe and of every human other is envious, and maliciously withholds the being we crave. It turns God and the human other into the model/obstacle and then into the scapegoat.

This rivalry for the fulfillment of lack is most vividly evident in the relation between the sexes. Agape, the generous love that comes from the divine fullness, was deformed to eros, the desire that lives in the power of lack, and sex became shameful (Gen 3:7). Male and female experienced sexual difference as a prohibition that masked envy and a lack that had to be overcome. The original unity of the sexes that Diotima tells of in the symbol of the primal hermaphrodite (Symp 203) dissolves and each experiences eros, "the bastard child of Wealth and Poverty." Concupiscence in its usual meaning of sexual lust, is, therefore, one of the first evidences of the deformation of desire, and plays an integral part in the subsequent development of mimetic desire in terms of misrepresentation of the prohibition. Sin as the attitude of concupiscence (ἐπιθυμία) has arrived on the scene.

Concupiscence transforms the prohibition into the principle of lack at the heart of eros and thus makes itself ultimately the love of death. The prohibition whose misrepresentation creates the sense of lack is essential to eroticism because it makes violation possible, and every erotic act is an act of violation.[15] Eros violates the self-possession of the other. There is no mutual giving in eros, only mutual taking, the "hungry mouth clamped on the other's breast." The deformation of desire into acquisitive and conflictual mimesis includes the corruption of sexuality into eroticism, which turns it from the service of life to the service of death.

We now expect the third stage of sin, as a state of affairs (ἁμαρτία) to appear, and we are not disappointed, as Adam and Eve fall to scapegoating God, one another, and the serpent (Gen 3:8-19), and thus the stage of the Sacred is

---

[15] Cf. G. Bataille, *Erotism.*

reached. The most important scapegoat is God whom Adam blames when he says, "The woman whom thou gavest to be with me, she gave me fruit of the tree and I ate" (Gen 3:12—RSV). In scapegoating God, Adam prefigures the crucifixion, as the driving out of the divine to preserve the myth of human beneficence. Adam's scapegoating of God turns God into the victim and thus, by the double transference, God becomes the primitive Sacred who threatens the curse and drives them out of paradise.

The text, however, reveals this process of sacralization. It is very precise in attributing the cause of the subsequent human misfortune. Each announcement of the curse is preceded by the emphatic, "because you have done this," and followed by the impersonal, "cursed are you / cursed is the ground" (Gen 3:14, 17). The culprits are actually guilty and the curse is the automatic result of the free acts of disobedience. The creatures bring it on themselves.

The divine causation is indirect and impersonal. Nevertheless, Adam blames God directly for his misfortune, and thus we have the first example of myth, the myth of the divine envy that scapegoats humanity, and the original sin of the idolization of God. The Bible, however, is not taken in; rather it enables us to trace the process of mythification and see its deceitfulness.

The serpent is the mythic representation of the divine envy, through which the scapegoating of God goes forward. It symbolizes and then conceals the source of the temptation in desire itself rather than in God. It is the classic symbol of the refusal of personal responsibility, which is the heart of the scapegoating phenomenon. The act of turning from the creator to the self is freely generated from within the self, but the mythic serpent presents the motive as coming from without, and ultimately from God, who gave the prohibition and the serpent to incite mimetic acquisitiveness.

The actual inner motive for sin is distrust of the constituting call of the divine prohibition on acquisitiveness—that is, lack of faith in God. The voice of desire insinuates the untrustworthiness of God and the self takes measures to secure itself by becoming God's mimetic rival. The result is that it becomes "as God" in the form of its own misbegotten image of the divine. The self becomes the monstrous double of its own misrepresentation of God. It becomes its own mimetic other, and seeks to possess itself as it is in the misprized divine other, either by becoming the other or absorbing the other into the self. By entering into the rivalry of metaphysical desire with "God," the self in fact mimes its own misunderstanding and thus turns God into an idol created by its own mimetic acquisitiveness. The myth of the serpent as scapegoat was invented to obscure this process from consciousness. In the serpent the self's own slander of God speaks.

The myth of the serpent, therefore, is also a scapegoating of the responsible self in the sense of the expulsion of responsibility onto an external fiction, and this scapegoating of the self is perhaps the most ironic moment in the story of the birth of consciousness. By refusing to acknowledge that the impulse to mimetic rivalry comes freely from within desire itself, we are unable to take responsibility for it. By driving it out into myth, we expel ourselves from ourselves and constitute ourselves as a myth to ourselves. The account of the passing of responsibility from Adam, to Eve, to the serpent, to God, is almost comic in its exaggeration (Gen 3:8-19), but it marks the serious moment of self-alienation by self-exoneration and scapegoating. It marks the moment of the idolization of God by the accusation that God is the ultimate source of the temptation to envy. God the idol is the model/obstacle who incited acquisitive desire, and the scapegoat who bears the blame for the violence that ensued.

The blaming of the serpent is the origin of mythology, and the Bible's way of signaling the advent of the whole apparatus of the Sacred. It is the first attempt to exonerate the perpetrators of the primal crime by blaming the victim (God). The cultural result is the deliberate self-deception and self-alienation of the double transference from which prohibition, ritual, and myth grow. The Bible, however, refuses to accept the ruse and assigns responsibility equally. Thus we have the first exposure of the surrogate victim mechanism and the first demythologization. All are guilty, "for God has shut up all in disobedience so that he might have mercy on all" (Rom 11:32; cf. 1 Cor 15:22).

Thus too begins the story of the dialectic between human self-righteousness and the divine judgment, seen most clearly in the very next story, of Cain and Abel (Gen 4:1-17). Cain denies responsibility for his brother's murder, but God marks him so that he may serve as a sign of responsibility for all. His progeny build the first city on the cursed ground of the brother's murder, but always there is the mark of Cain to remind them that the city is a system of sacred violence and to point them to the possibility of responsibility, repentance, and reconciliation with God.

The account of the expulsion from paradise might be perplexing in the context of the story, because here God seems to be scapegoating Adam and Eve (Gen 3:20-24). However, it is not a scapegoating because the victims really are guilty (Gen 3:17), and furthermore refuse to acknowledge their guilt. Because they do not take responsibility or repent, Adam and Eve must be expelled from paradise so that they cannot eat of the tree of life and so become immortal. We learn rather suddenly at the end of the story that there are in fact two trees in the garden (Gen 3:22-24). Only the tree of the knowledge of good and evil was forbidden (Gen 2:17), therefore we may presume that Adam and Eve would have had access to the tree of life had they obeyed the prohibition. Genesis 2:20-24, therefore, interprets the threat in Genesis 2:17, that if they eat they shall die, to mean that they shall be denied access to the tree of life. By their transgression Adam and Eve incurred death.

This is the background of Paul's statement that sin used the Law to deceive and kill Adam (Rom 7:11). According to the story they gained the knowledge of good and evil. According to our theory this "knowledge of good and evil" is acquisitive and conflictual mimesis with the divine. Before the transgression they knew only good—namely, that the creator is beneficent and generous, and free of envy. After the transgression they had imputed both evil and good to the creator in making God a rival. Thus faith as trust in the divine goodwill was at an end. Now the Law produced not faith but anxiety and rivalry with God and one another.

The sin of Adam and Eve was, therefore, the corruption of human desire to mimetic rivalry by using the prohibition to misprize the divine proscription on acquisitiveness as an expression of divine envy. This had the effect of turning God into an idol of sacred violence. The corruption of the relationship between the divine and the human corrupted the relationships between human beings. Mimetic desire broke out in the forms of envy, concupiscence, and sacred violence. This is the argument of the first three chapters of Romans.

Romans 1:18—3:20[16]

The keynote of the Letter is that only faith in the gospel can save both Jew and Greek, because the righteousness of God is given to this faith alone (Rom 1:16-17). This faith has the death of Christ at its center (Rom 3:25), and so it is not important that the terms "cross" and "crucify" (σταυρός and σταυρόω, respectively) do not occur in Romans. Romans 3:21-26 is the hinge on which the argument of the letter turns.[17] There Paul presents the death of Christ as the revelation of the two systems of the old and new creations respectively, and faith as the way to pass from one to the other. The whole argument unfolds from this faith in the death of Christ as the foundation of the new system of the righteousness of God.[18] From the vantage point of the new system, Paul sees the old under the curse of Adam, and interprets sin and the Law accordingly, demythifying sin by means of the Cross and desacralizing the Law by revealing how its basic intention has been corrupted. As he reads it, the story of Adam's sin is a symbolic account of the deviation of desire to sacred violence by means of the Law, and the corruption of the Law by the guile of desire. The results of this are idolatry, which begins with the idolization of God,

---

[16] See W. D. Davies, *Paul and Rabbinic Judaism*, 27-31. Davies reminds us of the relationship between the thought of this passage and the wisdom of Solomon. The significant passages in Wisd. are 2:24; 6:20; 6:23; 7:1ff.; 9:2; 10:1 2; 15:8; 13:1ff.; 14:12; 14:24-27; 12:23, 27; 16:28-29. There is also a remarkable reflection on the origin of idolatry in 14:12-31 that is very similar to Girard's theory of religion. It traces the origin of idolatry to the memorialization of a dead child by the father whose excessive grief causes the remembrance to escalate into worship, with the result that τόν ποτε νεκρὸν ἄνθρωπον νῦν ὡς θεὸν ἐτίμησεν (vs. 15). The transformation of a dead human into a God is the essence of the surrogate victim mechanism. This kind of religion leads to violent disorder, which nevertheless they call peace (ἀλλὰ καὶ ἐν μεγάλῳ ζῶντες ἀγνοίας πολέμῳ τὰ τοσαῦτα κακὰ εἰρήνην προσαγορεύουσιν—22).

[17] C. K. Barrett, *A Commentary on the Epistle to the Romans*, 72, "one of the great turning points of the epistle"; C. E. B. Cranfield, *The Epistle to the Romans 1*, 73, "the center and heart of the whole of Rom 1:16b—15:13"; O. Kuss, *Der Römerbrief*, 1 (1963), 110, "theologische und architectonische Mitte des Römerbriefs," cited by Michael Theobald, "Das Gottesbild des Paulus"; see 131, n. 1, for a good bibliography on the passage.

[18] On "righteousness" as world order, see H. H. Schmid, *Gerechtigkeit als Weltordnung;* idem. "Rechtfertigung als Schöpfungsgeschehen."

in the sense of the transformation of God from generous creator to envious rival and then scapegoat, and the construction of religion as the system of the primitive Sacred.

The pivot on which the action in the Adam story turns is the serpent, symbol of the possibility given along with its freedom for desire to corrupt itself. The origin of desire's desire for self-corruption lies beyond explanation in the freedom that is its being in the image of God. The temptation of freedom draws desire away from its proper divine pole to mimetic rivalry and the displacement of the divine pole by the human. The human pole had to become the divine, and in the course of this the human attributed to the divine the characteristics of its own mimetic rivalry and thus turned God into an idol by the double transference.

The corruption of desire took place as a free act in three stages, each of which is an element in idolatry. The first stage is the diversion of desire from the creator to the self, symbolized by Eve's turning to the serpent. The second stage is the desire to be like God—to mime one's own misrepresentation of the divine desire—by transgressing the limit so as to become the mimetic rival of the divine and the object of one's own desire as one imagines it in the divine, to be one's own creator as the source and object of one's own desire mediated through the creator. The third stage is to blame God for this process, and thereby turn God into the divine victim/scapegoat, and the source of the threat of the Sacred. This is the "qualitative leap" of sin, the free act of turning from God through God to the self, the free decision to misdirect desire to the solipsism of self-sufficiency, to desire one's own desire in everyone and everything, including the divine, and to turn God into the primitive Sacred.

The mediation of self-desire through the divine explains the dynamics of idolatry. The idol is the victim to whom I have transferred my own mimetic desire. I imagine that it desires what I desire and then I copy my own desire as I imagine it in the victim. But the idol is not therefore a purely private delusion, because the desire I attribute mimetically to it has been mimed from the human other, in the course of the swing from acquisitive to conflictual mimesis. Thus the idol as surrogate victim is the mirror that reflects back the conflictual mimesis of the group.

The idolization of God is the presupposition of the idolization of one's fellow human beings (Rom 1:24-32). One enters into the same mimetic rivalry with them as with God, and is "given over" to three forms of mimetic desire: the "desires of our hearts," "disgraceful passions," and the "failed mind" (ἀδόκιμος νοῦς). These are the pathologies of deviated desire in descending order, the consequences of which the first couple were "ashamed" (Gen 3:7). Sexuality is deformed to lust. The first form of this concupiscence is sexual transgression in general, the dishonoring of the body through fornication, exhibitionism, and sadomasochism of all kinds. Paul probably has in mind not only sexual licence but also the erotic violence of the arena—gladiatorial combats, naked athletes, and wrestling with wild beasts.

The next stage in this Gadarene descent is homosexuality understood as an explicit rather than an incidental perversion of the relationship with God and each other. The incidental violation of the body's modesty escalates into its intentional humiliation by perversion. The "desires of the heart" are those untrammeled by inhibition, but "disgraceful desires" are those that arise from deliberate perversion (Rom 1:24, 26). Thus corruption progresses from absence of restraint to active deformation, from passive to active corruption. As desire for the same sex, homosexuality reveals with special clarity the desire of the self for itself in the other, and the love of the self through the other.

Physical abuse is, however, merely symptomatic of a deeper corruption of desire that contaminates all human interactions, the murderous strife of the "failed mind" (ἀδόκιμος νοῦς). The "failed mind" is the third stage of corruption, and from it come the deeply destructive forces of disorder, the vices that destroy human community: "wickedness, evil, covetousness, malice . . . envy, murder, strife, deceit, malignity . . . gossips, slanderers, haters of God, insolent, haughty, boastful, inventors of evil, disobedient to parents, foolish, faithless, heartless, ruthless" (Rom 1:29-31).[19] It is not difficult to see how all of these vices stem from mimetic rivalry.[20] "The failed mind" is a mind enslaved to the deviated transcendence of mimetic rivalry in its most acute form, in which the object of desire is not merely physical but the intangible prizes of prestige and power. The "failed mind" desires not only to possess the other but to consume or destroy. It wishes not only to imitate the other, nor merely to possess itself in the other, but to destroy the other as the place where the self is alien to itself.

And all the while they know the primal prohibition (δικαίωμα) that those who do such things must die (Rom 1:32).[21] Genesis 2:15-17 is the first commandment to carry an explicit sanction of death, and Paul assumes it to be universally recognized; the failed mind of both Jew and gentile intuits it (Rom 2:15),[22] but submerges it in a context of wrongdoing (τὴν ἀλήθειαν ἐν ἀδικίᾳ κατεχόντων) (Rom 1:18). This is an apt description of what happens to the prohibition when desire makes it part of the structure of sacred violence, by turning it into the envious obstruction of the idolized God. The divinity of

---

[19] Cf. Philo, *Sacrif.* 32, which Colson and Whitaker call "probably the most formidable catalogue of bad qualities ever drawn up" (*LCL* 2,89). Cf. Wisd. 14:25ff. Philo presents the list as the work of the "Cain" type of mind, whose characteristic is to think that it alone is the source of all its benefits (*Cher.* 57, 63–66, 83) and to refuse to give thanks to God.

[20] In Hellenistic Jewish sources desire (ἐπιθυμία) was often said to be the root of all sin: Philo, *Spec Leg* 4.84, 130; *Dec* 142, 173.

[21] R. W. Thompson, "How is the Law Fulfilled in Us?," referring to Rom 8:4, 13:8-10, and Gal 5:13-16, argues that δικαίωμα means primarily the love of neighbor as the "just requirement" of the Law. In 1:32, therefore, we have the negative formulation of the same point: the interdiction of mimetic rivalry is the negative expression of the command to love the neighbor (13:10).

[22] Cf. το κρίμα in 2:2, which means essentially the same thing—namely, the condemnation due to transgression.

God that can be known from the created world (Rom 1:20) is, therefore, essentially the prohibition on mimetic rivalry in the form of the demand for the recognition of the true transcendence and generosity of God, expressed in Genesis 2:15-17.

Paul, therefore, reckons with this one fundamental commandment, the primal prohibition, which has been corrupted along with desire. As desire became rivalry, so the prohibition became a jealous obstruction. This is the key to Paul's understanding of the Mosaic Law. For him the Jewish interpretation of the Mosaic Law is the corrupt Adamic expression of the primal prohibition deformed by mimetic desire to the service of the primitive Sacred. The true, uncorrupted prohibition, on the other hand, is the one that we accept prior to the double transference onto the surrogate victim; it is the presacralized prohibition that arises from personal responsibility, which has been corrupted by being transferred to the Sacred and sanctioned by vengeance. The sanction of death that the uncorrupted prohibition carries is not vengeful but minatory. If we transgress it, we remove the proper limit that defines our creaturehood and prevents mimesis from becoming rivalrous and open the way to rivalry not only with God but with all other human beings. Paul calls the misrepresentation of the divine prohibition the refusal to give honor and thanks to God (Rom 1:21) and identifies it as the basis of the refusal to relate to one another in terms of respect and gratitude that results in the unleashing of mimetic rivalry with the ultimate outcome of death (Rom 1:24ff.).

The idolization of the prohibition into the obstacle is the basis of the spurious order of the "good violence" of the primitive Sacred. The prohibition was dissembled through the Sacred into a Law that provokes the envy it proscribes (Rom 7:7), because within the nexus of the Sacred we see it as the obstacle set up by the envy of God. Thus we refuse to own our envy and transfer it to the idolized God. Paul understands this configuration by reason of the Cross; he sees that mimetic desire uses the prohibition to transfer our violence to God, by misrepresenting the prohibition as a sign of divine envy, and so stimulates rather than prevents rivalry, and promotes the killing of surrogate victims in symbiosis with the sacrificial system. The individual expression of this pathology is the zealotry that Paul himself practiced, scapegoating the Christians in obedience to this system of deformed desire. Paul, therefore, accuses the current interpretation of the Law of using the Law to idolize God.

The unfolding of the consequences of this idolatry in Romans 1:18—3:20 is described as the revelation of the "wrath of God" (1:18). Paul refers to the wrath (ὀργή) ten times in Romans (1:18; 2:5, 8; 3:5; 4:15; 5:9; 9:22; 12:19; 13:4, 5), and only once outside this epistle, in 1 Thessalonians 2:16. The last text is a bitter indictment of the Jews that many commentators find impossible to attribute to Paul for the reason of its bitterness. There is no reason, however, to deny the statement to Paul and consequently no reason not to use

1 Thessalonians 2:14-16 to illuminate Romans 1:18ff.[23] In 1 Thessalonians 2:14-16 Paul uses traditional material from the theme of the persecution of the prophets to blame the Jews for the death of Christ. In Romans 1:18ff. he develops the consequences of idolatry under the rubric "the Jew first and also the Greek" (Rom 1:16, 2:9-10, 3:9),[24] which applies not only to the order of salvation but also to the order of sin. The order of sin or the wrath is the order of sacred violence.

The whole letter expounds how the transgression of the Jews in killing Christ produced "wealth for the cosmos" (Rom 11:12).[25] Therefore at the outset Paul argues that the Jews are first in sin! For the sake of the argument, however, which is directed primarily to Jews, he begins by making the point that salvation and sin encompass the whole world and there is no difference between Jew and Greek in this regard. All this world, in both its Jewish and gentile manifestations, is under the wrath of God, shut up in disobedience (Rom 11:32; Gal 3:22), sealed in the Sacred, because of the sin of Adam (Rom 5:12; 1 Cor 15:22). The Jews are in mind, therefore, from the beginning of the indictment in Romans 1:18.[26]

This wrath of God is revealed in the gospel; not just in the preaching but in the events on which the preaching is based.[27] This is clearly the sense of Romans 1:18, which must be taken as carrying on the thought of Romans 1:17 where the Gospel is the locus of revelation. Barth puts it succinctly; "The death of Jesus Christ on the Cross is the revelation of God's Wrath from heaven,"[28] and this must be taken seriously as the defining principle of the concept of the wrath. Accordingly, the wrath revealed in the gospel is not the divine vengeance that should have fallen on us falling instead on Jesus, but rather the divine nonresistance to human evil (cf. Matt 5:39), God's willingness to suffer violence rather than defend himself or retaliate. It is the permission granted

---

[23] K. Donfried, "Paul and Judaism"; W. D. Davies, "Paul and the People of Israel"; D. Schmidt, "Linguistic Evidence." Donfried (250–53) relates the discussion of 1 Thess 2:16 to the discussion of the term "wrath" in Romans.

[24] Cf. T. Donaldson, "The 'Curse of the Law,'" who says that for Paul the Jews, "the people of the Law, thus functions as a kind of representative sample of the whole. Their plight is no different from the plight of the whole of humankind, but through the operation of the Law in their situation that plight is thrown into sharp relief" (104). Donaldson says this apropos of Gal 3:13-14, but it is equally apt of Rom 1:18ff.

[25] The term παράπτωμα used in 11:12 to describe the act of sin of the Jews is the same term used in 5:15-18 to describe Adam's act of sin, which we all imitated. In 4:25 it describes that on account of which Christ died; διά with the acc. here must be taken to mean that on account of which, in the sense of that which caused the death. Barrett's translation is apt, "was delivered up because of the sins we committed, and raised up because of the justification that was to be granted us" (*Romans*, 99).

[26] Cranfield, *Romans 1*, 141–42. The force of διό in Rom 2:1 indicates that the indictment of the Jew that begins explicitly in Rom 2:1 follows logically from Rom 1:18-32.

[27] "The reality of the Wrath of God is only truly known when it is seen in its revelation in Gethsemane and on Golgotha" (*Cranfield, Romans 1*, 110).

[28] Karl Barth, *A Shorter Commentary on Romans*, 26.

us by God to afflict ourselves unknowingly; it is the divine nonresistance to human evil. It is God's unwillingness to intervene in the process of action and consequence in the human world by which we set up and operate the system of sacred violence, and so paradoxically a sign of love as the refusal to abridge our freedom and a respect for our choices even when they are catastrophic. One need not posit an absolutely reciprocal moral order to acknowledge that self-destructive activity takes place and that in a general sense we punish ourselves and each other. The Cross reveals this paradoxical wrath as God's acceptance of our free choice to destroy ourselves and each other, inasmuch as it is the supreme instance of this human rage against the good.[29] Wrath, therefore, is primarily sacred violence in its aspect of human vengeance.

The Cross first discloses the wrath in the structure of Judaism, which is Paul's exemplary instance of religion as violence. The Jews are the "vessels of wrath created for destruction" whose function is to reveal the wrath and the power of God (Rom 9:22).[30] That is why God has "borne them with patience"; their very existence down the ages, driving out and killing the prophets (1 Thess 2:15-16) was a testimony to the wrath that culminated in the Cross. Thus dialectically the Jews served the divine revelation, a theme to which I shall return at length.

Wrath has an essentially eschatological significance, but it is also at work in the world before the end, in the sacred violence of both the civil and the religious institutions. In Romans 13:4-5 the officers of the state serve God by promoting the good of the Christian, presumably in providing the provisional order within which Christians are to work out their salvation, and enforcing the vengeance that is part of this order "with a view to wrath" (εἰς ὀργήν), in the sense already described. One is to be subject to these authorities not only to avoid the sanctions of the wrath but also because of the dictates of conscience. In Romans 4:15 Paul states explicitly that the Law works wrath, which I take to mean that it is the basis of the sacred violence of zealous Judaism. The passages in which wrath is a present phenomenon refer, therefore, to institutionalized violence in the form of religious and civil vengeance (Rom 4:15, 9:22, 13:4-5), and to the abandonment to deformed desire that culminates in the violence of the failed mind whose prime instance is Jewish boasting (Rom 1:18—3:20).

The passages in which wrath is a future phenomenon seem to understand it as the eschatological divine vengeance (Rom 2:5,8; 5:9; 12:19; and to some extent 9:22), but there is no reason to see a change in the way the wrath

---

[29] The predominantly impersonal reference to "the wrath" confirms this interpretation. Only once is it referred to as "the wrath of God" (Rom 1:18), and soon thereafter described explicitly as God's giving us up to our own desires (1:23). All other references are simply to "the wrath." In the one case where wrath is God's direct response to human transgression, the text identifies it as a "human" mode of speaking (Rom 3:5).

[30] A. T. Hanson, "Vessels of Wrath or Instruments of Wrath? Romans IX. 22-3," 433–43, argues that the unbelieving Jews were the instruments by which the wrath of God was revealed.

functions. In the eschaton there will simply be a climax and a conclusion of the process of self-destruction that has been going on all the time, an end of the possibility of repentance and restoration. "The last judgement makes one be what one has been—irremediably."[31] God does not intervene to destroy the system of sacred violence, but rather provides us with an opportunity to escape from it.

Paul indicts the whole world but singles out the Jews as an acute example of sacred violence. The phrase "those who do such things" (οἱ τά τοιαῦτα πράσσοντες), which he repeats three times (Rom 1:32, 2:2-3 x2), is the transition to an explicit reference to the Jews. The "such things" that they do are chiefly the deeds of the "failed mind" (ἀδόκιμος νοῦς—Rom 1:28-32; cf. 2:21-24), and those who do them are now explicitly both gentiles and Jews (Rom 2:1). It is significant that Paul introduces the Jews explicitly only when the exposition of the development of sin has reached a climax in the "failed mind," although their presence has been implied all along.

In Romans 2 Paul's conception of the Law oscillates between the primal prohibition (Rom 1:32; 2:2-3)[32] and the Mosaic Law. In Rom 2: 1-11 he has the prohibition in mind because most of the references to the "work" are in the singular (ἔργου ἀγαθοῦ—7; τὸ κακόν—9; τὸ ἀγαθόν—10). This also seems to be the meaning of the τὸ ἔργον τοῦ νόμου γραπτὸν ἐν ταῖς καρδίαις ἀὐτῶν in Romans 2:15. The references in the plural must be interpreted in terms of this preponderance of the singular as nevertheless references to the primal prohibition. It could be that he has in mind the two valences of the primal prohibition, both the negative and the positive, so that when he says that the "gentiles do the *things* of the Law" (τὰ τοῦ νόμου—Rom 2:14) he still has the prohibition in mind. Therefore, the primal prohibition lies behind the text here and behind the tendency to summarize the Law in the great commandment or in the commandments against idolatry and envy, which are themselves essentially expressions, respectively, of the positive and negative valency of the prohibition (Rom 13:8-10; Gal 5:14; Rom 7:7).

In Romans 2:21-29, however, he has the Mosaic Law in mind, referring to it explicitly in Romans 2:21-23. The argument that what counts with God is deeds and not status, is a response to the Jewish insistence that their status as possessors of the Mosaic Law gives them a privileged position with reference to salvation.

Elsewhere Paul has argued that there are two worlds and that those who belong to the old world can only be saved by passing over into the new through

---

[31] Sartre, *Being and Nothingness*, 538.

[32] G. Klein, "Sündenverständnis und theologia crucis bei Paulus"; *Die von Gott gegebene Gesetz ist nicht einfach mit dem identisch, was der Jude zu erfüllen trachtet* (257). He refers also to Stuhlmacher's argument that the spiritual intention of the Law achieves its goal only when Christ liberates its life-preserving function. Stuhlmacher calls this new Torah the Zion Torah as distinct from the Sinai Torah; cf. P. Stuhlmacher, "Das Gesetz als Thema biblischer Theologie."

the act of faith in Christ (Gal 6:14-15)—that is, that there is no "natural" knowledge of God of the kind implied in this part of Romans. The explanation of this apparent aberration is that he argues on the two levels inherent in the symbol of Adam, that of the group and that of the individual, of phylogeny and ontogeny. On the level of the group the two worlds are mutually exclusive, but on the level of the individual they overlap. In the old world there are both Jew and gentile individuals who desire "glory and immortality through the patience of a good work" (Rom 2:7) and that is their form of saving faith. They show that they still intuit the presence of the primal prohibition and seek the true transcendence of God. This places the Mosaic Law on the same basis as other ethical codes, as one among many expressions of the primal prohibition, one of several sources of moral insight, and part of the ethical debate that goes on in the world (Rom 2:15b). Because the Law incorporates the primal prohibition, it is possible for the gentiles to do the Law without having the Law, because their own sources also incorporate it.

This shows that Paul does have a real place for the doctrine of creation in his theology. The old world that has fallen prey to violence nevertheless remains God's world and the primal prohibition by which God maintains Godhood can still be discerned through all the distortions of sacred violence. This is evident also from the way Paul reasons morally.[33] He does not give the Mosaic Law a place of honor among the moral sanctions he invokes, but appeals to a wide range of rational and pragmatic sanctions at the center of which is the theological sanction of the love commandment, which he takes to be the central thrust of the Mosaic Law and the positive form of the primal prohibition. By loving God and the neighbor one observes the original prohibition in the sense that one ceases from mimetic rivalry with God and the other, and replaces it with the good mimesis of love.

The larger point that he is making in the context of the argument in Romans 1:18—3:20 is that the Jews and the gentiles are in the same situation and that the election of the chosen people does not exonerate individual transgressors. In all groups there are transgressors as well as those who try to observe the primal prohibition, and the desire of the latter counts with God in their favor.

All of this takes place within the old system, which is, therefore, not totally corrupt, but mixed. In Girardian terms this means that even within the system of sacred violence there are those who withhold their vote from the scapegoating consensus. Parts of the Old Testament and the Greek tragedies are pre-Christian instances of the disclosure of the possibility of the nonviolent system grounded in the original goodness of the creation. The new creation based on the uncorrupted prohibition is mostly evident, however, on the individual rather than the group level, although the emerging, nonexclusive

[33] R. Hamerton-Kelly, "Sacred Violence and 'Works of Law.'"

Christian community, as a vanguard of the new creation, is a hopeful anticipation of a world beyond sacred violence. Faith in the Cross, therefore, redeems the Law by restoring the prohibition to its original loving intention, by lifting it out of the Jewish context of sacred violence, and by enabling a new, nonsacrificial reading of the Torah.

Structurally speaking this means that there are two founding mechanisms at work, sacred violence and divine love, and the latter is logically prior to the former. In Genesis the announcement that we are created in the image and likeness of God and commanded to be co-creators (Gen 1:26-31) precedes the account of the fall. In the experience of the individual, the possibility of good mimesis precedes the corruption of mimesis to rivalry. Freedom grounds both of these possibilities, and the fact that we realize the negative does not erase the possibility of the positive. If this were not the case, the creation would be tantamount to the fall and Paul would be a Gnostic dualist. Romans 2 shows that this is not the case.

Desire in itself is good, and its imitative structure makes possible the vocation to imitate God as co-creators (Gen 1:28-30).[34] As Paul read the Torah the first word of God to humankind is this commandment to act like God, to be a pro-creator and to exercise universal dominion. This is the implication of being in the divine image. As the image of God (2 Cor 3:18; Wisd 7:25; cf. Prov 8:22; Sir 24)[35] the human replicates the divine on the earthly level, but always subject to the divine sovereignty, which is maintained by attracting to itself all of human desire (Deut 6:4 / Mark 12:29-30), and setting the limits to that desire through prohibition. There is, therefore, a good creative mimesis of God, and to this we shall return.

In conclusion, as he reaffirms the equality of Jew and gentile in sin, Paul says that the Law, now in the sense of the Old Testament in general, speaks especially to those under the Law (Rom 3:19-20) so that the Jews should be especially aware of the fact that the purpose of the Law in their present circumstances is to uncover the hidden work of sin. The Gospel reveals that the old age in general and the way of life based on the Mosaic Law in particular are interlocking systems of mimetic violence. The concluding emphatic statement that the Law speaks to those under the Law (Rom 3:19) confirms that for Paul the Jew is first in sin. Jew and gentile are equal in sin, but the Jew is more equal than the gentile! The Judaism that Paul has in mind is the acute example of

---

[34] R. Samuel ben Nahman understands our point completely and his famous logion in Gen Rab 9.7 could be Girard in a nutshell: " 'And behold it was very good.' This is the evil impulse! Is then the evil impulse good? Yet were it not for the evil impulse no man would build a house, nor marry a wife, nor engage in trade. Solomon said 'All labor and all excelling in work is a man's rivalry with his neighbor (Ecclesiastes 4:4).' " Quoted from W. D. Davies, *Paul and Rabbinic Judaism*, 22.

[35] R. G. Hamerton-Kelly, *Pre-Existence, Wisdom, and the Son of Man*, 172.

the pathology of sacred violence consequent to Adam's sin of mimetic rivalry with the divine.

The argument of Romans 1:18—3:20 shows that Paul is having trouble with the doctrine of election. His adherence to it makes it impossible for him to give up the idea that the Jews play a special role in the divine plan of salvation, but the only role he can find for them in the wake of their rejection of the Messiah is the negative one of being the rejectors and, therefore, first in sin—as they also are first in salvation, by the fact that Jesus and his initial followers were Jews.

As Paul understands the claim to election, it is based on the superiority of the moral insight which the Torah provides (Rom 2:17-20). However, his belief that the prohibition on mimetic desire, which constitutes the basic intent of the Torah, is universally known, entails that there is no essential difference between the Mosaic Law and other codes of behavior, and that it is possible for people to observe the prohibition without knowing the Mosaic Law. This undermines the Jewish claim to election based on the exclusiveness and superiority of the Torah. Consequently the only remaining basis for the claim that the Jews are elect and called to play a special role in the plan of salvation is that they disclose sacred violence, especially by their rejection of the Messiah. We shall return to this dialectical interpretation of election in the next chapter.

Romans 7:7-25

Paul applies the consequences of this reading of Adam's sin to the doctrine of the Mosaic Law in Romans 7:7-13, where he continues to think of the δικαίωμα τοῦ θεοῦ (Rom 1:32; cf. 8:4) as the basic intention of the Mosaic Law. Consonant with Jewish tradition he identifies the fundamental thrust of the Law with the tenth commandment of the decalogue, the proscription against envy,[36] which in his mind corresponds by reason of its place as the last commandment, with the first commandment, the prohibition on idolatry. We have seen how the primal prohibition is a proscription on envy, and how it was misused by desire to turn the divine into a rival, that is, to idolize God. In Romans 1:18—3:20 Paul had both commandments—the first, against idolatry, and the last, against envy—in mind as he wrote, while here he focuses on the last, taking it as the δικαίωμα. He uses the terms νόμος and ἐντολή interchangeably as he reads the decalogue as an expression of the

---

[36] 4 Macc 2:6; G. Theissen, *Psychological Aspects,* 204–5; R. Weber, "Die Geschichte des Gesetzes und des Ich in Römer 7, 7–8,4: Einige Überlegungen zum Zuzammenhang von Heilsgeschichte und Anthropologie im Blick auf die theologische Grundstellung des paulinischen Denkens" (154–55).

primal prohibition.[37] Νόμος is the Law as a whole and ἐντολή is the tenth summary commandment, which expresses the δικαίωμα. The νόμος is the ἐντολή writ large and the ἐντολή is the νόμος in a nutshell.

The Mosaic Law is not the same as sin because it expresses the δικαίωμα, the divine defense against mimetic rivalry. Speaking representatively, in the person of Adam, Paul gives us an allegorical summary of the temptation story in which he assigns specific theological identities to the characters in the narrative. Adam is Paul and everyman; the prohibition is the basic intention of the decalogue expressed in its first and last injunctions; and the serpent is sin that tricked everyman into transgressing the prohibition and thus caused mimetic desire to break out in him (κατειργάσατο εν ἐμοὶ πᾶσαν ἐπιθυμίαν—Rom 7:8).

According to our analysis of the Genesis story, the serpent symbolized the temptation of desire to deform itself that arises freely within desire. In the present passage Paul telescopes temptation and sin because the sinful yielding to temptation is already a fait accompli in his case. The prohibition is an essential instrument of this deformation because without it, desire could not have formed the idea that God was enviously keeping something from it. The temptation presented by the prohibition is, therefore, as I have argued, the temptation to mimetic rivalry with God. Thus Paul can write, "But sin taking its opportunity through the prohibition, worked all kinds of wrong desire in me" (Rom 7:8)—that is, it provoked mimetic rivalry with God. Sin is, therefore, the free self-deformation of desire to idolatry, in the sense of turning God into a mimetic rival. It was not the prohibition but sinful desire that caused his spiritual death, and even in this circumstance the goodness of the prohibition was manifest in that it made sin appear more sinful and thus brought it to light (Rom 7:13).

The Law, therefore, remains "holy, just, and good" because it expresses the primal prohibition (Rom 7:12), especially in its first and last injunctions, and because it exposes sin. However, the fact that Paul recognizes this does not automatically mean that he approves the current religion based on obedience to the Mosaic Law. On the contrary, the realization of the goodness of the Law highlights the extent to which it is being misused in Judaism. Sin manipulated the commandment in order to create not only deformed desire but also the whole structure of the Sacred, or, less symbolically, desire deformed itself with reference to God and thus created a religion in which God is an idol and the prohibition is the instrument of that idolization.

In the following famous passage (Rom 7:14-25), still speaking representatively, but now as a representative specifically of the religious person, Paul gives an account of the plight of the sinner caught in the coils of the Sacred,

---

[37] R. Weber, ibid., 156–58, reads the relationship between ἐντολή and νόμος in roughly the same way as I do. Specifically, he does not see them as synonyms as so many other commentators do.

and confronted by the holy command. He confesses that he did not know what he was doing when as a Jew he tried to obey the command. The sacred system created by sin blinded him to the real consequences of his actions. He thought he was doing the good, and according to the sacral interpretation of the Law within which he lived he was doing the good. Now, however, from the viewpoint of his conversion and the Cross he sees that he was deceived and self-deceived. Sin used the Law to deceive him, by constructing the sacred community of sin and death within which his desire for God was deformed continuously into the service of self. His will was not weak but warped by mimesis, the deviated desire that dwelt in his religious identity as a Jew. He thought he was serving the one God of Abraham but he was really serving the idol of sacred violence. "Wretched man that I am! Who will deliver me from the body of this death?" (Rom 7:24). For Paul, from this point of view the body of death is the Jewish religious system.

Paul refers to his individual self in this passage, but that self is the representative Jewish self, given identity by his membership in the community of the Law. When he says that nothing good dwells in his flesh, we cannot ignore the strong allusion to his Jewish identity present in the term "flesh" (Rom 11:14; Phil 3:4). Just as the serpent used the good prohibition to deceive and enslave Adam in the coils of sacred violence, so deformed desire uses the good Law to do the same to the Jew. It achieves this by creating a system of sacred violence within which good intentions have bad outcomes.

This is a severe indictment of Judaism. In effect Paul accuses his ancestral religion of being a system of sacred violence in which sin misuses the Law as part of its strategy to dominate all humanity. Thus Paul preserves himself from the Marcionite heresy at the expense of Judaism; he saves the Torah at the expense of Judaism; he accuses Judaism of a sinful distortion of the primal divine prohibition, and of being, as a result, a structure of sacred violence.

Paul, therefore, reads the story of the fall as a study in the nature and origin of mimetic desire and of the system of sacred violence. This hermeneutical method is similar to Philo's who internalized the story and read it as a psychological allegory; Adam stands for the mind (νοῦς), Eve the senses (ἄισθησις), and the serpent either pleasure (ἡδονή) or desire (ἐπιθυμία).[38] The main difference, apart from the obvious ones, is that Paul understands the ego mimetically while Philo understands it substantively. Paul's ego is not the stable and self-sufficient entity that a theory like Philo's demands, but is constituted by mimetic interaction.[39] The fact that I would not have known sin if the

---

[38] *Leg All* 2.5, 24, 38, 72, 74; *Opif* 157; *Quaes Gen* 1.47–8. G. Theissen, *Psychological Aspects*, 206–7.

[39] Cf. M. Borch-Jacobsen, *The Freudian Subject*. Cf. "His [the believer's] continuity and identity also rest outside himself, in his participation in the heavenly world and in his communication with the Word of his creator, which is always challenging him anew to leave his own past behind and

prohibition had not confronted me shows that for Paul the "other" is essential to the constitution of the ego. This does not mean that self-consciousness comes only through sin, but simply that this negative experience shows the mimetic structure of the self.

Romans 5:12-21

Whereas in chapters 1-3 and 7, Paul distinguishes between the primal prohibition and the Mosaic Law, while nevertheless treating them as one, here he invokes their separation in time to signal the difference in their function. Sin entered the world through Adam's transgression of the prohibition and was in the world before the Law of Moses was promulgated. The primal prohibition made sin actual, the Mosaic Law "charges sin to our account" (ἁμαρτία . . . ἐλλογεῖται), and thereby identifies our state as one of sacred violence. Paul makes the latter point explicitly when he says that the Law was given "for the sake of trespasses" (τῶν παραβάσεων χάριν—Gal 3:19) and to make possible "the knowledge of sin" (ἐπίγνωσις ἁμαρτίας—Rom 3:20b). The function of the Law was to bring sin to the level of awareness and thereby help contain it (Rom 7:13; Gal 3:21-5). This means that its role in the crucifixion is the culminating service of the Law, by which it reveals sin as the structure of sacred violence. Thus it revealed the system of the old world to be the system of the Sacred and a realm of death. Paradoxically, in killing Christ the Law performed its most important act of disclosure, and fulfilled its purpose.

The celebrated ἐφ' ᾧ πάντες ἥμαρτον (Rom 5:12) should, therefore, be read in the way favored by the Eastern church (Photius).[40] The ᾧ refers to θάνατος, and the ἐπί means "with respect to which." Thus the clause reads, "and thus death penetrated to all men, with respect to which all sinned." This means that subsequent to Adam all sin was committed within the context of death, which is the system of the Sacred.

In terms of the difference between agape and eros, sin, as the deformation of the former to the latter, is the love of death. I shall return to the phenomenology of eros as the love of death, but for the time being it is sufficient to note that eros is constituted by a necessary lack—the obstacle of the model/obstacle of desire—and that this need for lack is a love of death. Instead of accepting death with the proper humility of hope in God, as the postlapsarian mark of creaturehood, anxiety causes us to affirm it erotically. The erotic love of death is denial by preemption.[41]

---

which drives him forward into the future of his Lord . . . it means being involved in the world-wide conflict between *civitas dei* and *civitas terrena*" (E. Käsemann, *Perspectives on Paul,* 27).

[40] Cranfield, *Romans 1,* 275–76.

[41] The early Christian ascetic attitude to sex was determined by the view that childbearing in the service of the city was a service of death, providing food for the sarcophagus in a vain attempt to keep this world from passing away (Peter Brown, *The Body and Society*).

Adam's sin is unique (Rom 5:14) because it established the system of sacred violence, just as Christ's obedience is unique in establishing the system of grace. In this sense Adam is the type of Christ. In the period between Adam and Moses death reigned in unconsciousness; we went to death thinking that it was our fate, and we killed victims thinking it was necessary for order. Then Moses brought the Torah as the beginning of our enlightenment. The story of Adam told us of the deformation of desire to violence, the decalogue brought the prohibition to our attention again, and we were able to understand how as a result of Adam's sin we are in the kingdom of death, the realm of the Sacred, knowing good and evil, but not the way to the tree of life. From the Torah we learn that once we knew only good, but now we know evil too, and death; we learn how we and the world lost our innocence, and of the violence within and around us in the order of the Sacred.

To sin with reference to death, therefore, is to live in the world of sacred violence that is cemented and sustained by the brother's blood, and covered over by our erotic love of death. Every act within this system is a "sin with reference to death" because it is part of the conspiracy to kill and cover up the body of the founding victim. Adam set up this system, therefore his sin is unique; we all freely collaborate with it, therefore his sin is typical.

We must imagine Adam and Eve blaming it all on that first mythological scapegoat the snake, even as they left the garden grumbling at the injustice of God who refused to accept their alibi. We must imagine the city of Cain full of the self-righteous who maintained order by the ruse of the surrogate victim, transferring their violence and mythologizing away their responsibility. That all men sinned with reference to death means, therefore, that in the city of Cain the "default" position of desire is mimetic violence and scapegoating. Adam's sin is unique because it laid the foundation of the system of sacred violence, and it is typical because it took the form of the depraved mimesis that binds us to one another in rivalry. Thus the *massa perditionis* consists in mimetic enthrallment to Adam and each other, miming his mimetic rivalry with God in rivalry with one another; and the way out is the *imitatio Christi,* the last Adam (1 Cor 11:1, 15:45-48). One can only escape by a leap that posits at one bound both sin and faith as the acknowledgment of the limit, a leap that cracks the mimetic cement of the city of death.

Adam's trespass established the realm of sacred violence and Christ's obedience established the kingdom of God. The following passage (Rom 5:15-21) contrasts these two spheres,[42] with the remedy of grace being far more effective than the disease of sin. Such a contrasting of Adam and Christ was characteristic of Paul's theology (cf. 1 Cor 15:20-28, 44-49; Phil 2:6-11). He may have been influenced to take up this pattern by its use by proto-Gnostics; it is also an expression of the basic design of the "two ages" teaching of apocalypticism;

---

[42] Cf. H. Weder, "Gesetz und Sünde," 357–76.

but it is not necessary to settle the question of outside influence in order to understand the meaning of the imagery. Paul naturally thinks of Adam and Christ when he thinks of the widest horizon of salvation in space and time. Adam and Christ represent the whole human race and the whole of human history, as the symbolic beginning and end of all.

At the end of the passage, almost as an afterthought, we are told that the Law "slipped in alongside" (παρεισῆλθεν) to increase the trespass, but that where the trespass increased, grace increased all the more (Rom 5:20). Thus he reminds us of the role of the Mosaic Law, not just to "charge sin to our account" but also, in the hands of sin, to incite it.

Sin and the Law

The link between sin and the Law is easily understood if we keep the Genesis story in mind. Sin is the free act of desire by which it uses the prohibition to deform itself to mimetic rivalry, and God into the idolatrous model/obstacle. In the Adam story it used what should have inhibited rivalry with God to instigate it.

It is well known that a prohibition incites transgression. Desire finds it hard to tolerate frustration, and a prohibition is an objective symbol of frustration, therefore it actually incites desire for the thing proscribed. According to our theory, this is because every prohibition is the expression of the desire of another to possess the prohibited thing, and that incites mimetic rivalry. Therefore, the problem is not that obedience to the Mosaic Law makes one proud and independent of God, as the traditional Lutheran exegesis holds, but that it actually tempts one to transgress, in the sense that it tempts desire to rivalry. Paul does not say that the proscription on mimetic desire made him proud of his ability to obey the Law, but that it caused more mimetic desire in him than he would otherwise have felt and consequently enmeshed him in a religious system of sacred violence. Allowing sin to do this was a free choice on our part. We were deceived by sin, but willingly deceived (Rom 7:11), and therefore, when we are informed of the deception by the disclosure of the Cross we can remedy its results by faith.

Although Paul focuses the whole discussion on proscription of desire in the tenth commandment, and does not say that the proscriptions on killing, stealing, adultery, and perjury made him a murderer, thief, adulterer, and false witness, he does accuse the Jewish community of these transgressions (Rom 2:17-29), and thus, by implication himself also. These are all manifestations of mimetic rivalry within the system of sacred violence.

Nevertheless, even within the realm of sacred violence that it helped to found, the Law has a positive function. The chief functions of the Mosaic Law with reference to sin are: to bring it to the level of consciousness (Rom 3:20b; 5:13), to work wrath (Rom 4:15), to cause sin to multiply (Rom 5:20), to bring it to life (Rom 7:7-8), and to contain it until Christ came (Gal 3:19-22). Its role is thus primarily diagnostic rather than analgesic. It brings sin to the level of consciousness by telling us the story of Adam. It was the Torah that told us of our fall into the Sacred and called the misuse of the prohibition to our attention again. It works wrath and causes sin to multiply precisely by means of the sacred context in which we are caught and by which it brings sin to life constantly by continuing the deception under which we commit sacred violence. Nevertheless, it contained mimetic rivalry by means of the structures of the Sacred, transforming the bad violence of acquisitive mimesis into the good violence of conflictual mimesis through the instrumentalities of the surrogate victim and the double transference. Thus the Law both revealed and contained the ravages of sin until the coming of Christ and the disclosure of the Cross (Gal 4:1-11).

It was diagnostic and prophylactic but not analgesic, despite the fact that it told the story of our fall. The full meaning of that story could not be understood before the disclosure of the Cross. Without that disclosure its revelations of sin were not properly understood, and so, according to Paul, the Jewish interpretation missed the true meaning of Torah as the prohibition of mimetic rivalry and turned it into something that incited rather than interdicted desire.

For Paul, therefore, the Jews treat the Torah as analgesic because they do not appreciate its diagnostic function, which exposes our plight under the Sacred and points to faith in Christ as the way out. They do this by means of sacrifice, which refuses the diagnosis of our responsibility for violence and transfers it to the victim. Kierkegaard expressed this in his meditation on anxiety: Anxiety is the human substitute for the real acknowledgment of sin, and sacrifice is the ritual of that anxiety.[43]

The Jews of Paul's experience do not even reflect skeptically on sacrifice in light of the failure demonstrated by repetition, because they are in thrall to anxiety. Anxiety in this Kierkegaardian sense is the attitude of those within the sacred system. Desire misused the prohibition to set up the system; the Jews misuse the Mosaic Law to the same end. This raises acutely the question of the place of Judaism and the Jewish people in the plan of salvation, a question much on Paul's mind, and to which I shall return.

The Metaphors for Sin

Metaphors give us access to the deeper levels of experience, and open them up to reflection.[44] One remarkable thing about Paul's usage is his overwhelming preference among all the words available to designate sin, for the term ἁμαρτία

---

43 *The Concept of Anxiety,* 104.
44 P. Ricoeur, *The Symbolism of Evil.*

(= "a state of affairs, the system of sacred violence"—p. 88) and his frequent use of it in the singular, giving the impression that he thought of sin as a single being or entity. This diverges from the traditional Old Testament and Jewish idea of sin as a *deed* of disobedience or transgression. Paul does, however, from time to time give ἁμαρτία the nature of a deed, showing that the Old Testament influence is not entirely absent, but this causes a conceptual confusion that needs to be cleared up if we are to understand his teaching.[45]

Emphasizing the "deed" rather than the "entity" conception of sin, Röhser calls the abstractions in Romans 5–7—sin, death, grace, and Law—"abstract-personifications," thereby specifically denying any mythological background to them. Sin is the essence (*Inbegriff*) of human misdoing, which develops its own dynamic and becomes a reality that stands over against one destructively as something that one has produced oneself.[46] While his concern to safeguard the element of human responsibility in the Pauline doctrine of sin, and thus to recognize its continuity with the Old Testament, is on target, Röhser does not do justice to the ability of the Pauline concept to combine personal responsibility with the transpersonal aspects of sin. He fails because he does not take sufficient account of the apocalyptic matrix of the imagery and the predominance in Paul's mind of the Adam story. He does not follow up clues that he himself uncovers—namely, that Paul's preference for the term ἁμαρτία locates him in the tradition of Jewish apocalyptic, and especially in the apocalyptic traditions about Adam and Eve (Apoc Mos 32[47]; cf. Wisd 4:20; 4 Ezr 7:35; Apoc El 41;7f.; 1 Tim 5:24; 4(6) Esr 16:66).[48]

I have already argued that for Paul sin is an activity, the deformation of desire to rivalry (φθόνος), an attitude, the concupiscence of mimetic desire (ἐπιθυμία), and a state of affairs (ἁμαρτία), the system of sacred violence that results from mimetic rivalry. The key to an understanding of the Pauline use of ἁμαρτία is the figure of the serpent as the symbol of deformed desire. Desire actively deforms itself, and as a result imprisons itself in the realm of the Sacred, where it is constantly dominated, deceived, and violated (indwelt) by the power of its own deformation lodged by the double transference in the instrumentalities of the Sacred. This explanation satisfies the need to account for both the "act" and the "entity" function of the concept. In Paul ἁμαρτία is, therefore, not a mythic entity, but on the contrary, a demythification that reveals personal responsibility for sin by revealing the intrigue of desire in its game of self-deception.

In terms of the apocalyptic notion of the two worlds, the world of sin is well described as ἁμαρτία, in the sense of the sphere of sacred violence in which the

---

[45] Röhser, *Metaphorik und Personifikation*, 15–16.
[46] Ibid., 142–43.
[47] R. H. Charles, *Apocrypha and Pseudepigrapha*, 149.
[48] Röhser, *Metaphorik und Personifikation*, 14.

acts and attitudes of deformed desire take place all the time. Thus the imagery of apocalyptic, interpreted mimetically, in the light of the Adam story, takes account of Röhser's concern by uniting the "deed" and the "state" elements in the Pauline usage of ἁμαρτία.

When we look more closely at the metaphors that Paul uses for sin, we find this interpretation confirmed. Paul favors certain metaphors among the general biblical and pagan metaphors for sin—burden, stain, debt, sickness, guilt, poison—which disclose the general cultural consciousness. The specific metaphors Paul uses are: *domination*—master and slave, political overlord, military commander, which together make one category (Rom 6; 7:14); *deception* (Rom 7:11); and *indwelling* (Rom 7:17).[49]

The *domination* (master/slave) metaphor is a commonplace of Hellenistic moral philosophy, especially the Stoic-Cynic philosophy (Epic. *Diss* 4.1; 2.123), and well attested in the Hellenistic Judaism of Philo (*Quod Lib*) 21–25; 156–59). It describes the possible enslavement of the mind by the passions. Much of Paul's usage of ἐπιθυμία seems to fit this category (Gal 5:16-17, 24; cf. Rom 7:5), but he also uses the master/slave metaphor on a broader front—as part of the metaphor that describes salvation as adoption out of slavery (Rom 8:15-17; Gal 4:6-7)—and so one might seek for the root of the metaphor in the practices relating to slavery in the Greco-Roman world. The purchasing of a slave with a view to adoption, or manumission by adoption, is not well attested. There is, however, in Paul's scriptural background the understanding of the exodus as an adoption out of slavery (Exod 6:7), as well as the Jesus tradition of "Abba" in which the Lord invites his followers to regard God not as master but as adoptive father (Rom 8:15-17).[50] It is probably these factors combined with the more general image of sin as the enslaver of reason to the passions that constitute the full range of meaning of Paul's master/slave metaphor.

The background of the *deception* metaphor is the fall story. The pagan view that desire deceives reason (Plato *Leg* 9.863b; Dio Chrys *Or* 8.21; Epic. *Diss* 4.1.2; cf. Philo *Quaes Ex* 1.15) is also in the background, but Paul's account is dominated by the Adam story in which the serpent symbolizes deliberate self-deception. In 2 Corinthians 11:3 the serpent is the symbol of the Judaizers who attempt to deceive, and in Romans 7:11 sin uses the Law for this purpose. Sin, therefore, is not personified as a mythological demon, but symbolized by means of the serpent figure from the traditional story. It is a case of typology rather than mythology or rhetorical personification.

The *indwelling* (οἰκέω ἐν . . .) metaphor is attested in parallel Hellenistic Jewish sources (T.Dan 5:1; T.Benj 6:4; Wisd 1:4; Philo *Fug* 117) and probably derives ultimately from the experience of inspiration and ecstasy. The striking thing about the Pauline usage is that both Christ (or the Spirit) and sin are

---

[49] Ibid., 101–26.

[50] R. G. Hamerton-Kelly, *God the Father*, 85–86.

described in the same way as indwelling a person. They are mutually exclusive rivals for the same dwelling space (Rom 7:17; cf. Gal 2:20). Paul thinks of the two states as analogous, and the two indwelling powers as rivals.

All of these metaphors are transformations of sacrificial violence, more or less concealing the founding mechanism. To the extent that they are metaphors of malaise, they have advanced from the sheer mythology of good violence in the direction of diagnosis. The general cultural metaphors—burden, stain, debt, sickness, guilt, poison—indicate a solitary affliction (with the possible exception of debt, where an other is necessary to complete the image). They conceal therefore the mimetic nature of the affliction by obscuring the relational nature of the deviated desire. This is due to the fact that they symbolize the resultant state of affairs rather than the process by which it came into being. They are strictly speaking metaphors of the system of violence rather than of the oscillation of mimetic desire, and to that extent they are myths.

The Pauline metaphors—master, deceiver, indweller—are all metaphors of relation, and therefore, we must show that Paul's understanding of the structure of the subject is relational, or in our terms, mimetic, before we can be satisfied with our analysis of his metaphors for sin.

The Mimetic Structure of the Pauline Subject

There is something of a consensus that Paul's concept of human being is dynamic and relational rather than static and ontological, more influenced by the Hebrew Bible than by the Orphic hymns. Bultmann's magisterial exposition remains authoritative and provides the foundation for my mimetic account.[51] For Bultmann's Paul the most comprehensive term for the human subject is "body" (σῶμα), a term that is interchangeable with the personal pronoun "I," and the essence of the structure of *soma* is self-relatedness:

> Man is called *soma* in respect to his being able to make himself the object of his own action or to experience himself as the subject to whom something happens...as having a relationship to himself—as being able in a certain sense to distinguish himself from himself.[52]

In this state subjects can either be at one with themselves or estranged from themselves.

This is also the subject of Heideggerian existentialism for whom the relation to the self is fundamental and immediate, and attainable by the exercise of the

---

51 Bultmann, *Theology 1,* 190–239.
52 Ibid., 195–96.

will to resist the alienating power of external forces.[53] The outside power that usurps control of the *soma* from itself is the "flesh" (Rom 8:13, cf. 6:12; Gal 5:16, 24). Sometimes the *soma* is thought of as so utterly subject to the "flesh" that the term *soma* is used as if it were "flesh," as in Romans 7:14, 18, 23, 24.

Bultmann believes that the self-relatedness of the human subject is what distinguishes it from all other creatures. However, the more encompassing relationship for Paul, as for the whole biblical tradition, is the relationship of all created things to the creator. Human self-relatedness is, therefore, a relation within a relation, and we need to go further than Bultmann to understand the nature of the subject within these two relationships. He was content to stop with the existentialist subject and the possibility of immediate self-presence. Paul, however, makes the primacy of the relationship to the divine paradigmatic of the constitution of the subject, and this means that self-presence is mediate and not immediate. Like all things, which exist mediately, "from, through, and for" God (Rom 11:36), the self is present to itself mediately rather than immediately. The structure of the self is triangular.

The evidence that Bultmann cites for his version of the subject are the four texts that tell of self-reflexive action: Paul pommels and subdues his body (1 Cor 9:27); he can give his body to be burned (1 Cor 13:3); he can yield himself to the service of sin or of God (Rom 6:12; 12:1); and he can expend himself for Christ (Phil 1:20). These do prove that the subject is reflexive, but one may ask whether they are sufficient to make this unmediated reflexivity central to the constitution of the subject.

The statement that marriage partners do not rule over themselves but belong to one another (1 Cor 7:4), which Bultmann believes supports this view, seems to point to the mimetic rather than the existentialist version of the subject.[54] Therefore, the place to look for the structure of the Pauline subject is the discussion of sexual relationship, and here again the Adam story is at work, and especially the idea of the corruption of agape to eros by the fall into concupiscence.

1 Corinthians 6:13-20 is a good example of Paul's understanding of the triangularity of the structure of the subject as disclosed in sexual relation. The Adam story is in the background as the reference to the "one flesh" shows (1 Cor 6:16 / Gen 2:24). "The body (σῶμα) is not for fornication, but for the Lord, and the Lord for the body" (1 Cor 6:13) means that the subject as desire can be corrupt or pure, depending on its object, and when pure its object is Christ himself. The metaphor is sexual union. The self and the Lord are related as sexual partners are related, in mutually self-giving love, agapaically

---

[53] Hans Jonas ("The Abyss of the Will") takes this mode of interpretation to an extreme in an exposition of the plight described in Rom 7:14-25 as the inevitable self-alienation that the externalization of moral aspiration in written Law entails.

[54] *Theology 1*, 196.

rather than erotically. The self loves the Lord by doing what the Lord desires, and the Lord loves the self by doing what the self desires. This is the structure of agapaic love, to be patterned nonrivalrously on the desire of the other, and thus to be properly and creatively mimetic. Therefore we can say that in agape the self and the Lord constitute each other mimetically.

Union with a prostitute is the other, erotic form of mimetic desire. To be united to a prostitute is to be one body with her, and to be united to the Lord is to be one spirit with the Lord (1 Cor 6:16-17). The change from body to spirit is not significant, because both terms signify the essential person (1 Cor 2:11). The analogy between the two unions is best understood as alternative forms of mimetic desire. In the union with the prostitute the subject sins against itself (1 Cor 6:18) in the sense that desire deforms itself to acquisitiveness and attempts to possess itself by displacing the other. Fornication denies the otherness of the other by making him or her the servant of its own desire in the attempt to fill the erotic lack.

In the union with Christ, the self of the Christian is like the shrine of the temple in which the Spirit of God dwells, with the result that the self does not create itself but receives itself as the gift of the Spirit (1 Cor 6:19), and the Spirit is formed by the self in which it dwells. Fornication is the erotic mimesis of self-creation, while faith is the true imitation of Christ that is openness to the divine agape.

Therefore, we have the relational structure of the self set out mimetically. One relates to the self properly when one relates through the desire for Christ that comes back to the self as Christ's desire for the self, and thus constitutes the self agapaically. One relates to the self improperly when one relates through the desire for a prostitute, which comes back to the self as its own desire now inflated by its colonization of another and constitutes the self erotically. The former desire satisfies, the latter leaves the self empty, and thus compels it to more conquests. This is fornication and it is the opposite of faith, and the sin against the self.

The agapaic mimesis of faith is especially evident in the account of Paul's conversion in Galatians 2:19-21. As a result of the act of identification with the crucified, Paul can say, "I live, but no longer I, Christ rather lives in me; and the life I now live in flesh I live by faith in the Son of God who loved me and gave himself for me" (Gal 2:20). Faith means that the self-absorbed subject is replaced by the Christ subject, but in such a way that the subject can still say "I live." The oscillation between the dying of the subject as itself and the living of the subject not as itself but as Christ makes perfect sense mimetically. Christ lives in me because I imitate him in the sense of his desire becoming my desire (1 Cor 2:16b), and my desire becoming his, in the sense that "he loved me and gave himself for me." Thus I love myself in Christ and as Christ loves me. Christ lives in me and I live in him because we share the same desire, and thus acquisitive and conflictual desire becomes generous and consensual desire.

I shall return to this theme of the reformation of desire through the restoration of the divine pole, as well as to the theme of the imitation of Christ. At present I wish only to establish the fact that the Pauline subject is primarily constituted mediately with reference to the other as model/obstacle or as creator God, rather than immediately by the relationship to itself. The self-presence is mediated mimetically either through the human model/obstacle or through the divine creator. There is no immediate self-presence, except in the extreme pathology of sin when the subject has swallowed the obstacle and become its own idol, and then it is in a state of deception disturbed by violent dreams.

There are other indicators of the mimetic subject in Paul. In Romans 7:7 he says that the subject would not have known sin had the Law not said, "You shall not desire." Thus desire was awakened from without by the prohibition that the subject understood as an expression of desire to be imitated. The clearest other indicators, however, are the relational nature of the metaphors for sin.

The metaphors of mastery, deception, and indwelling, we now see, point us to the mimetic constitution of the self. The movement from the solitary afflictions of the general cultural metaphors, through the apocalyptic image of the ledgers of sins, to the fully reciprocal Pauline metaphors of mastery, deception, and indwelling, is the movement from myth to gospel, from cover-up to disclosure of the true nature of sin as interpersonal mimetic violence.

Sin as master indicates the powerlessness of desire in the grip of acquisitive mimesis. It is forced by its own inner dynamic to imitate the desire of the other, and so is caught in the coils of rivalry. Sin as deceiver symbolizes the self-deception of desire about the divine envy and the deviousness of conflictual mimesis in covering over the true origin of violence in the self by means of the double transference. Indeed, deception is an apt name for the whole system of sacred violence. Indwelling sin, finally, describes the obscure awareness that despite the veils this violence has deep roots within the subject.

The System of Sin

The mimetic nature of the subject means that its communal context is determinative. The subject is not the self-sufficient individual but the communally embedded self. Paul does not forget the deed-character of sin, and the idea of personal responsibility (Rom 6:16), but he correlates it closely with sin's transpersonal dimension, in the sense that individuals declare membership in one or the other community—either of sin, death, Law, the wrath, or of grace, life, love, and Christ—by their actions. Actions are part either of the mimesis of violence or the mimesis of love, and take place in the system of sacred violence or in the system of holy love.

If Paul has two systems or communities in mind, why does he not say, "I dwell in sin," rather than "sin dwells in me"? Because the two systems are founded on two kinds of mimesis, and mimesis is both internal and external.

It constitutes the self by means of the other, the inner by means of the outer, and the individual by means of the group. In terms of mimesis one can talk of the sin that dwells in me as the sin that I dwell in, because the "in me" is the other whom I imitate and whose desires constitute my desires. My inmost self is the inmost other; I dwell in the group and the group dwells in me.

Acquisitive and conflictual mimesis, and the consequent setting up of the system of the Sacred by the double transference is, therefore, the non-metaphorical content of all the metaphors for sin; sin as mimesis masters me, as double transference it deceives me, and as the Sacred it indwells me. It is of more than just historical interest that this combination of universalism and individualism is characteristic of apocalyptic thought.[55]

The notion of sin as a sphere of power is part of the metaphor of mastery,[56] and of the imagery of the apocalyptic literature. Sin is a "world" that envelops the subject and in which death is active. The Law is the instrumentality by which this power of death is set in motion with eschatological force.[57] Romans 1:18-31 presupposes an order in which sin and disaster are automatically correlated, and such a constellation has been identified in the Old Testament by Koch.[58] He calls it a *schicksalswirkende Tatsphere* because the emphasis is not on the individual deed but on the whole system, that works virtually automatically, as in the Wisdom tradition. In early Judaism the recompense comes sooner rather than later, in the form of death and destruction (Prov 13:6; Sir 21:2, 27:10).

Clearly Paul's concept of the wrath expresses this idea. The notion of the sphere of transgression and automatic recompense confirms my argument that the wrath is to be understood as the self-inflicted alienation and deception of the order of sacred violence, and the state of anxiety and vulnerability that underlies the uneasy conscience of sinful humanity.

Up to this point my analysis has shown that Paul identified his experience of Judaism as the experience of this sphere of sin as the system of sacred violence. We must now consider more closely his explicit teaching on the relationship between Christ and Israel.

---

[55] P. Vielhauer in J. C. Beker, *The Apostle Paul*, 135.
[56] Cf. L. Schottroff, "Die Schreckensherrschaft der Sünde und die Befreiung durch Christus."
[57] Röhser, *Metaphorik und Personifikation*, 142.
[58] K. Koch, *Um das Prinzip der Vergeltung in Religion und Recht des Alten Testaments* (1972), cited by Röhser, *Metaphorik*, 142.

5

Sacred Violence
and the Jews
Beloved Enemies in the
Plan of Salvation

Κατὰ μὲν τὸ εὐαγγέλιον ἐχθροὶ δι' ὑμᾶς, κατὰ δὲ τὴν ἐκλογὴν
ἀγαπητοὶ διὰ τοὺς πατέρας.

(Rom 11:28)[1]

Watson has characterized Paul's theology as "an ideology legitimating separation," which arose out of the experience of rejection, and was motivated
by hostility toward the society that had rejected it. It is part of the attempt to
transform a movement into a sect.[2] There is some truth in this sociological
description, because Paul does think on the level of the groups, but it is for the
most part wide of the mark. To call Paul's theology an ideology is a question
begging reduction of one frame of reference to another, and to call his idea of
the church sectarian is unsupported by the evidence of the texts. His treatment
of the relationship of Israel and the church is a theological discourse about
social groups that are defined theologically, not sociologically. Paul's central
category is the theological category of election.

The sociological template, therefore, does not cover the Pauline phenomena, excepting insofar as he does at times think on the level of the group. When
he does he uses symbols like the traditional "Adam" and the innovative "flesh."
The ultimate horizon of these symbols is the whole human race, but the specific instance in his experience is Judaism. We have already examined the role
of Adam, and so we turn to the term "flesh" (σάρξ). To live according to the
flesh is to live in a way that conflicts with the will of God. All the human race

---

[1] "On the one hand, according to the gospel they are enemies because of you. On the other,
according to election they are beloved, because of the patriarchs."

[2] F. Watson, *Paul, Judaism and the Gentiles,* 48.

does so to one extent or another, but in Paul's experience the chief example of this mode of life is life based on the Mosaic Law as interpreted by the Judaism he confronted. Just as the Jews are "first in sin," so they are first in the "flesh."

Jewish Life as the Prime Instance of Life "according to the Flesh"

Robert Jewett advanced our understanding of the Pauline term "flesh" considerably when he pointed out that its primary semantic field is the conflict with the Judaizers.[3] The Pauline use of the term "flesh" originated in the polemical situation in Galatia, as a metaphor from circumcision and a metonymy of the whole way of life that it signified. The metaphor is forged "before our eyes" in the transition to the Sarah/Hagar allegory at Galatians 4:21, where the former stands for life in the Spirit and the latter for life in the flesh, Christian and Jewish existence respectively.[4] Jewett posits a third stage of development in Galatians 5 where the term is generalized further to apply to common sensuality. We do not find this third stage as clearly delineated as Jewett does; it seems rather that throughout Galatians "flesh" describes the Jewish way of life as a threat to Pauline "freedom." Thus "flesh" is a metaphor coined in a situation of polemics and persecution, on the basis of the literal fact of circumcision, to designate the Jewish way of life as an active threat to life based on the Pauline gospel.

Paul's usage of "flesh" (σάρξ) and the phrase "according to the flesh" (κατὰ σάρκα—18 times) in the authentic Letters might tentatively be classified as follows: (1) to refer to the Jewish way of life[5]; (2) to refer to natural human life in this world[6]; (3) to refer to the Hellenistic denigration of the human body as compared with the mind or the soul.[7]

(1) Bultmann pointed the way to understanding the term σάρξ in Paul as referring primarily to Jewish life when he wrote:

> To the category of conduct "according to the flesh" belongs above all zealous fulfillment of the Torah: it does so because a man supposes he can thereby achieve righteousness before God by his own strength. The Galatian Christians who want to adopt the Torah and be circumcised are indignantly asked; "Having begun with the Spirit, are you now ending with the flesh?"—ending, that is, not in sensual passions but in observance of the Torah (Gal 3:3). In fact, not only zeal for the

---

[3] R. Jewett, *Paul's Anthropological Terms*, 95–101. Cf. *TDNT*, VII, 125–35.

[4] Jewett, *Paul's Terms*, 113–14.

[5] Rom 1:3, 3:20, 4:1, 7:5, 18, 25; 8:3(x3), 4, 5, 6, 8, 9, 12, 13, 9:3, 5, 8, 11:14; 1 Cor 10:18; 2 Cor 1:17, 5:16(x2), 10:2, 3, 11:18; Gal 2:16, 3:3, 4:23, 29, 6:12, 13; Phil 3:3, 4(x2).

[6] Rom 2:28, 6:19; 1 Cor 1:26, 29, 5:5, 6:16, 7:28, 15:39(x2), 50; 2 Cor 4:11, 7:5, 10:3, 12:7; Gal 1:16, 4:13, 14; Phil 1:22, 24; Phlm 16.

[7] 2 Cor 7:1 (probably non-Pauline); Gal 5:13, 16, 17, 19, 24; 6:8; Rom 13:14. The last two are probably the only ones that can plausibly be given a Hellenistic meaning, but not necessarily.

Law but also pride in all the pious Israelite's merits and titles of honor belong to the attitude of the flesh—or, the Torah and the merits and dignities of Israel fall within the concept "flesh" as belonging to the sphere of the visibly occurring and the historically demonstrable. [Phil 3:3-7][8]

Most commentators recognize that the "flesh" includes Jewish religious attitudes, whether legalism or exclusionism,[9] in its purview, but because they do not give sufficient weight to exclusionism, they do not see that the Jewish component is determinative for the meaning of the term.

Paul described life as a Jew as a "trusting in the flesh" (Phil 3:3-4) or a "boasting according to the flesh" (2 Cor 11:18-23), which he now regards as "rubbish" (Phil 3:8) and "foolishness" (2 Cor 11:16ff.). In 2 Cor 11:16ff. he parodies the opponents' status claims; while they boast of a way of life described by the credentials "Hebrew, Israelite, seed of Abraham, servant of Christ," he boasts of his catastrophes and sufferings.[10] Paul's experience of his own violent zeal as a "perfect righteousness" (Phil 3:6)[11] is the probable starting point for the reflection that led to the dire conviction that the hearts of those who live in the Mosaic way have been hardened by God (cf. Rom 11:7); he once felt good about persecuting Christians and destroying the church!

In Romans 9–11 he begins by calling the Jews "my brothers, my kinsmen according to the flesh" (κατὰ σάρκα—Rom 9:3), which is at first sight a neutral use like the apparently neutral use in Romans 1:3 and 4:1, to designate genetic identity. However, the phrase designates membership in a group that shares both a cultural and a genetic inheritance, since the term "brothers" identifies a fellow member of the covenant community.[12] Furthermore, when Paul wishes to indicate genetic human life he uses ἐν σάρκι, which he deliberately contrasts

---

[8] R. Bultmann, *Theology 1*, 240.

[9] E.g., G. Bornkamm, *Paul*, 133; C. K. Barrett, *A Commentary on the Second Epistle to the Corinthians*, 170; V. P. Furnish, *II Corinthians*, 312, also includes a brief summary of the usage of κατὰ σάρκα.

[10] If Paul's claim to Jewish status were bogus, as Maccoby (*The Mythmaker*) maintains, the irony of a passage like this would be undecipherably complex and ultimately lame. Only a madman would parody dignities that he never had; but then Maccoby comes close to saying that Paul was mad.

[11] Although it is fashionable, ever since W. Kümmel, *Römer 7 und die Bekehrung des Paulus*, to read this as a psychological statement that makes it impossible to interpret Rom 7:14-25 as autobiographical in any sense, we must demur and follow interpreters like Calvin and J. B. Lightfoot, who take ἄμεμπτος in the formal rather than the psychological sense. See G. R. Horsley, *New Documents Illustrating Early Christianity*, 141, on ἄμεμπτως. It and the adjective are widely attested in honorific inscriptions and epitaphs, suggesting that it is a well-known cliché for externally faultless behavior, with no serious claim to psychological accuracy. On the other hand, it should not be emptied entirely of psychological force in the Pauline context. Looking back on his Jewish life from the other side of his conversion, he saw the moral numbness caused by the system and confesses it ironically. He really did think he was blameless, but in fact was simply self-deceived. Now he understands that he did not know what he was doing (Rom 7:15a), and can refer to his former state by means of an honorific cliché.

[12] Cranfield, *Romans 2*, 458–59.

with κατὰ σάρκα; "for we walk in the flesh (ἐν σάρκι) but we do not fight according to the flesh (κατὰ σάρκα)" (2 Cor 10:3; Gal 2:20). Κατὰ σάρκα has, therefore, not just the connotation of being a human, but of being human in a particular way, and that particular way is, in the Pauline context, the Jewish way. And this is also the meaning in Romans 1:3 and 4:1.

The messiah comes from the Jews "according to the flesh" (κατὰ σάρκα— Rom 9:5) which, in the light of our argumentation so far, means that he was born a Jew, with the emphasis not on the genetic but on the cultural force of Jewishness; he was born into the Jewish way of life. As Paul says elsewhere, he was "born under the Law," not as a matter of status but "in order that he might purchase freedom for us who were under the Law" (Gal 4:4). He came "in the likeness of sinful flesh" in order that God might condemn sin in the flesh (Rom 8:3). "Flesh," therefore, means the Jewish community rejecting Christ and persecuting Christians despite—and in our dialectical interpretation "because of"—their special gifts and status. In Romans 11:14, and this is decisive, Paul refers to the Jews simply as "my flesh" (τὴν σάρκα μοῦ): "to the extent that I am an apostle of the gentiles I glorify my vocation, in the hope that I might make my flesh jealous and save some of them." Here "flesh" is the Mosaic Jews whom Paul wishes to convert (cf. Rom 7:18).[13]

The accusation that Paul is "walking according to the flesh" in 2 Cor 10:2-3 makes best sense if taken as an accusation that he like his opponents claims Jewish status.[14] This is confirmed by the enigmatic statement in 2 Corinthians 11:12, "What I am doing I shall continue to do, in order to destroy the opportunity of those who desire an opportunity to maintain that in the work of boasting they are doing exactly the same thing as I am doing." What Paul is alleged to be doing that is "exactly the same" as his opponents is boasting in his Jewish credentials, and what he will continue to do in order to deprive them of grounds for this accusation is not use his Jewish right to financial support (2 Cor 10:9b, cf. 1 Cor 9:9), and not base his claim to authority on status or Law, but on the fact that he is their founding apostle (1 Cor 10:13-18).

Furnish draws attention to the fact that in 2 Corinthians rhetorical questions cluster in chapters 10–13 and 1–3, suggesting that the same situation of conflict is behind both sections.[15] In any case the use of "flesh" in 2 Corinthians 1:17 makes good sense if interpreted against a background of conflict with the same prestige-conscious Jewish opponents as in 2 Corinthians 10-13, as another reference to the Jewish way of life.

---

[13] Cranfield (ibid.) points out that "flesh" is an accepted term for "family" or "clan" in the LXX, esp. Gen 37:27; Lev 18:6, 25:49; Judg 9:2; 2 Sam 5:1.

[14] Cf. Gal 5:11, where it seems some even thought he still demanded circumcision. There is a strong similarity between 2 Cor 11:1-12 and Gal 1, suggesting the same kind of opponents in both places.

[15] V. Furnish, *2 Corinthians,* 134. In any case, Letter E (chap. 10–13) and Letter D (chap. 1–9) have been judged, on broader grounds, to have the same opponents in view. Ibid., 50–52.

In 2 Corinthians 1:17-22 Paul's correspondents are unhappy because he apparently changed his mind about his plans to visit them. In defense he says two things; he was not acting with levity, and he does not make his decisions "according to the flesh" (κατὰ σάρκα). The former statement in the aorist tense refers to the matter under discussion—he did not change his plans lightly; the latter statement in the present tense describes his habitual activity—he never makes his decisions "according to the flesh." The content of the concept of a decision according to the flesh is saying yes and no at the same time. The usual translation of "according to the flesh" here is "like a worldly man" (RSV) or some such rendition that takes the phrase to mean "humanity in general." There is, however, no reason to make self-contradiction especially characteristic of the human condition in general, while there is good reason to see it as characteristic of the Judaizers. They could be accused of saying yes and no at the same time; "yes you are free, no you are not; yes you are justified by faith in Christ and not by works of the Law, no you cannot disobey the Law's requirements."

Furthermore, the comparatively heavy theological justification given in 2 Corinthians 1:18-22 is overdone if all Paul wants to maintain is that he has good spiritual reasons for his decisions. A polemical situation, however, would call forth such a justification, and since the contents show that it is aimed at the Judaizers, it is reasonable to interpret it as a reply to them, from which we can discover per contra their position. The passage defends the sufficiency of the work of Christ in which all the promises of God are fulfilled and concludes with an assurance that his readers are all established by God and should not let themselves be shaken by criticism, because they have the gift of the Spirit.

It responds, therefore, to a Judaizing argument for continuance in the Jewish way of life, intended to shake the confidence of the Pauline Christians, and says that such a course is self-contradictory, unlike the straightforward gospel of Paul, who never says both yes and no, because in his gospel sounds only the yes of promises fulfilled.

2 Corinthians 5:16 also supports this interpretation (cf. 2 Cor 11:18)[16]; it says that from the moment of his conversion Paul has regarded no one from

---

[16] R. G. Hamerton-Kelly, "A Girardian Interpretation of Paul." I argued there that knowledge according to the flesh is knowledge "from within the coils of mimetic rivalry, characterized by the 'works of the flesh.'" (78). Our present argument identifies those mimetic coils as the Jewish way of life seen from the Pauline point of view. Furnish (*2 Corinthians,* 324) identifies the opponents here ("who boast in the face and not in the heart"—2 Cor 5:12) with the people in 2 Cor 11:18 and 22 who boast in the flesh—that is, in Abrahamic descent, apostolic accomplishments, and visions. Here Furnish thinks their visions are in mind because Paul mentions that in 2 Cor 5:13. This does not mean that the other two aspects of their boasting, the specifically Jewish ones, are not in view also. C. K. Barrett (*Second Epistle to the Corinthians,* 170) argues well that "a legalist, Judaizing, view would also involve knowledge according to the flesh." Both Furnish and Barrett take the broader meaning of "flesh" as "self-regarding" or "this-worldly" as primary and the Jewish meaning as a subtype; Paul actually reverses this order, taking the specific experience of Judaism as primary and the general category as a logical subtype.

a Jewish point of view (κατὰ σάρκα), even though once he regarded Christ in that way (cf. Rom 9:5).[17] The larger context of the statement runs from 2 Corinthians 2:14 through 6:10, and its theme is the apostolic office.[18] The immediate context begins in 2 Corinthians 5:12 where we learn that the subject of the passage is the difference between Paul and those who boast in their Jewish status. In 2 Corinthians 5:14-15 Paul gives us an insight into his conversion experience, which he describes elsewhere as "through the Law dying to the Law" (Gal 2:19) and which tells us exactly why he will not regard anyone from the Jewish point of view. In his conversion he came to the conviction that "if one has died for all, then all have died,"[19] and in his case died to the Jewish way of life. Christ died because Jews like Paul were so zealous and judged Christ from a Jewish point of view as a transgressor of the Law.

He interprets this death for us, morally and not sacrificially: because of it we are to live no longer in the Jewish way, which he describes as living "for oneself," but in the Christian way, which is living for Christ (2 Cor 5:15). Then follows with perfect consistency the statement "therefore we regard no one from the Jewish point of view (κατὰ σάρκα); even if once we regarded Christ himself in this way, we do so no longer." We may paraphrase it as follows: "We once saw everyone in terms of whether they were Jew or gentile, whether, if Jews, they obeyed the whole Law or not. This caused us to kill Christ and persecute Christians. Now that is no longer possible for us, because in Christ the new creation has come, and the chief mark of the new creation is reconciliation between God and humanity whose sign is the reconciliation between Jew and gentile" (2 Cor 5:16-17). Paul, therefore, experienced a change in the criteria by which he evaluated people, commensurate with the conversion from one order of reality to another—that is, from the system of sacred violence to the system of love and reconciliation.

Paul's understanding of the link between the Jewish way of life, his own activity as a persecutor, and the death of Christ, also explains the culminating

---

[17] Furnish, *2 Corinthians,* 313, argues that 2 Cor 5:16 and Rom 9:5 are not comparable because in the latter Christ is explicitly identified as the messiah of Israel by means of the article. The context here makes clear that the Jewishness of Christ is as much in view as in Rom 9, and so the absence of the article should not be taken to mean that the Jewishness of his identity is being denied. That would be an illegitimate argument from silence. Furnish also provides the evidence for taking κατὰ σάρκα adverbially rather than adjectivally.

[18] J. L. Martyn, "Epistemology at the Turn of the Ages," Martyn's argument that Paul has in mind an old and a new epistemology is right in that claim, but wrong in what he makes of it, because he does not take seriously enough the statement that Paul "once knew Jesus according to the flesh." His reconstruction of fleshly knowledge quite ignores this statement.

[19] Hamerton-Kelly, "A Girardian Interpretation of Paul," 77: "The only sense one can make out of the conclusion that all have died if one has died for them, is that the natural mimesis is being interpreted in a special way, as the imitation of Christ in his death." Furnish (*2 Corinthians,* 310) reminds us that Paul is interpreting the tradition that Christ's death was "for our sins" (1 Cor 15:3), or "for us" (Rom 5:8, 1 Thess 5:10). Paul's interpretation is moral, not sacrificial: Christ's death for us lays a moral obligation upon us to imitate him.

affirmation, "[God] made him who knew no sin to be sin for us, in order that in him we might become the righteousness of God" (2 Cor 5:21). The "sin" that God made him is Jewishness, elsewhere called "the likeness of sinful flesh" (Rom 8:3; cf. Gal 4:4-5). There is no precedent in Paul's thought for the death of Christ as a sin offering, but there is precedent for the identification between sin and the flesh (Rom 8:3). Somebody, we presume, had made the argument that since Jesus was a Jew, Christians should be proud to become Jewish too, to which Paul replies that Jesus' Jewishness had been a temporary sojourn under sin for our sake, so that through this work of his we might become the community of the righteousness of God, rather than the community of "one's own righteousness" (Phil 3:9).

Other evidence for this interpretation is 1 Corinthians 10:18 where the generation of the wilderness is "Israel according to the flesh," as distinct from the church, which is Israel according to the Spirit[20]; Romans 3:20 where Paul alters the "everything living" (πὰς ζῶν) of LXX Psalm 142:2b), which is a perfectly good translation of MT Psalm 143:2b כל־חי ("all living") to "all flesh" (πάσα σάρξ = כול בשר), to apply the quotation to the Jewish way of life,[21] to make the point that the role of the Law in the Jewish way of life is chiefly to bring home the knowledge of sin (Gal 2:16).[22]

(2) The neutral uses of "the flesh" are: the cliché "flesh and blood" (Gal 1:16; 1 Cor 15:50), the reference to the flesh in connection with illness (Gal 4:13-14; 2 Cor 12:7); the designation of life in this world (1 Cor 1:26, 7:28; 2 Cor 10:3; Phlm 16); and the references to mortality and weakness (1 Cor 5:5, 6:16; 2 Cor 4:11, 7:5; Rom 6:19). Three texts are on the way from the neutral to the significant meaning: 1 Corinthians 15:39 is semantically on the border because it says that flesh cannot be used without further semantic specification, that it always implies an environment from which it gets its specific meaning; Philippians 1:22, 24 should be understood in the light of 2 Corinthians 5:6ff.

---

[20] H. Conzelmann, *1 Corinthians*, 172 n. 29, compares the κατὰ σάρκα here with Rom 9:5. It is more than just a historical example, however, but a contrast between the lesser Israel and the greater, in the form of an argument from the lesser to the greater, "If the Israel of the flesh . . . then how much more the Israel of the Spirit."

[21] כול בשר occurs in the Qumran texts with a negative moral connotation (CD 1:2, 2:20, 3:6, 1QM 4:3). Meyer describes it as "arrogant humanity" (*TDNT,* VII 112). In 1 QS 11:9 those outside the community are called "the fellowship of the flesh of iniquity." It is unlikely that Paul had this Qumran usage in mind; in any case, his usage is a reversal of Qumran's; "flesh" refers not to the wicked outsiders but to the "righteous" insiders.

[22] Jewett, *Anthropological Terms*, 98, says that Paul made the change "because he wished to counter the Judaizers' claim that circumcised flesh was acceptable as righteous before God" (98). By Jewett's reckoning this is a very early stage of the metaphorical extension of the term to the Jewish way of life; in any case the full metaphoric meaning is implicit in this text and beginning to emerge. Jewett approaches my interpretation of "flesh" as the Jewish way of life but does not quite reach it because he is detoured by the notion that "works of the Law" mean religious self-justification in the Lutheran sense; using this as the analogue, he concludes that "flesh" means self-justification (97). This is a good example of how a methodologically correct insistence on historical concreteness can be derailed at the last moment by theological apologetic.

where flesh is the same as body and denotes the relative separation from the Lord compared to his immediate presence in the next world; and Romans 2:28 ("circumcision in the flesh") is a bridge to the significant usage that Jewett draws to our attention.

(3) The "Hellenistic" uses are sparse and can be shown to be semantically dominated by the Jewish meaning. Galatians 5 is the only possible semantic home for the "Hellenistic" interpretation.[23] The discussion begins in Galatians 4:21 ff. with the setting up of the contrast between the Judaizers and the Pauline Christians in terms of the difference between Hagar and Sarah, between the slave and the free woman. Paul describes Hagar's children as "according to the flesh," and Sarah's as "through promise" (Gal 4:23), or "according to the Spirit" (Gal 4:29). Furthermore, as then so now the former persecutes the latter. Thus we have an antinomy set up between the persecuting Judaizers and the persecuted Paulinists that is presented in terms of the antinomy between the flesh and the Spirit.

The larger topic under discussion is moral and spiritual freedom (Gal 4:31—5:1) and the possible misuse of this freedom; but before and more important than freedom's possible misuse is the threat that it might be lost altogether by acceptance of the Judaizers' restrictions. True Christian morality is "faith working through love" (Gal 5:6) and not observance of the Mosaic Law. Having established that under no circumstances are Christians to surrender or abridge their moral liberty by accepting any part of the Jewish way of life, Paul considers the possible moral misuse of that freedom by "giving opportunity to the flesh" (Gal 5:13).

It is critical to note that the first example Paul gives of this "opportunity to the flesh" is not fornication or anything else having to do with sensuality but rather the failure to serve one another in love, the "biting and devouring" of one another (Gal 5:13-15)—that is, behavior characteristic of those engaged in a bitter and threatening dispute. "Giving opportunity to the flesh," means primarily, behaving like the Judaizers.

With this context in mind we notice the unexpected contrast in Galatians 5:18 between being led by the Spirit and being under Law,[24] presented as the summation of the foregoing series of antinomies between "walking in the Spirit and fulfilling the desire of the flesh . . . the desire of the Spirit and the desire of the flesh" (Gal 5:16-17). It seems reasonable to identify Spirit with Pauline freedom and flesh with Judaizing bondage. The argument is, therefore, very specific in its terms and it continues the argument of the whole Epistle against Judaizing.

---

[23] Jewett, *Anthropological Terms,* 101, says that "Paul breaks off the argument against the nomists [at this point] and turns to a new set of problems."

[24] Cf. Rom 6:14 where being under Law and being under sin are equated in a way that makes the continuation of the argument in Galatians perfectly understandable.

Between the antinomies and their summation occurs a statement that seems to generalize the point into a universal moral norm: "These are opposed to one another so that you cannot do what you like" (Gal 5:17b), which interpreters take as an indication that the problem here is libertinism, not Judaizing. However, why should Paul suddenly generalize? It is much sounder method to assume that he is consistently arguing against Judaizing. On this assumption the insistence that the Spirit and the flesh are opposed to each other means that one cannot be a Christian and a Jew at the same time, in the spirit of the warning in Galatians 5:4—"you are cut off from Christ, you who are justified in the Law, you have fallen out of grace!" So the one liberty you do not have is the liberty to Judaize (Gal 2:14b), because the two ways of life are mutually exclusive. The phrase "the works of the flesh" that introduces the list of vices (Gal 5:19) is a variation on the phrase "works of Law" that is a major theme setter in the epistle (Gal 2:15-21).

That the list of the "works of the flesh" begins with sexual transgressions does not mean that it cannot be intended as a description of life under the Law. It is a formal rather than a specific description, traditional rather than contingent. We have an example of the same thing in Romans 1:18—3:20 where under the rubric "the Jew first and also the Greek" (Rom 1:16; 2:9-10) Paul begins the description of the ravages of sin with sexual transgressions and works up to the more serious travesties of personal relationship. Although Jews are not explicitly introduced before Romans 2:1 they are, nevertheless, in mind from Romans 1:18 on,[25] and in Romans 2:17–29 are accused of the kinds of transgressions covered by this list in Galatians. One does not, therefore, have to be able to assign a direct target for every accusation of vice. The list intends to give a general impression of life under the Mosaic Law, a Law whose chief function is to bring sin to light (Rom 3:20), to cause sin to increase (Rom 5:20), and to make sin more sinful (Rom 7:13b).

At the end of the list of virtues (Gal 5:22–23) Paul indicates again that he has in mind the particular contrast between the Mosaic Law and the morality of freedom, and not the general contrast between legalist and libertine types of moral reasoning, when he says "the Law is not against such people" (Gal 5:23),[26] in the sense that it has nothing to accuse them of because they fulfil the divine will, which is the basic intention of the Law. They are not under the Mosaic Law, but they nevertheless fulfil the divine will (Gal 5:14,18).

How do they fulfil the divine will? With Christ they have "crucified the flesh with its passions and desires" (Gal 5:24), a summary of the whole process of salvation as seen by Paul, as a process of participating in the crucifixion by

---

[25] Cranfield, *Romans 1,* 141–42. The force of διό in Rom 2:1 indicates that the indictment of the Jew that begins explicitly in Rom 2:1 follows logically from Rom 1:18-32.

[26] I take τῶν τοιούτων as masculine rather than neuter (against H. D. Betz, *Galatians* 288–89) because Paul had 18 in mind when he dictated it, and because of the specification in 24; those not under the Law are those who have crucified the flesh—that is, the Jewish way of life.

renouncing the mimetic rivalry that so characterizes the Jewish way of life as represented by the Judaizers (Gal 2:19; Rom 7:7).

In the closing message of Galatians written by the apostle's own hand, he confirms our interpretation by claiming that the Judaizers want only to glory in the flesh of their victims, a pun on the term "flesh" that refers both to the fact of circumcision and the Jewish way of life (Gal 6:13). He goes on, however, to make the concern about Jewishness or its opposite trivial by comparison with the new creation, and again because of the Christian's mimesis of the crucifixion: "Far be it from me to boast save in the Cross of Christ, by which the world is crucified to me and I to the world. For neither circumcision nor uncircumcision counts for anything, but only new creation" (Gal 6:14-15). Thus Paul expresses his experience of co-crucifixion as the end of the Jewish way of life for him, and that ending as the chief instance of the ending of the significance of all claims to status based on the old world. Uncircumcision, the position opposed to the Judaizers, is as irrelevant as the position they advocate! Life according to the Spirit is the life of the new creation beyond the divisions of mimetic rivalry and sacrificial distinctions.

Paul's special use of the term "flesh," therefore, has the Judaizers in the foreground as the most significant instance of the life of all humanity within the realm of sacred violence. For this reason Judaism bears the brunt of his critique, but that does not mean that it is the only place where the rivalrous mimesis occurs. It is merely a synecdoche of the human race in thrall to the Sacred. It is also a synecdoche for all the world under the electing grace of God.

The Dialectical Role of the Jews in
the History of Salvation

In the light of this paradox, how are we to understand the role of Israel in the plan of salvation? To answer this question we now turn to the classic passage on Christ and Israel in Romans 9–11.

This passage belongs with Galatians as an equally thorough if less polemical treatment of the matter. Romans 9–11 has been regarded as a self-contained section that records "sermons" that the apostle might have preached to Jewish audiences,[27] and thus essentially unintegrated into the thought of the epistle. It has also been regarded as the heart of the letter, inasmuch as Paul's chief concern was precisely the relationship between Christ and Israel, and the place of the gentiles in the covenant.[28] I find the latter view more likely than the former, although I cannot accept it altogether. Nevertheless, the passage in question is well integrated into the overall argument and close to the heart of Paul's

---

[27] R. Scroggs, "Paul as Rhetorician."
[28] K. Stendahl, *Paul among Jews and Gentiles.*

concern. For this reason Romans 9–11 will be the focus of our inquiry into Paul's more systematic thought on the role of Israel in the plan of salvation.

Preliminary Summary

It might be helpful to set out as a guide to the exposition the principles that we have discovered through a reading of the text.

For Paul the Jews are God's appointed servants of sacred violence and their rejection of Christ served the plan of salvation; by saying no they said yes. Therefore, although they have been temporarily rejected and placed under the wrath (Rom 11:15; cf. Rom 9:22), their election stands unimpaired and they continue to play a pivotal role in God's purpose (Rom 11:11-12). That is to say, the Jews are "dialectically" in God's service, inasmuch as they perpetrate sacred violence in order to reveal it.

Israel's service is dialectical because it takes the form of opposition to God for the sake of God; "according to the [logic of] the gospel they are God's enemies for your sake; but according to the [logic of] election they are [God's] beloved for the sake of the patriarchs" (Rom 11:28). The Jews are God's beloved enemies; but they are beloved before they are enemies, and they will continue to be beloved after they cease to be enemies. God says both yes and no to Israel; but God's yes includes and swallows up God's no. Israel says both no and yes to God, and the two answers are in fact one; by killing Christ and driving out the missionaries to the gentiles, the Jews revealed the founding mechanism and propelled the gospel across the world, providing the initial point of contact in a new city by means of their synagogues and then providing the motivation to take the gospel to the gentiles by their driving out and persecuting the apostles. In this understanding Paul is at one with the Acts in its portrayal of the typical missionary experience of welcome and then ejection.

"If their transgression (παράπτωμα—cf. Rom 5:15) is wealth to the world, and their loss gain to the gentiles, how much more will their fulfillment be!" (Rom 11:12). Their transgression is wealth, their loss is gain, and the ultimate fulfillment of their election—namely, the eschatological acceptance of Christ—will be "life from the dead" (Rom 11:15). This emotionally complex and easily misunderstood argument unfolds against a background of opposition from Judaizers (Rom 9:30—10:4; 12:9—13:10; cf. Gal 2:11—3:14), the accusation that Paul's teaching is univocally anti-Jewish (Rom 9:1-2), and a gentile arrogance over the apparent rejection of Israel (Rom 11:13-24). I shall try to expound it fairly, but in order for that to be possible, it must be emphatically established at the outset that all happens according to God's plan, which is a plan to effect mercy for all the world, and that even in their refusal the Jews are God's beloved and God's elect servants in carrying out this plan.

The foregoing argument could be dangerous if we do not emphasize that the plan of salvation, according to Paul, is guided by the divine mercy (Rom

9:15). In the hands of the secular ideologue, it easily becomes a warrant for anti-Semitism; in the hands of the theological partisan, a justification for anti-Judaism. However, it can be responsibly expounded if one keeps in mind that everything in this plan—both the negative and the positive elements—expresses the loving mercy of God in service of human salvation, and if one treats it as an irreducibly theological argument.

The explanation is emphatically theological, having to do with God and God's purpose of mercy, with the mystery of the death of God's Son at the hands of God's beloved Israel, with the revelation of the founding mechanism and the possibility of the renunciation of vengeance and the return of the world to God. This means that for Paul the issue between Christ and Israel, between Jews and Christians, is an irreducibly theological one, that secularized members of both groups might easily misunderstand by reading it ideologically or politically.

The nub of Paul's explanation of the role of Israel in the mystery of salvation is that all that has happened concerning Christ, including the Jewish refusal, has been willed by God as the plan for the salvation of the world.[29] It took place "according to the scriptures" (καθὼς γέγραπται—Rom 9:13, 33; 10:15; 11:8, 26; Μωϋσῆς [ἡ γραφή, Ὠσηέ, Ἡσαΐας, Δαυίδ, ὁ χρηματισμός] λέγει [γράφει]—Rom 9:15, 17, 25, 27, 29; 10:5-8, 16, 19, 20-21; 11:2, 4, 9). In these terms Paul expresses his understanding of the continuity of the plan of salvation with the faith of Israel and the God of Abraham, and his conviction that both the negative and the positive actions of the drama of salvation happened according to that plan, and that the Jewish refusal did not discredit God's word or dishonor God's promise (Rom 9:6). Thus Paul makes any Marcionite interpretation impossible; the God of Jesus Christ is one and the same God as promised Abraham, instructed Moses, and through them entered into the covenant that established Israel as a nation.

The first link to the Old Testament history of Israel is paradoxically through the rejected prophets who went unheeded and unaccepted (1 Thess 2:14-16; cf. Gal 1:15; Mark 12:1-12 par.). Jeremiah, the prophet of the first fall of Jerusalem, seems to have been on Paul's mind when he described himself as having been called from his mother's womb (Gal 1:15; cf. Jer 1:5). Elijah (Rom 11:2-10) and Isaiah of Jerusalem suggest to him the idea of the remnant that remains positively committed to God's plan in the midst of the unbelief and persecution of the opposition (Rom 9:27-29). In 1 Thessalonians 2:15-16 he expressly says that the Jews killed Jesus in the same spirit in which they killed the prophets and drove out the Christians. Thus the rejectors are an integral part of the process of salvation. They serve God by saying no to God's messengers and plan.

---

[29] Barrett, *Romans*, 193–94.

The Argument in Romans 9–11

Paul begins by passionately insisting that he remains a Jew and that his soul is scored with grief at the Jewish refusal of Jesus (Rom 9:1-5). Such an asseveration suggests that he is responding to an accusation that he has turned against his own people and is preaching anti-Judaism. There are several not surprising indications of such response to his work, and he is trying now to correct it. Thus he begins by reciting the marks of Israel's preeminence in the history of God's plan of salvation, to the climax in the Jewishness of Jesus. He also begins to make clear his conviction that he as a Jew who believes in Christ is part of the remnant of Israel that has traditionally been central to the plan of salvation.

In the light of this history it cannot be that God has suddenly changed the modus operandi and that the divine plan will now be fulfilled apart from Israel. Rather as one understanding of the plan gives place to another, Israel remains at the center of the action. The version that has all of Israel accepting the Messiah first and then the rest of the world, which Paul might once have held, must give way to the majority of Israel rejecting the messiah, a remnant of Israel accepting the messiah, then a fixed number of gentiles, and then all the world, in the eschatological dénouement.

The first step in the exposition of this revised scheme of salvation history is to establish the idea of the remnant and its scriptural warrant (Rom 9:6-17). As in the case of the rejected prophets who revealed God's plan, both the rejectors and the rejected are necessary. The rejectors are the ones who cause the remnant to come into being, thus the plan goes forward with the participation of all Israel, both the rejected and the rejectors.

Paul begins by invoking the story of the divine election of the patriarchs and showing that it was selective—Isaac not Ishmael, Jacob not Esau. In response to the complaint that this divine election is unjust, Paul invokes the story of the exodus, and the answer to this complaint based on that story is definitive for the whole explanation. He first affirms that both the election and the rejection are in the service of God's mercy (Rom 9:15) and then presents the figure of the Pharaoh as an exemplar of the rejectors who serve God's plan. Pharaoh served God's plan of salvation because his resistance enabled God to display saving power and to spread abroad the knowledge of it. "I raised you up for this very purpose, to show my power through you, and to spread my name through all the earth" (Rom 9:17 / Exod 9:16; cf. Exod 4:21; 7:3; 9:12; 10:20).

The Pharaoh, therefore, served to spread the "gospel" of God's saving power by his resistance to it, and in this regard he is like those Jews who refuse Jesus. If the Pharaoh had not resisted, the liberation of Israel might have gone unnoticed by the world for whose sake it was ultimately undertaken. Since the liberation of Israel from Egypt was ever only a metonymy of the salvation of the world, the Pharaoh's role was critical in making this known. In the same way the refusing Jews serve to make the Cross known as the extension of the exodus to the world, and the realization of the promise implied by that liberation of the part for the whole, in the synecdoche of salvation. Jewish refusal of Christ is an integral part of the plan of divine mercy for the world. Therefore God still works through all Israel by means of the conflict between the rejected and the rejectors.

Predestination and Free Will (Rom 9:17-29)

The argument is complicated by the problem of predestination and free will (Rom 9:17-29) expressed in the fact that the Pharaoh's resistance is said to be the result of God's "hardening" (Rom 9:18) rather than the Pharaoh's free choice. This confirms the objection that God is unjust, because God assigns blame where there is no freedom of choice. Paul's response to this renewed complaint—that God the potter can make vessels for destruction if he pleases—lacks sensitivity if viewed from any other than the theological point of view (Rom 9:20-23). From the theological point of view, however, it is unexceptionable. He appeals to the well-known image of the potter and the clay (Is 29:16; 45:9; Jer 18:6; Wisd 12:12; 15:7; 2 Tim 2:20) to make the point that the creator can do what the creator wills with the creature and that creatures are not in a position to question the creator on the matter of their own creation. This is theologically self-evident; the creature owes its being to the creator and cannot complain that it is this creature rather than that; what it in fact is, is the immutable limit of what it might be, and God is free by right and by power to create whatever creature for whatever purpose he sees fit.

In this case, because vessels of wrath are in question, we must reemphasize that that purpose is defined by the mercy at the heart of the plan of salvation. God's purpose will always be merciful and conduce to the salvation of the world and the fulfillment of the creature. Therefore, to participate in this work of God is the joy of creatures whether they are vessels made for honor or dishonor, of mercy or of wrath. In either or both capacities the purpose of the creature's creation is fulfilled and one could only object to one's lot if one did not trust God to know what is best for one and to be able to provide the absolute fulfillment of bliss that the divine mercy promises. The Pharaoh, therefore, is also one of God's beloved enemies who performs one of the harder tasks in the history of salvation. This means that there is a special class of people within the process of salvation history who serve God negatively. The Pharaoh and the rejecting Jews are special agents with a special task.

Why then are they called "vessels of wrath made for destruction" and distinguished from the "vessels of mercy prepared beforehand for glory" (9:22-23)? Do the members of the respective classes have any choice in the matter or do we have here the doctrine of a double predestination (*praedestinatio gemina*), to hell and to heaven? The answer must be given in terms of the whole exposition, at the end of which it is said that all Israel will be saved (Rom 11:26). This means either that the rejecting Jews cannot be included among the vessels created for destruction, or that the phrase "vessels of wrath made for destruction" must be taken loosely, in the sense that while they perform their negative task, they seem to be vessels created for destruction, but are not so in fact.

There are other hints to support the latter interpretation. In Romans 9:22-23 God patiently bears with transgressors in the hope that they will repent (Rom 2:4; 3:26). This means that there is always the possibility that they, having done their strange work, will freely choose faith in Christ and so escape destruction. This is further indicated by the fact that Cranfield[30] points out, that while Paul says God prepared the vessels intended for glory beforehand (προητοίμασεν—aorist indicative active), those intended for wrath are merely "made" (κατηρτισμένα—perfect passive participle), and suggests that this means that God actively predestines the former while the latter are merely said to be in a state ripe for destruction without implying that they were made for that purpose, or will in fact be destroyed—that is, that they were created for a menial task but not necessarily to be destroyed.

Within the plan of salvation, therefore, there is a group of Jews that performs the noble task of accepting Christ and another that performs the menial task of rejecting him. All, however, are chosen for their roles and all, therefore, belong to the elect. This means that we must resist the temptation to generalize the double election beyond the narrow confines of the plan of salvation to the whole human race. Election to the negative task in the plan of salvation does not entail that there is in general a double predestination for all humanity. The Pharaoh and the rejecting Jews remain obedient parts of God's plan and so will eventually be saved, because they were appointed to their negative role for the special purposes of the plan of salvation, which needed contrasting roles for its fulfillment. They are confusingly called the "vessels made for destruction," but that does not mean that they will in fact be destroyed.

When we do apply the implications of this argument to all of humanity, we find a single and not a double predestination, and in the light of Romans 11:32 (cf. Rom 5:15; 1 Cor 15:21-22) a single predestination that is universal and inclusive. The purpose of the dialectic in the plan of salvation is the salvation of all the world. In Christ all are chosen for glory (Rom 8:29-30), inasmuch as he is the representative of us all in whom God has chosen to love us all. To have faith is to claim that election, and in due course all rejectors, inside and outside the plan, will come to faith. The Jews, therefore, within the purview of the plan of salvation accept and reject Christ for the sake of the salvation of the world.

The argument continues (Rom 9:30—10:21) by explaining what form the hardening of Israel took in terms of the plan. The rejectors pursued righteousness in the wrong way, by works rather than by faith, and therefore they stumbled over the stone God laid in Zion. "Behold I am laying in Zion a stone of stumbling and a rock of scandal, and he who believes in him will

---

[30] Cranfield, *Romans 2*, 495–96.

not be put to shame" (Rom 9:33), suggests that God directly causes Israel to be scandalized. The context, however, suggests that their decision to pursue righteousness in the wrong way is a free choice, even though it was what caused them to stumble over the stone that God had laid to trip them up.

The paradox of predestination at the macro level and free will at the micro level is operative here. The classes of rejectors and acceptors are predestined according to the plan, but the subjective choice of which class to belong to seems to the individual to be a free choice. This is a well-known feature of the traditional reflection on predestination and free will, which I cannot explore further here. It seems as if the divine purpose and human freedom interact in such a way as always to preserve the freedom of the human will.

The symbolism of the stone is multilayered because the quotation from Isaiah 28:16 is a reference to the remnant, into which Paul has inserted from Isaiah 8:14 the reference to stumbling.[31] Thus he identifies the crucified Jesus as the heart of the remnant, the stone laid in Zion on which the other members of the remnant are founded (cf. 1 Cor 3:11), and over which the rejecting Jews stumble.

The remnant is constituted by faith. "He who has faith shall not be in haste" (Is 28:16) is its motto. The stone therefore symbolizes a community based on faith in God through the Cross of Christ and patient trust in God's purpose. To have faith is to see the primal prohibition as a sign of God's trustworthiness, not as an indication of God's envy. Faith is to interpret the Cross aright, as the revelation of sacred violence, and to transfer from the community of the sacred to the community of faith. Christ is the end and goal of the Law in the sense that the faith that his death evokes is the real purpose of the primal prohibition (Rom 10:4).

Despite the fact that they were instrumental in the crucifixion of Christ, God has not abandoned the people (Rom 11:1-36). "I ask therefore, 'Has God abandoned his people?' Not at all!" And the evidence Paul brings for this is his own conversion; "For even I am an Israelite, of the seed of Abraham, of the tribe of Benjamin" (Rom 11:1). In this way Paul begins the summary of the argument for the two contrasting roles within the one plan of salvation, roles played by the accepting remnant and the rejecting majority, respectively.

By referring to himself he identifies himself with the remnant, and takes a further step in the argument. The remnant is the evidence that God has not rejected the people; therefore, the rejectors are related to the plan of God through the remnant and not directly. They are accepted by God only because they are the rejectors of this particular remnant. Thus they are dialectically related through the rejection of faith.

---

[31] Cf. 1 Pet 2:6, 8, where the same collocation of the two Isaiah texts occurs, leading some to suggest that it was a common property of the early church rather than a Pauline formulation.

Another feature of the remnant, which was mentioned in Romans 9:24, comes to the fore here—namely, that unlike its traditional predecessor, this remnant is made up of gentiles as well as Jews. It comprises the whole motley membership of the Pauline churches. This explains the purpose of the allegory of the wild and domestic figs (Rom 11:13-24). The remnant of Israel is the root stock into which the gentiles have been grafted, because the domestic branches have given up their places. It also explains why the order of salvation now runs: remnant of Israel—gentiles—all of Israel, in the sense that the gentiles are entering and thus changing the traditional remnant of Israel into an inclusive unit (Rom 11:25). Nevertheless, all this change does not mean that the gentiles have replaced Israel as the apple of God's eye. This is the point that Paul makes in the climactic conclusion of the exposition of the plan of salvation in Romans 11:25-36.

The reasoning in this crucial passage (Rom 11:25-36) is, as so often in Paul, extremely compressed. The first part is clear: the plan of salvation (μυστήριον) includes a hardening of part of Israel until a fixed number of gentiles have come to faith in Christ; then all of Israel will come to faith as well and be saved. That this faith is Christian faith is evident from the comparison in Romans 11:30-31: just as gentile disobedience has been turned to obedience because of the Jewish refusal that forced the gospel out into the world, so Jewish disobedience will be turned to obedience by the "mercy shown to [the gentiles]." The mercy shown to the gentiles is inclusion in the remnant through faith in the gospel, and since there is no other way into this salvation, the Jews will believe the gospel and be saved at the end of history.

The concluding statement of the first part of this section: "For God has shut up all people in unbelief in order that he may have mercy on all" (Rom 11:32) is an allusion to Adamic solidarity in sacred violence and Christic solidarity in salvation. The Jewish refusal is the sign that the chosen people are not excluded by election from participation in the sin of Adam, and by the same token are not excluded by rejection from participation in the grace of Christ.

The "all" in this formula should probably be taken to refer to the level of the group rather than the individual, in the sense of the group as a whole whoever is part of it at that time. By the same reasoning the statement in Romans 11:26, "and thus all Israel will be saved," should be read in this context to mean "Israel as a whole" but not necessarily every individual Jew,[32] just as one might say that all the church will be saved and yet understand that there will be individual members who are not, because of their moral failure. It is significant that in Romans 11:32 Paul does not say that everyone will be saved, only that God will have mercy on all. The point he is making is that the only basis on which God has a relationship with the world is mercy.

---

[32] Cranfield, *Romans 2;* Barrett, *Romans;* E. Käsemann, *An die Römer,* loc. cit.

The point being emphasized is that the Jews as a group have not been rejected by God, because of their role in the death of Christ. In that role they were engaged in a "strange work" on behalf of God's mercy, revealing the founding mechanism of the primitive Sacred. Therefore if their status is to be any different from that of other groups before the judgment throne of God, it would be more rather than less favorable. Despite the dreadful deed and the relentless refusal, "the gifts and the call of God are irrevocable" (Rom 11:29) and "Israel as a whole will be saved."

Paul ends this subtle exposition with a confession in praise of the wisdom of God and the obscurity of the divine working in the world (Rom 11:33-36). It is ultimately beyond human comprehension, and, therefore, we infer, his own explanation, so laboriously presented, is to be read with that caveat in mind. Thus he closes with a disclaimer comparable to the one that ended the discussion of the "flesh" in Galatians (Gal 6:14-15), a disclaimer that relativizes the status of his argument with reference to the ineffable reality of the new creation beyond the structures of sacred violence. In this way he prevents his own theology from becoming just another myth of mimetic rivalry.

We have already said that this is a dangerous and easily misunderstood doctrine. Either one misses the point that the part of Israel that refuses the messiah does so to fulfil God's purpose and therefore is not to be regarded as cast off by God, or one is unable to tolerate the fine balance between freedom of individual choice and the divine predestination. On the one hand Paul holds that God caused the Jewish refusal, and on the other that the Jews are nevertheless guilty and under the wrath (1 Thess 2:16) until they too, like the remnant, come to the righteousness not of "works of Law"—which killed Christ and expelled the gospel—but of faith. At the same time God's gifts and call remain irrevocable and persist even under the wrath, and the proof of this is that certain Jews, like Paul, respond to the gospel on behalf of those who have the strange work of refusal to do. Just as in the time of Isaiah, the remnant represents the people.

One can only understand this doctrine theologically. It is appropriately called a mystery (Rom 11:25) and should not be carelessly revealed. Unfortunately it cannot be kept only to the mature; therefore we must make determined efforts to interpret it properly. According to Paul the Jews have performed a hard service for the world; they unveiled the founding mechanism of sacred violence once and for all in the crucifixion of Christ and the refusal of the gospel. In that work they represented all of us, and exposed the darkest shame of us all. Therefore, we hate them and load upon them the very violence that they uncovered in us. When we call them the "Christ killers," pretending thereby that we, of course, are on Christ's side, and would not have participated in this crucifixion had we been on hand, we treat them as they treated Christ and thereby show that we are their mimetic doubles, and more than that, that we have taken their place and they have taken Christ's. This is the theological cause of the continuing Christlike suffering of Jews at the hands of Christians, a mimetic reversal of roles that Paul in his robust theology of the divine purpose sought to forestall.

Both the positive and the negative poles of the drama of salvation are necessary until the end of history; Christians must continue to accept the messiah and Jews to reject him. In the dialectic of that relationship between the two groups each must accept the necessity of the other if they are to avoid the devastating mimetic rivalry that has marked the history of the relationship up to now. That means that Christians must affirm the Jewish existence of the Jews, because it is as such that they serve the divine purpose. The dark side of this is that that service is the service of the negative pole; the darker side is that mimesis causes the two roles to interact resulting in mutual recrimination and violence when power permits. The record shows more such violence on the part of Christians. This may be due to the lack of opportunity on the part of Jews because of their exclusion from political power. The record of the state of Israel under the pressures of state responsibility does not suggest that Jews are inherently less violent than gentiles, or that the Jewish religion less militant than others.

The Problematic of the Doctrine of Election

Having said all this in favor of Paul's doctrine of election, I must confess that I find it a dangerous doctrine that should be radically reversed. Election is an integral part of a theology that sees God revealed in history, specifically the history of groups, some of which are favored and others of which are abhorred. According to my theory such doctrines, which identify groups as especially beloved of the divinity, are ploys of the primitive Sacred. They are essential components in the victimage machine, justifying the expulsion of victims and the remorseless pursuit of enemies.

Since election is a myth of scapegoating, if Paul had carried through to the end the project of demythification started by the Cross, he would have decoded not only the scapegoating myth of gentile exclusion based on the misinterpretation of Torah, but also the myth of election, since they are aspects of the same myth of the sacred group. Paul did not, however, do that, but on the contrary used the myth of election to explain a central feature of his field of concern. In this regard, therefore, we must judge him to have failed to draw the logical conclusions from his insight into the sacred violence of Judaism.

We have suggested that he failed to draw this conclusion because of nostalgia. He could not bring himself consistently to accept the fact that since the crucifixion and resurrection his Jewishness and the Jewishness of Jesus were not negatively significant but rather simply insignificant. We have seen evidence that he could accept this, notably the fact that he could refer to Jesus' Jewishness as the "likeness of sinful flesh" (Rom 8:3) and ethnic identity as insignificant (1 Cor 9:19-23). However, when it came to the question of whether

God had rejected Israel because Israel had rejected the Messiah, he could not accept an affirmative answer, but adapted the doctrine of election, logically discredited by his own theology of the Cross, to serve the ingenious argument that Israel served God by rejecting God's Messiah and persecuting God's prophets.

This makes God responsible for the persecution of the divine messengers and for the murder of the Son, and is, therefore, simply a form of the sacrificial doctrine of the atonement, by which we shift responsibility for our sins onto the divine. Paul wanted to maintain that the saving events were caused by God, that God was acting for the salvation of the world in the life, death, and resurrection of Christ. Judaism was integrally a part of those events, and so it was impossible on historical grounds to deny the significance of the Jewish role. It was from Paul's point of view a negative role and so his options were to identify the source of the negativity as simple human perversity of the kind that the theory of sacred violence reveals, or to say that this perversity was divinely inspired. If he had chosen the former option, he would effectively have dissolved the doctrine of election. In that case Jewish rejection of Jesus and the gentiles would have been simple sacred violence. By choosing the latter option, however, he lapsed into mythology, and covered up the responsibility of the Jews as representatives of us all by blaming God for their rejection of Christ. This is simply a form of the sacrificial doctrine of the atonement to the effect that God persecuted the Son because of humanity's sin. This God is the primitive Sacred, who takes part with the group in the killing of the victim.

There is, therefore, a major flaw and inconsistency in Paul's thought. It is no wonder that Jews are for the most part unconvinced by the far-fetched dialectical argument that makes them the divinely appointed killers of Christ. It would be better simply to identify them in that role as the representatives not of God but of us all, bringing to light the sacred violence of the world.

6

Sacred Violence and the Law of Moses

The Prohibition Perverted

Τὸ οὖν ἀγαθὸν ἐμοὶ ἐγένετο θάνατος; μὴ γένοιτο. ἀλλὰ ἡ
ἁμαρτία, ἵνα φανῇ ἁμαρτία, διὰ τοῦ ἀγαθοῦ μοι κατεργαγομένη
θάνατου

(Rom 7:13)[1]

Within the order of the Sacred, Law is the myth of vengeance (see pp. 29–34 above). The Mosaic Law operates within that order and, therefore, is an extension of the sacrificial system and an instrument of sacred violence. In that capacity it cursed and crucified Christ, and scapegoats the gentiles. Such a negative judgment could lead to the Marcionite conclusion that the God of Israel is a demon from which faith in Christ delivers us, but that would be a mistake. Although Paul never invokes the Mosaic Law as such as a guide to moral conduct for the Christian,[2] and does not believe that it was ever intended to be a way of salvation (Gal 3:11, 18), he does acknowledge it as an expression of the primal prohibition and identifies love for God and neighbor as its basic thrust and faith as its fulfillment. Before it was diverted to the service of sacred violence, the divine Law was the prohibition of mimetic rivalry and the injunction to love God and the neighbor, the two sides of the coin of the primal prohibition. According to Paul, Judaism distorted it into the ideology of Jewish separatism and made it the instrument of mimetic rivalry. The Cross redeems it to its originally intended purpose.

---

[1] "Did the good thing, therefore, cause my death? Not at all! Sin, rather, in order that it might appear as sin, contrived my death by means of the good thing."

[2] R. G. Hamerton-Kelly, "Sacred Violence and Works of Law."

In terms of the Adam story, the Law makes faith possible by prohibiting rivalry with the creator and therefore making it necessary for the creature to trust the creator. Since we cannot know good and evil we must trust that God is not envious and allow God to act for us in that regard. Faith is to accept this fact of our dependence on the divine goodness, to be satisfied with innocence and immortality, and to accept the prohibition as a sign of God's solicitude for the integrity of human desire. As primal prohibition, the Law points the way to the tree of life by standing as a barrier to the tree of the knowledge of good and evil, and thus guards our innocence and our immortality. In this sense the Law serves faith, and is "holy, just, and good" (Rom 7:12); but it has been wrested by desire to the service of mimetic rivalry, and within the sphere of sacred violence serves the power of vengeance and death.

Paul, therefore, radically opposes the Mosaic Law in the name of the divine Law, in a strategy of "using the Law to overcome the Law." Strictly speaking he confronts one interpretation of the Law with another, the interpretation from the point of view of holy nation/holy place with the interpretation from the viewpoint of the Cross.

In Paul's thinking the Mosaic Law is a metonymy for the Jewish way of life characterized by exclusionism and violence. Paul's opposition to it is not based on a theoretical assessment of the Jewish sources or a general assumption about the status of the Law,[3] but on his own experience. I have argued that Paul's conversion was a death to the Law by means of the Law, in the sense that the Law drove him to persecute Christians and in the course of that he came by revelation to see that the same impulse to fulfil the Mosaic Law had made him a persecutor and had killed Christ. After his conversion he experienced persecution at the hands of Jewish and Jewish-Christian zealots, which he interpreted in the light of the Cross. His is not, therefore, the judicious assessment of a scholar but the living reaction of a victim. One may protest that this does injustice to Judaism, and that may be the case in that it does not take the whole range of the religion into account, but one cannot deny that this is the way Judaism impinged on Paul.

The Torah in Contemporaneous Judaism[4]

The Law that Paul identified as an instrument of violence was to its adherents a manifestation of the love of God. The term "Torah" has a wider meaning than strictly law in the sense of ordinances, a meaning that approaches that

---

[3] Therefore knowledge of the general understanding of the status of the Law in the messianic age (e.g., W. D. Davies, "Paul and the People of Israel," 4–5) or of the gentile estimate of the Law (e.g., L. Gaston, *Paul and the Torah*) is only indirectly relevant. One must not allow the background to overshadow the foreground.

[4] See W. D. Davies, "Law in First-Century Judaism."

of "revelation." The Torah reveals the nature of God, and provides the basis for the covenant relationship between God and the people. It was both the civil and the religious Law of the community, and shaped the whole of life. The temple was central to its concern and most of its injunctions pertained to the activities of the priests. It was also the principle of order in the universe, a written expression of the Law of nature and the creative wisdom of God. It was one of the preexistent things.

W. D. Davies argues that for Paul, Christ as the Messiah replaced the Torah in the life of a Pharisee for whom the Messiah had come.[5] This means that faith's interpretation of the death of Christ both repudiated and restored the Torah. It repudiated those aspects of Torah that served violence, its service of exclusionism and moralism, and it restored the nature of Torah as revelation of the loving grace of God. To faith in Christ the Torah revealed the deformation of the prohibition, and the possibility of its reestablishment as the command to love God and neighbor.

This repudiation and restoration, in turn, reduces distinctions of race, class, and sex to relative unimportance (Gal 3:28), stops the sacrificial practice of scapegoating, both in its ritual and its actual forms (Rom 3:24-25), and changes moralism into toleration (Gal 5:13-15; 6:2; Rom 14–15). In this recasting of the Torah one can see also the presence of the Jesus tradition in the reduction of the Torah to the commandment to love God and neighbor (Matt 22:34-40/Mk 12:28-34/Lk 10:25-28). Paul, therefore, got the positive side of his theology of the Law from the tradition and the negative side from his experience. The negative side is, therefore, the most characteristically Pauline facet.

The Social Function of the Law

The traditional Protestant reading of Paul's attitude to the Law, taking its cue from Luther, has Paul repudiating the Law, because it created a mode of piety that relied on the moral strength of the pious to obey the Law and thus justify themselves before God. This is the notorious "works righteousness" of traditional Lutheranism, under which slogan Protestants were able to criticize both Catholics and Jews.[6] Luther's late medieval anguish of conscience, influenced as much by the general psychic shock of the black death—vividly represented in the late fifteenth-century portrayals of the crucified as a grotesque, of which the famous Isenheim altar of Matthäus Grunewald is an example—as by his own psychological scrupulosity, was used as a principle for the interpretation of Paul. Because Luther could not find peace for his conscience by means of the

---

[5] W. D. Davies, *Paul and Rabbinic Judaism,* 147–76.
[6] E. P. Sanders, *Paul and Palestinian Judaism,* 33–59.

penitential system, the ancient Jew under the regime of the Law must have experienced the same frustration.

Although this interpretation is not without support in the Pauline text, it has to be modified in the light of recent reinterpretations of the situation of Paul's relationship to Judaism, which are more firmly based in a knowledge of the Judaism of that time. The balance between Paul's rejection of the Law on the one hand and its acceptance on the other is a fine one, and can best be maintained if we identify precisely what the defect was that Paul spotted in the Law. I believe that, at the deepest level, what Paul experienced was the servitude of the Law to sacred violence, but this servitude appears on the surface in various forms to which we must pay attention. One of these forms is surely the uneasy conscience of traditional Lutheranism, but there are other more fundamental forms.

The first blow to the traditional Lutheran interpretation was struck from within the Lutheran establishment by Krister Stendahl who argued that the chief concern of the Apostle was not the question of the justification of the individual conscience but the matter of the conditions on which the gentiles might be included in the people of the God of Israel.[7] This was followed by a second blow from the secular historical establishment by E. P. Sanders, who argued on the basis of the Jewish sources that Judaism was not the kind of religion to cause anguish of conscience.[8] It was not a religion of "works right-eousness" at all, but rather a "covenantal nomism" in which the standing of a member of the covenant was conditioned by the grace of having been born into the covenant, and the obedience to the Law was simply a way of indicat-ing one's intention to maintain that standing. There was a lively penitential system and a realistic attitude to the human capacity to fulfil the Law. Paul left Judaism not for negative but for positive reasons, not because of flaws he saw in Judaism but because of the overwhelming advantage he saw in Christ. Accord-ing to Sanders, if Luther were right, then Paul had seriously misunderstood, or deliberately misrepresented, his ancestral religion. According to Stendahl, Luther simply interpreted Paul anachronistically. Both of them, however, miss the cruciality of the Cross as the disclosure of violence both in his religion and in his heart, and therefore underestimate the negative reasons for Paul's break with Judaism.

The most promising new understanding of the Law in Paul sees it as the definer of the socio-religious group and its boundaries. From this point of view we can see the violence of the Law's scapegoating most clearly. Life according to the Law is primarily a sociological rather than a psychological category. J. D. G. Dunn has argued that Paul criticizes only the "social function" of the

---

[7] K. Stendahl, *Paul among Jews and Gentiles*.

[8] E. P. Sanders, *Paul and Palestinian Judaism*.

Law and not its role in a "works righteousness."[9] Referring to the work of the social anthropologists Hans Mol and Mary Douglas, Dunn argues that ritual serves to mark the boundary of a group, and that circumcision and kosher laws performed this function for the Jews of the Greco-Roman world. Dunn's argument was anticipated in part by J. Tyson who, without recourse to extrabiblical disciplines like anthropology, concluded that "works of the Law" referred to "nomistic service" in the sense of the Jewish way of life, which Paul opposes to Christian existence marked by possession of the Spirit and miracles (Gal 3:5).[10] He based this conclusion on Lohmeyer's examination of the use of the pertinent terminology in the LXX, and "nomistic service" is his translation of Lohmeyer's *Dienst des Gesetzes*.[11]

The phrase "works of the Law" in Galatians 3:10 therefore means "obligations set by Law," or "the religious system determined by Law," and not the deeds of moral and religious practice that earn the approval of God. The Qumran community is a good example of this view of the Law. The "deeds of the Law" marked the life of the members as distinctive (1QS 5:21, 23; 6:18) and identified the community of the end of time (4QFlor. 1:1–7). Likewise, the "boasting" in the Law in Romans 2:17 and 23 does not refer to the piety that relies on achievement but to the use of the Law as the mark of divine favor regardless of the moral conduct of the individual member of the covenant—that is, the substitution of ritual for moral qualifications.

In its social function the Mosaic Law thus creates the community of the Law, and it is important that all discussions of the Law should include the notion of the community that it forms. Life according to the Law is not primarily a psychological category but a sociological one; the alternatives of Law and grace, Moses and Christ, are expressed primarily in terms of communities rather than states of conscience. Paul's criticism of the Law is, therefore, a criticism of certain features of the Jewish community, inasmuch as they are the result of a certain interpretation of the Mosaic Law.

Two Communities or Two Worlds?

If the social function of the Mosaic Law is the target of Paul's criticism, one could conclude that the argument is about the relative merits of two communities, and that it is nothing more than a sectarian squabble. J. L. Martyn[12] shows, however, that what is at stake are not two sects but two worlds, and thus corroborates our analysis in terms of the systems of sacred violence and

---

[9] J. D. G. Dunn, "Works of the Law"; cf. R. G. Hamerton-Kelly, "Sacred Violence and the Curse of the Law."

[10] J. Tyson, "Works of Law in Galatians."

[11] Ibid., 425, n. 13.

[12] J. L. Martyn, "Apocalyptic Antinomies."

divine love, respectively. Paul suffers a "loss of world" as he goes over from the side of the executioner to the side of the victim, because from the point of view of his "new world" he sees the current interpretation of the Mosaic Law as a distortion of the divine command within the structures of the old world's sacred violence.

The convention of "pairs of opposites" current in the philosophical thinking of Paul's day controls the argument in Galatians. According to that convention the cosmos is structured by what Aristotle might have called "tanantia." Ben Sira mentions the theory in 33:15, "all the works of the Most High are in pairs, one the opposite of the other." Paul denies the ultimate reality of this opposition in Galatians 6:13 where he speaks of "the cross of our Lord Jesus Christ, by which the world has been crucified to me, and I to the world. For neither is circumcision anything, nor is uncircumcision anything, but rather what is something is the New Creation"[13] (Martyn's translation). Martyn summarizes as follows:

> Perhaps in this final paragraph Paul is telling the Galatians that the whole of his epistle is not about the better of two mystagogues, or even about the better of two ways, and certainly not about the failure of Judaism. He is saying, rather, that the letter is about the death of one world, and the advent of another. With regard to the former, the death of the cosmos, perhaps Paul is telling the Galatians that one knows the old world to have died, because one knows that its fundamental structures are gone, that those fundamental structures of the cosmos were certain identifiable pairs of opposites, and that, given the situation among their congregations in Galatia, the pair of opposites whose departure calls for emphasis is that of circumcision and uncircumcision.[14]

The death of the world of opposites is a good way of describing the move beyond mimetic rivalry and the structure of sacred violence. The "pairs of opposites" are derived from the primary opposition between the group and the victim. They are the taboos and ritual differentiations, the myths and metaphors of the primitive Sacred. The "apocalyptic antinomy" is their transformation by the death and resurrection of Christ, into the distinction between

---

[13] In the parallel formulations in Gal 5:6 and 1 Cor 7:19 the place of "new creation" is taken by "faith working through love" and "observance of the commandments of God," respectively. Faith working through love should be taken as the equivalent of new creation. It describes the motivation for moral activity in the new order. The context in 1 Cor 7 is the exhortation not to change one's social status in view of the imminence of the end of history; it is not status that matters but obedience to the commandments. The present time is conditioned by the expectation of the new creation and the proleptic presence of its power. In view of this context, we may put 1 Cor 7:19 in the same category as the other two formulations. The observance of the commandments of God is to take place in the power of the new creation, as faith working by love, and not as the means of cultural exclusionism. The commandments in question are not the Mosaic commandments but the divinely inspired injunctions of the apostle himself.

[14] J. L. Martyn, "Apocalyptic Antinomies," 414.

sacred violence and the new creation. Thus for faith in Christ there is a new order based on the freedom of faith working by love and opposed to the present Jerusalem, which is characterized by differentiations of the system of sacred violence exemplified by the temple and the sacrificial system, as the Sarah and Hagar passage in Galatians 4:21—5:1 shows. The new creation is precisely a breakout from the system of mimetic violence theoretically represented as opposites and practically expressed in scapegoating the gentiles. The opposites to which Paul specifically denies reality are the cultural products of the Mosaic Law as upholder of the antinomies of sacred order.

This also means, as we have seen, that for Paul the church is not another sect, but the community of the new creation. It is ontologically beyond the world of opposites, and so is not a rival religion to Judaism, but a new and inclusive community. It is possible to construe this claim as just another ploy in the game of sectarian rivalry. Unfortunately, Christians down the ages have certainly read it as such and used it to justify themselves and delegitimize the Jews. Paul left himself open to such an interpretation, but he did not intend it. He would have been appalled to see the community of the end of time becoming just another sect in time, subject to the delusions of sacred violence. He believed that the Spirit of the new community of the Cross was a manifestation in time of the future of the nonviolent God.

The Law and the Flesh

Paul ranks the Jewish interpretation of the Mosaic Law with the things of the old world, and specifically with the "flesh." This can be seen quite vividly in Galatians 5:16-18, where the old opposites of flesh and Law are so realigned that the opposite of the flesh is not the Law but the Spirit, and the Law is shown to be in alliance with the flesh rather than its opposite. The Law and the flesh signify the same thing—namely, existence within the old world of sacred violence. No longer does the Law curb the passions of the flesh, rather it exacerbates them and conspires with them against the Spirit.

I have already argued that "flesh" is primarily a symbol for Jewish religious existence. This line of interpretation is corroborated in Romans 7–8, where Paul addresses "those under the Law" (Rom 7:1) and says that the state of being under the Law is the same as being "in the flesh" (ἐν τῇ σαρκί—Rom 7:5).[15] In this realm the three negative forces are sin, Law, and death. Sin uses the Law to cause death (Rom 7:5), as the serpent used the prohibition. This prohibition is expressed in the tenth Mosaic commandment against envy,

---

[15] Cf. 2 Cor 10:3 where it means simply "as a human being." Here the meaning "under the Law" is specified by 7:1.

which was a traditional summary of the Law.[16] The Mosaic Law, therefore, contains the primal prohibition, understood as an injunction against envy, and just as the serpent used that prohibition to produce envy, so sin uses the Mosaic Law to produce the system of sacred violence built on envy, life "according to the flesh."

The Law is an expression of the primal prohibition and so is good, just, and holy, but its function and effect is to make sin more sinful, by serving as its instrument of sacred violence, just as the primal prohibition served the serpent (Rom 7:12-13). This is the dialectical role of the Jews in the plan of salvation operating at a level of greater specificity. In Romans 9–11 Paul thinks of Israel as a whole doing dark service to God by rejecting the messiah; here the Mosaic Law does that same service by enabling sin to commit violence, to "be more sinful," and thus eventually to reveal the founding mechanism through the crucifixion.

It does this in two stages, by provoking envy and then by organizing that envy into the structure of sacred violence by means of the surrogate victim mechanism. Romans 7:14-25 is an explanation of how life "in the flesh"— in the system of sacred violence, under sin working through Law—feels to its subject. Paul speaks autobiographically but intends his experience to be representative,[17] and describes a life characterized by achieving the opposite of what one wills, an instance of how the Law makes sin more sinful (Rom 7:13). The Law is spiritual in itself, but like the self it is in thrall to sin[18] in the sense of being a part of the system of sacred violence. The self in this situation literally does not know what it is doing (Rom 7:15a); not in the sense that I do not understand my actions, because I cannot carry out my intentions ('ακρασία),[19] but in the sense that I really do not know what is going on, because I am being deceived by sin (Rom 7:11). The agent of my action in this situation is the sin "that dwells in me"; namely, "in my flesh" (τοῦτ' ἔστιν ἐν τῇ σαρκί μου) (Rom 7:18). In the light of my argument this might be paraphrased, "no good thing dwells in me, that is, in my culturally embedded (Jewish) self." Deception by sin, which is really self-deception, is, therefore, the hallmark of the Jewish religious life in its role as the paradigm of sacred violence that is

---

[16] In Hellenistic Jewish sources, desire (ἐπιθυμία) was often said to be the root of all sin: Philo, *Spec Leg* 4.84, 130; *Dec* 142, 173. From *Spec Leg* 4.84 it is clear that desire means more than merely sexual desire: "Desire is . . . the source of all evil, of robbery, plunder, not paying one's debts, slander and complaining, seduction, adultery, murder, and other crimes against the individual or the state, against holy and profane things" (cited from G. Theissen, *Psychological Aspects*, 204–5; cf. 4 Macc. 2:6); cf. R. Weber, "Die Geschichte des Gesetzes und des Ich," 154–55.

[17] J. C. Beker, *Paul the Apostle*, 326–43; W. D. Davies, *Paul and Rabbinic Judaism*, 25–26; E. P. Sanders, *Paul, the Law, and the Jewish People*, 89, n. 33.

[18] The fact that he uses σάρκινος rather than σαρκικός in Rom 7:14b is of no consequence in view of the context; it is just a stylistic variation and should not be taken to mean that he has the sensuous dimension rather than the psychological or sociological in view here (Käsemann, *An die Römer*, 191).

[19] H. Hommel, "Das 7. Kapital des Römerbriefs."

the primitive essence of all religion. Life in the community of the Law is a life of nescience concerning the founding mechanism.

Paul describes, therefore, a sociological phenomenon of deviated purpose rather than a psychological phenomenon of the weak will. The deviation of purpose is caused by the social dynamics of the Sacred rather than the psychological dynamics of frustration. The self that is both "I" and "my flesh" is the culturally embedded self, and in Paul's case, a Jewish self. As such it is enmeshed in a social nexus that turns good will to evil action. In this nexus a robust will produces well-intentioned actions that miss the mark.

The prime example of this in Paul's life is his persecution of the Christians, which was, as far as we know, not an act of uncontrollable rage, but rather the rational pursuit of a religious goal according to the ethos of his Jewish community. In doing this he really did not know that he was doing evil by doing good, because sin deceived him through the Law, with the result that he saw religious envy as divine obligation. Insofar as he wanted to be doing God's will, he could be said to have rejoiced in God's Law with his mind (Rom 7:22; cf. Rom 10:2),[20] but insofar as he tried to do that will through the Jewish community, he found his desire thwarted. Sacred violence turned the Mosaic Law (ἕτερος νόμος—Rom 7:23, cf. Rom 13:8) into the enemy of his desire to do the Law of God; it made the Law serve the opposite of its intended purpose.

On this understanding of "flesh" as the system of violence in its Jewish manifestation, the passages in Romans 8 on the Spirit and the flesh make perfect sense. Romans 7:25 is a resume of the problem that introduces the triumphant presentation of the solution. "The Law of sin and death" (Rom 8:2) is the Mosaic Law[21] and the "sinful flesh" in whose likeness Christ came (Rom 8:3) is the Jewish way of life (cf. Gal 4:5). Christ condemned sin in

---

[20] The Law of God affirmed by the mind or inner person is the essence of the Law thought of as the primal prohibition of Gen 2:15-17 and spoken of in Rom 7:7, 1:32, and 2:15. R. W. Thompson ("How is the Law Fulfilled in Us?") referring to Rom 8:4, 13:8-10, and Gal 5:13-16, argues that δικαίωμα refers primarily to the love of neighbor as the "just requirement" of the Law. In Rom 1:32, therefore, we have the negative formulation of the same point: the interdiction on mimetic rivalry is the negative expression of the command to love the neighbor. Also P. Stuhlmacher, *Versöhnung, Gesetz, und Gerechtigkeit*, 188, n. 46.

[21] Cranfield, *Romans*, 373–74, connects Rom 8:1-2 with Rom 7:1-6, by means of ἄρα in Rom 8:1. Rom 7:6, in turn, refers back to Rom 6:14—οὐ γάρ ἐστε ὑπὸ νόμον. On these grounds alone the νόμος τῆς ἁμαρτίας καὶ τοῦ θανάτου is the written Law of Moses, presented in Rom 7:6 in contrast to the newness of the Spirit. Cranfield, nevertheless, understands νόμος metaphorically in this phrase, as a symbol for the power of sin, presented as a travesty of the Law of God; it means the same thing as ὁ ἕτερος νόμος in Rom 7:23 (364–65). C. K. Barrett, *Romans*, 155, however, agrees with me that it is "evidently the Law of Moses, seized and perverted by sin and consequently leading to death." E. Lohse, P. von der Osten-Sacken, and E. Käsemann also support this interpretation, as reported by L. Keck, "The Law and 'the Law of Sin and Death.'" Keck does not share this view but, while taking the phrase to mean the same as the ἕτερον νόμον of 7:23, understands it to signify "a structure of power, which one inevitably obeys. It is not really a bondage of the will but a bondage of the self which is free enough to will but not free enough to achieve what is willed" (49). Keck generalizes too soon! He ignores the fact that the existence Paul has in mind is Jewish existence.

this most acute manifestation, and set us free (cf. Gal 5:1, 13) by being born a Jew and being scapegoated by the Law (Gal 4:4-5; 1 Thess 2:15). The primal prohibition (δικαίωμα) of the Law, which Adam was the first to transgress and allow to fall into the hands of sin, is fulfilled in those of us who no longer live as Jews, "who do not walk according to the flesh but according to the Spirit" (Rom 8:4).[22]

If one reads "Jewish way of life" for every occurrence of "the flesh" in Romans 8:1-17, the passage makes consistent sense. Thus, the "mind of the flesh" that is "enmity with God" is the Jewish mind (cf. Rom 5:10; 11:28), and the point of saying that it cannot subject itself to the Law of God is precisely to make the distinction between the Law of God as expressed in the fundamental prohibition, the δικαίωμα of Romans 8:4 and 1:32, and the Law of Moses (cf. Gal 5:17) that produces the sin it intends to prevent. The Law of God is fulfilled by those in the Spirit because they receive and obey the inspired commandments of God (1 Cor 7:19; 14:37), walk in the Spirit under the "Law of Christ" (Gal 6:2; 1 Cor 9:21), and fulfil the fundamental intention of God's Law, which is "faith working through love" (Gal 5:6, 14).

Just as "flesh" designates a way of life in a particular community, so does Spirit; the Spirit dwells in the community (ἐν ὑμῖν—Rom 8:9) just as sin dwells in the flesh in Romans 7:18 (ἐν τῇ σαρκί μου)[23]; that is, the Spirit dwells primarily in the community, and in individuals only to the extent that they are part of the community. All the verbs and pronouns referring to the action or locus of the Spirit in Romans 8:1-17 are plural, with the exception of 8:2 where the first person singular is representative in the same way as in Romans 7, and in 8:9b, which is a brief reference to the individual within a context that is overwhelmingly oriented to the group. For Paul the Spirit, therefore, describes the quality of life in the Christian community and as such is a perfect counterpart to the flesh as the quality of life in the Jewish community.

The image of Adam begins to assert control over Paul's thought again as the exposition of salvation approaches a climax in Romans 8:18-25 with a vision of the restored creation as the reversal of the curse on Adam in Genesis 3:17-19. This accounts for the fact that Paul begins to generalize the contrast between the Jewish and Christian ways of life, expressed as the contrast between flesh and Spirit, into a contrast between mortality and immortality, expressed as the contrast between the body and the divine Spirit (Rom 8:10-11). By the same token, in Romans 8:12-13 he generalizes the reference of "according to the flesh," which is parallel here to "the deeds of the body," to mean the evil things one does in this world under the influence of sin that is at work everywhere, in "the Jew first and also in the Greek" (Rom 1:16; 2:9-10).

---

[22] The metaphor of the walk may allude to the rabbinic designation of the Law as Halakah, literally, "the way."

[23] The ἐν ἐμοί of 7:18 is specified by the ἐν σαρκί. The linking word is ὀικεῖ.

There is a correspondence between the beginning of the exposition in Romans 1:18—3:20 and the end here in Romans 8:12-25; there we have the consequences of Adam's trespass and here we have the consequences of Christ's obedience, a symmetry set out in Romans 5:12-21. For Paul sin begins with Adam and concentrates its focus in the Jewish way of life; salvation begins in Christ under the conditions of the Jewish way of life and broadens its focus to Adam again. This explains why here at the limit of the exposition of the course of salvation Paul does at last generalize the meaning of flesh and use it as parallel with body to describe the human condition under sin. Romans 8:12-13 is, however, one of only three places in the Pauline corpus where flesh has this generalized negative meaning (cf. Gal 6:8, Rom 13:14). The negative connotation that it has here is an extension of the specific negativity it has when referring, as it does in the majority of cases, to the Jewish way of life.

Love, Law, and Vengeance

Law is the judicial transformation of the prohibition originally sanctioned by the threat of the recurrence of mimetic violence dissembled as the vengeance of the god. The element of reciprocity in Law is therefore a transformation of vengeance, and for this reason I have called law the myth of vengeance. Law is, therefore, essentially mimetic violence transformed into divine vengeance and then rationalized as retributive justice. In Paul's Judaism, Law had not yet been fully rationalized and still rested on the idea of the divine vengeance. The Law was still sacred.

The one explicit discussion of the Law in relation to vengeance occurs in Romans 12:9—13:10. Paul exhorts his readers to love sincerely, be forbearing and sympathetic, and especially not to take vengeance by rendering evil for evil. They must leave vengeance to God who has promised to repay, and as they recognize the divine monopoly on eschatological vengeance so they must recognize the state's monopoly on vengeance in this world. The reciprocity of legal obligation is, however, only an imperfect image of the generosity of love that overflows the bounds of the quid pro quo.

This acceptance of the divine and civic monopolies of vengeance could indicate that Paul's God is still the primitive Sacred, and God's order still the order of sacred violence, but that would be a misunderstanding. There are two clues in the immediate context to a proper understanding. One is the reference to sacrifice at the beginning of the chapter, and the other is the phrase in Romans 12:19, "give place to the wrath" (δότε τόπον τῇ ὀργῇ). Furthermore, Paul's teaching must be placed in the larger context of the Jesus tradition as recorded in Matthew 5:33-48 if it is to be fully comprehensible.

Romans 12:1-2 opens the ethical section of the letter by placing the image of sacrifice as a rubric over the discussion. It is, therefore, not substitutionary sacrifice that the image has in mind but rather self-dedication to God. Sacrifice is a metaphor for moral self-dedication and not a ruse for shifting responsibility on to a substitute. Thus the logic of substitution has been reversed, and instead of being a device for escaping responsibility, sacrifice is here a metaphor for the acceptance of responsibility before God. The metaphor is based on the "thanksgiving" element in sacrifice as an image of the moral dedication to God that acknowledges the creator as the "other" who constitutes the self by relationship.

The noetic element is prominent in the passage—such self-sacrifice is reasonable (λογικός) and renews the mind (ἀνακαίνωσις τοῦ νοός)—and this gives the following exhortation (Rom 12:3-8)—to maintain the proper order in the community—a moral rather than a sacral basis. In the realm of the Sacred, order is the effect of the filtered violence of ritual and prohibition; here it is to be the result of moral discernment by the renewed mind. Its mark is precisely the rational curb on rivalry by the responsible acceptance of the differentiated functions of an ordered society. In this Christian community the differentiation that is normally achieved by the threat of the vengeance of the god institutionalized in the law is to be achieved by rational self-restraint (φρονεῖν εἰς τὸ σωφρονεῖν—Rom 12:3). Therefore, not only the explicit image of sacrifice but also the deep logic of the passage attests the dialectical influence of the logic of the Sacred. The passage is in dialogue with sacrificial logic, correcting it in the light of the Cross, and redescribing sacrifice as self-sacrifice in thanksgiving, and order as the free acceptance of prudential constraints, rather than the fearful observance of divine sanctions.

This deep logic continues to form the text in the section on vengeance and love (Rom 12:9—13:10), and thus establishes a presumption in favor of a non-vengeful interpretation of God's action despite the quotation "vengeance is mine, I shall repay" (Rom 12:19; cf. Deut 32:35). The key to the interpretation is the phrase "give place to the wrath" (δότε τόπον τῇ ὀργῇ) in Romans 12:19. It specifies the meaning of the quotation from Deuteronomy 32:35. The vengeance of God is the wrath of God that operates when it is given place. The phrase "give place to" clearly means that the wrath operates apart from human participation. It could also connote, however, that the wrath works independently of God's action, in the sense set out in Romans 1:18-32. There are several indications that the two passages are related. The sinners in Romans 1:18-23 knew the godhead of God rationally from the evidence of creation, but irrationally refused to acknowledge it by giving thanks, and for this reason Romans 12:1-2 urges the rational worship of self-sacrifice. The result of the refusal in Romans 1:18-32 was the "reprobate mind" (ἀδόκιμος νοῦς—Rom 1:28), and for this reason Romans 12:1-2 describes the renewed mind as able to discern the will of God (δοκιμάζειν . . . τὸ θέλημα τοῦ θεοῦ—Rom 12:2). Romans 12, therefore, describes a reversal of the deleterious effects of the refusal of Romans 1, against the background of the presentation of the working of wrath in Romans 1.

The wrath works by self-inflicted harm. God gives sinners up to the consequences of their self-destructive actions, described as the activity of perverse desire (Rom 1:24-31). Thus there is no actual violence in God, and the quotation, "vengeance is mine, I shall repay" must, therefore, be taken loosely.[24] The vengeance of God is to give sinners their own way and not to mitigate the consequences of their freely chosen desires. This is the same understanding of judgment as we find in John 3:19 and in Dante's affirmation that there is no one in hell who does not freely choose to be there. The wrath is the consequence of living willingly in the system of sacred violence.

The presumption against active divine vengeance is confirmed by another intertextual comparison, with the Jesus tradition as recorded in Matthew 5:33-48. This passage contains the second triad of the six "antitheses" that follow the declaration that Jesus came to fulfil the Law and illustrate the "better righteousness" (Matt 5:17-20).[25] The three topics of the second triad are oaths, retaliation, and love of enemies. The inclusion of the prohibition on oaths with the other two items is odd, until one realizes that the essence of the oath is to call down upon oneself the divine vengeance if one proves false.[26] This concept of the oath is also integral to political order, part of the threat of sacred violence that undergirds it. In ancient Greece, for instance, there were official divine guardians of the oath, the θειοὶ ὅρκιοι, who linked people together by the threat of vengeance and were invoked by both sides to an agreement.[27] One might also recall the phrase "to cut a covenant" and the allusion that it makes to the sacrifice that traditionally accompanied agreements. The message was not simply that if one reneges, one will have one's throat cut like the victim, but the much more complex communication that the order that guarantees the agreement is based on the sacrificial victim and that to dishonor that order is to threaten the return of violence in the form of the vengeance of the god.

The concept of the oath, therefore, depends upon the assumption that God is vengeful, and for this reason it is included in the triad with the injunction not to fulfil the *ius talionis* and the injunction to love one's enemies, whose deeper purpose is to deny that God is vengeful. The larger passage is counteracting the generative power of sacred violence, and the section on oaths is no less a part of that strategy than its more explicit companions. Indeed, the final statement that whatever is more than the simple yes or no is of the evil one (or, realm) (τὸ δὲ περισσὸν τούτων ἐκ τοῦ πονηροῦ ἐστιν—Matt 5:37) shows that the text

---

[24] In the same way as the statement in the latter part of the quotation that one heaps burning coals on the head of one's enemies must be taken loosely.

[25] On the organization into triads, see W. D. Davies and D. C. Allison, *The Gospel according to St. Matthew 1*, 504.

[26] Cf. Thomas Hobbes, *Leviathan* (1839) 179 (in *OED*): "Which swearing or oath, is a form of speech added to a promise; by which he that promiseth signifieth that unless he perform, he renounceth the mercy of his God, or calleth to him for vengeance on himself."

[27] *TDNT,* 5, 458.

also thinks in terms of the realm of sacred violence and of the proper location of the oath in that realm.

There is a formal similarity between Matthew 5:43-48, the injunction to love one's enemies, and Romans 13:8-10, the statement on love as the fulfillment of the Law.[28] Both passages have the structure of injunction, reason, and discussion:

	Matt 5:43-48	**Rom 13:8-10**
Injunction:	Love your enemy	Owe only the debt of love
Reason:	To be sons of your father	Because this fulfils the Law
Discussion:	If you love your friends only, what do you do that is extraordinary.	Since love does no harm to the neighbor, it is the fulfillment of the Law.

This is a common literary structure, nevertheless its occurrence in these two passages suggests a link between them at the level of tradition. The presentation in Matthew 5:43–48 identifies the enemies as persecutors of the church (Matt 5:44), and the command to love one's enemies in the Pauline passage implies the nature of the enemies as persecutors. This tradition also lies behind Romans 12:14, 17-20; 1 Corinthians 4:12-13, and 1 Thessalonians 5:15,[29] where persecutors are in mind. This application would have been especially appropriate to Paul the former persecutor (cf. Rom 5:10). The theological basis for this inclusive love—that God includes both the good and the bad in the purview of generosity (Matt 5:45)—would also have been especially serviceable to the Pauline theme of the inclusion of the gentiles.

It would seem, therefore, that the understanding of the nature of the divine love is basically the same in the Matthean and the Pauline traditions. The divine love is not vengeful. This is the disclosure of the Cross; vengeance is human violence that finally breaks against God, and at the point of the Cross is disclosed, so that our minds might be renewed by the disclosure and we might take rational responsibility for our violence.

From vengeance Paul turns to exhort his readers to be obedient to the established authorities and to render to every legitimate creditor his or her due—that is, to observe the reciprocities of obligation. The emphasis on the reciprocity of obligation shows that he is aware of the fact that the civil order is based on the threat of vengeance (Rom 13:4-5). He must, therefore, address the question whether the rejection of vengeance on the part of the Christian entails the rejection of the authority of the state. His answer is that it does not, because the state serves the good of the Christian

---

[28] Davies and Allison, *St. Matthew*, 548–66.

[29] Ibid., 551–52.

by providing the provisional order within which one can work out one's salvation. There is no practical alternative at present to the order of sacred violence.

Implicit in the argument is the claim to a state monopoly on violence. At the generative level, this acknowledges the inevitability of the order of sacred violence. We cannot escape its structures this side of the eschaton, we can only withhold willing cooperation beyond what is absolutely necessary. At the historical level it indicates that there were those in the community who felt justified in opposing state authority. The Roman congregation included the same kind of "zealots" as we identified in Galatia.[30] They advocated resistance to the Roman authorities, especially in the matters of taxes and tolls (Rom 13:7), vengeance against Rome for its oppression of the Jews, and against Christian gentiles who did not observe the Law. They are the ones primarily in mind in Romans 12:19, who are not to avenge themselves but to make place for the wrath, and especially they are not to use the imagined right to revenge to oppose the state.

Like so much of Paul's writing, the argument is fundamentally an interpretation of texts from the Old Testament (Lev 19:18; Deut 32:35; Prov 25:21-22). Vengeance is forbidden in several Old Testament and Jewish texts (Lev 19:18a; Prov 20:22; 24:29; cf. 2 Chron 28:8-15; Sir 28:1-7; T. Gad 6:7; 1 QS 10:17; CD 9:2-5),[31] but they all explicitly or implicitly restrict the range of application to fellow Jews. The evangelical injunction in Matthew 5:43-44, which is reiterated in Romans 12:17-18, is that this restriction must be lifted and that vengeance is forbidden against anyone, and love commanded for all (πάντων ἀνθρώπων).

Most prominent among these Old Testament texts is Leviticus 19:18, which clearly restricts nonvengeance to fellow Israelites, and which probably lies behind Romans 12:19. Paul ignores the restriction and, in addition, makes another point altogether—namely, that the individual should not take vengeance into his own hands. In the LXX Leviticus 19:18 reads: "Your own hand shall not vindicate [you], and you shall not bear a grudge against the sons of your people, but you shall love your neighbor as yourself " (καὶ οὐκ ἐκδικᾶταί σου ἡ χείρ, καὶ οὐ μηνιεῖς τοῖς υἱοῖς τοῦ λαοῦ σου καὶ ἀγαπήσεις τὸν πλησίον σου ὡς σεαυτόν).[32] The LXX emphasizes the prohibition on private vengeance by introducing into the translation the clarifying note *"your own hand"* (ἡ χείρ

---

[30] Marcus Borg ("A New Context for Romans 13," 205–18) places the section from 12:14 through 13:7 in the historical context of the "zealot" movement.

[31] Cranfield, *Romans 2*, 647; W. Klassen, *Love of Enemies*. Klassen's attempt to present the OT and Jewish teaching on revenge as essentially the same as that of the NT does not succeed. At best he can show only occasional texts that are liberal in this regard.

[32] I note, in passing, that the term μηνίω sounds the note of Achilles' wrath in the opening line of the *Iliad* (μῆνιν ἄειδε, θεά, πηληϊάδεω Ἀχιλῆος) alluding to the best-known instance of revenge in the culture, an allusion that Paul and his readers, who probably read the LXX and not the Hebrew, would have picked up.

σοῦ) and Romans 12:19 adopts this interpretation alluding to Leviticus 19:18a by saying "do not vindicate *yourselves*" (μὴ ἑαυτοὺς ἐκδικοῦντες). Thus Paul defends the state's monopoly on vindication. In this world the state has the monopoly on vengeance, and therefore the zealots should not seek to vindicate themselves against the state, but rather leave vengeance to God in the sense of giving place to the wrath.

But the order of reciprocity in the state is only provisional and imperfect, and the true order is the order of love (agape) that rests upon an impossible reciprocity. Thus Leviticus 19:18 takes us from the prohibition on private vengeance to the injunction to love the neighbor. Romans 13:8-10, having confirmed the authority of the civil powers and the duty of ordered obedience within the structure of reciprocal duty, takes up the question of the relationship between love and the Mosaic Law. The civil law prohibits private vengeance on the basis of the constitutional prerogative, and the Mosaic Law prohibits it against one's fellow Jews on the basis of the divine prerogative; but the real answer to the problem of vengeance is the love that fulfils all law, both divine and human.

Therefore, the argument comes to a climax and conclusion in the impossible reciprocity of love, the *debitum indelibile*. After we have discharged all our human and divine obligations, we will still owe the debt of love. "Owe no one anything, excepting to love one another; for he who loves has fulfilled the other law" (μηδενὶ μηδὲν ὀφείλετε, εἰ μὴ τὸ ἀλλήλους ἀγαπᾶν· ὁ γὰρ ἀγαπῶν τὸν ἕτερον νόμον πεπλήρωκεν—Rom 13:8). Contrary to the usual translation of this last verse, "for he who loves the neighbor has fulfilled the Law," I translate "for he who loves has fulfilled the other Law," taking ἕτερον with νόμον as the object of πεπλήρωκεν rather than as an adjective used as a substantive as the object of ἀγαπῶν. On this reading the "other Law" is "other" by comparison with the civil law Paul has just been discussing in Romans 13:1-7; that is, it is the Mosaic Law.[33] Paul is saying that both types of law, the civil and the religious, are fulfilled by the insatiable reciprocity of love.

Love breaks the bounds of reciprocity. It is the one obligation that we can never discharge, and as such points to the new creation; it is the opening in the otherwise closed system of Law based on vengeance. "Owe no

---

[33] W. Marxsen,("Der ἕτερος νόμος: Rom. 13:8") argues that the phrase refers to the Mosaic Law as compared with the civil law of Rome alluded to in μηδενὶ μηδὲν ὀφείλετε, against Cranfield (*Romans 2,* 675–76) who takes ἕτερον as the object of ἀγαπᾶν, "along with the great majority of interpreters from the earliest times to the present day." The consensus does not, however, explain why at 13:10 Paul uses the more usual word for neighbor, ὁ πλησίος, which is the word used in LXX Lev 19:18. Marxsen argues plausibly that the phrase τὸν πλησίον ἀγαπᾶν ("to love the neighbor") was a fixed phrase in the early tradition based on Lev 19:18, and that when this fact is put together with the significantly greater frequency of the adjectival compared to the substantive use of ἕτερος by Paul, one cannot accept the reading of the consensus.

one anything, except [the obligation] to love one another" (Rom 13:8) expresses the point that love sums up and transforms the Law from a system of vengeance into a provisional structure for the expression of love in this world. The exposition reaches a climax in the quotation of Leviticus 19:18, which is presented as an alternative to vengeance. The prohibition of vengeance now applies to all people, not just to one's fellow Israelites. The issue all along has been the transformation of the basis of order from the reciprocity of vengeance into the open-endedness of love. Thus the Law has been fulfilled, and been shown to point beyond itself to the new order of the new creation.

The Law and the "Powers"

In the light of our theory that the Law is the myth of vengeance and the instrument of sacred violence, it is easy to grasp the force of Paul's identification of the Law with the "powers" of this world. The powers are the mythological transformations of the founding mechanism of which the Law, in its current Jewish interpretation, is an integral part, the mythic reifications that disguise the real source of violence. They are the monsters of mimetic rivalry on the macrocosmic scale, in terms of which we alienate our death wish and use it to reinforce order in the world. They reify the patriotic lie, institutional hypocrisy, and the personal envy that we cannot own. Had the powers understood the divine plan of salvation, they would not have crucified the Lord of glory, because by so doing they forfeited the anonymity on which their effectiveness depends (1 Cor 2:8). Once the founding mechanism has been revealed in the epiphany of violence on the Cross, it begins to lose its effectiveness.

The immediate source of this insight is Paul's conversion, but the imagery in which he expresses it comes from Jewish apocalyptic. The divine plan of salvation (μυστήριον) in 1 Corinthians 2:8 is a translation of a technical term in the apocalyptic literature. The general notion of spiritual powers behind human actions is typical of that genre, as is the dualism between the present evil age and the future age of blessing. The pairs of opposites that Martyn identifies are counterparts within the old world of this macro-opposition between the ages. They are the principles and products of mimetic rivalry and sacrificial violence. In the terms of the Galatian debate, they are circumcision and uncircumcision, an opposition that the gospel of the new creation declares obsolete by its message of the reconciliation of rivals in the new creation (2 Cor 5:16-21; cf. Col 1:16-20).

The clearest identification of the Law with the powers occurs in Galatians 3:21—4:11, where they are called "elements" (στοιχεῖαι). Wink has shown that while the basic meaning of this term—the simplest form of a substance or phenomenon—is more or less fixed, it readily takes a wide range of more specific meanings from the context. The dominant basic meanings in the work of Philo, for instance, are the four elements of Empedocles—earth, air, fire, and water—on the one hand, and the letters of the alphabet, on the other.[34]

In the Galatian context the elements are part of the "curse" from which Christ redeemed us by becoming a curse in our stead, of the pedagogues, supervisors, and stewards that control us as if we were minor children, of the Law from whose power we needed to be redeemed in order to receive the status of adopted heirs, and of slavery to false gods. The signs of slavery to this world are ritual observances of "days, months, seasons, years" (Gal 4:10). There is no evidence to support the claim that the Galatian opponents actively promoted worship of the four Empedoclean elements, although such worship is known to have taken place in the ancient world, nor that the "elements" represent spiritual powers of an angelic or demonic kind that had to be supplicated or appeased, nor that the reference to the observance of special days indicates a cult of the calendar.[35]

Martyn has pointed the way to the proper understanding of Paul's meaning in saying that Christ has delivered us from bondage to the elements, by uncovering the pattern of opposites by which the argument in Galatians is structured. In the immediate context we have the celebrated antinomies of Jew/Greek, bond/free, male/female, whose validity is denied (Gal 3:28). In Galatians 4:25 Paul gives us a clue to the presence of this device when he uses the term συστοιχέω. Συστοιχεῖαι is the term for tables, and συστοιχεῖαι τῶν ἐναντίοτων refers to tables of opposites (Arist *Metaph* 986a). These opposites characterize the structure of the old world, about which Paul says in Galatians 6:14-15 that it has passed away as a result of a threefold crucifixion—of Christ, Paul, and the cosmos—in consequence of which he denies the sectarian nature of his position, for which neither circumcision nor uncircumcision means anything. To yield to the demands of the Judaizers is, therefore, simply to resuscitate the old creation (cf. 2:18), by returning to the elemental antithetical structure of things. This explanation is preferable because it coheres so well with the overall theology of the letter.

The passage in question (Gal 3:21—4:11) mixes Jewish and pagan material in its portrayal of the world of sacred violence, showing that Paul regards the religious situation in the old creation to be fundamentally uniform. The pagan's enthrallment to "beings that are by nature not divine" (Gal 4:8) is in the same category as the Jew's imprisonment under the Law (Gal 3:22; 4:4-5).[36] And, by the same token, to make Christianity an anti-Jewish sect would be to succumb to the same slavery by falling back into the pattern of rivalry. Paul, therefore, adapted the general concept of the "elements" to the

---

[34] W. Wink, *Naming the Powers.*

[35] P. Vielhauer, "Gesetzesdienst und Stoicheiadienst."

[36] Ibid., 552–53.

specific meaning of the religious phenomena of the old world, both pagan and Jewish—that is, to the structures of sacred violence.

Faith as the Fulfillment of the Law

I have often noted that Paul regards the Mosaic Law as enduringly valid when properly interpreted, because it contains the primal prohibition. The fact that current Jewish interpretation could summarize the intention of the Law in the tenth commandment against envy shows that there were inklings of this interpretation among the rabbis of that time. The Cross enabled Paul to develop these inklings into a full-fledged new interpretation of what it means to fulfil the Law. Despite its misuse by sacred violence, the Law in its essence is not alien to the divine purpose; therefore it must be fulfilled, but in a sense different from the current Jewish way. Faith is the way to fulfil the essential purpose of the Law.

In Romans 9:30—10:4 Paul faced the unthinkable situation for a Jew of having to conclude that the Law had been the instrument of sin and yet being unable to give up the conviction that the Law was given by God and is therefore holy, just, and good (Rom 7:12). We have already seen that one of the ways he answers that question is to say that the Law was hijacked by sin to the service of sacred violence. This is a mythic way of saying that we use our freedom to misuse the Law by making what was intended to be a bulwark against mimetic rivalry into an instrument of rivalry and scapegoating.

The crucifixion and resurrection fulfils or ends the Law for "everyone who has faith" (Rom 10:4). There is an intimate connection between faith and this denouement of the Law. The Adam story is once again a guide to Paul's meaning here. The purpose of the primal prohibition was to ensure that the relationship between the creature and the creator would be one of trust. Excluded from the knowledge of good and evil, shut up in innocence, the creature could only trust the creator. Thus it makes sense to say that the purpose of the Law is faith. Desire misinterpreted the divine motive and misused the Law to incite envy; the death of Christ reveals this and makes possible a return to the proper understanding of the Law. Those who accept Christ's revelation and return from the state of "knowing good and evil" to the state of innocence and trust—from "works" to faith—therefore fulfil the original purpose of the Law.

To pursue the Law of righteousness by works is to transgress rather than to observe the Law. In terms of the Adam story, it is to transgress the limit of the knowledge of good and evil by entering into mimetic rivalry with God. On this side of the line we are innocent, knowing only good and therefore trusting God in all matters because lacking the knowledge to make decisions for ourselves. We are like little children, and our observance of the prohibition guards our innocence and maintains our faith. Over the line we have declared our lack of confidence in the divine good will, and our suspicion that the prohibition guards God's privilege rather than our paradise. This is what Israel did when it pursued the fulfillment of the Law by works and not by faith (Rom 9:31-32), and manifested an uninformed zeal (Rom 10:2). The Cross revealed the structure of sacred violence in which Israel lived as a result of this misinterpretation of the Law, but Israel found the Cross a stumbling block rather than a salvation (Rom 9:33).

So Christ is the fulfillment of the Law because faith based on the Cross is the trust in God by renunciation of acquisitive mimesis that the prohibition originally intended. Τέλος cannot mean "end" because the Law, in the sense of the primary prohibition, continues to be the norm of righteousness, in the sense of nonacquisitive mimesis, as the determinant element in the structure of faith. Faith is trust in the creator and contentment with innocence; therefore, faith is the fulfillment and goal of the Law.

Elsewhere Paul calls this fundamental thrust of the Law to faith its δικαίωμα (Rom 1:32; 8:4; cf. 2:26; 5:18),[37] a term that can only be understood within the context of the Adam story. It has a negative and a positive force in Paul; it is the sentence of death upon transgressors (Rom 1:32) and the command to love God and the neighbor (Rom 8:4; cf. Rom 13:10b), the two sides of the coin of the primal prohibition. It corresponds to the primal prohibition that threatened death (Gen 2:17b) and secured access to life (Gen 2:16; cf. 3:22b). In Romans 2, where the Adam story continues to control the argument, the several words used to refer to the function of the Law within the Adamic horizon of all humanity—τὸ κρίμα (Rom 2:2-3), τὸ ἔργον ἀγαθόν (Rom 2:7), ἡ ἀδικία (Rom 2:8), τὸ κακόν (Rom 2:9), τὸ ἀγαθόν (Rom 2:10), τὸ ἔργον (Rom 2:15)—all refer to the primal prohibition, which is present to the consciousness of every human creature by virtue of the order of creation.

Thus the fulfillment of the Law is the faith that trusts God and restores the primal prohibition to its true role as the guardian of creaturehood by inhibiting mimetic rivalry with God.

At issue, therefore, are two different interpretations of Torah, one that caused the death of Christ and one that prevents such violence. They are respectively the Mosaic reading and the reading through faith in the Cross of Christ. Therefore, faith is the fulfillment of Torah also in the sense that it provides a way to read it according to its real intention.

Having given us an example of how the hermeneutic of the Cross reads Genesis (the Adam story), Paul also gives us in 2 Corinthians 3:1-18 an example of how it reads Exodus (34:33-34). He contrasts the two interpretations as "word" and "Spirit" respectively, and calls the latter a "new covenant" (2 Cor 3:6). Using a possibly preexisting midrash on the veil of Moses (Exod 34:33-34), he boldly reinterprets the meaning of the term "veil" to mean something like "a veil of ignorance," and the phrase "turn to the Lord" (Exod 34:34) to

---

[37] In Rom 5:16 it is the equivalent of δικαίωσις (Bauer), as in Rom 5:18.

mean "turn in faith to the Lord Jesus." This enables him to read the Exodus passage as saying that the present Jewish reading of the Law of Moses fails to understand it because it is hampered by a veil of ignorance (cf. Rom 10:2), which is removed only when one turns to the Lord Jesus in faith (2 Cor 3:16 / Exod 34:34).

This imagery controls the exposition right up to the end of 2 Corinthians 5, linking the theme of the shining face with the original light of creation now breaking forth from the face of Christ to create the new world of agape (2 Cor 4:6; 5:17). A grand soteriological category like "new creation" therefore has as its practical application a way of reading Torah that at last enables one to see its revelation as the disclosure of sacred violence and the command for agape love. This way of reading the Torah sees beneath the words to the basic purpose of faith and love.

For Paul, the reading of the Torah by his Jewish contemporaries on the other hand brings death because like a veil of ignorance it comes between its readers and Christ. The letters of the text function to obscure rather than to reveal the true goal and purpose of the Law, which is to point to faith in Christ by revealing the sin of Adam and the victimage on which the world is based. If the Mosaic Jews were to read Moses in the light of the crucifixion, they would see the revelation of the distortion of the primal prohibition by the faithlessness of Adam, and understand how it is that the Law brings death—that is, they would read it as Paul read it. By the same token if Christians were to read the Torah in the Jewish way, they would lose sight of the one whom the Law cursed and crucified. The Law kills because the Mosaic interpretation covers up the surrogate victim mechanism and spins the sacred web of self-delusion through observance of holy rules and rituals. The veil of Moses is the web of the double transference.

Susan Handelman took 2 Corinthians 3 as an example of how patristic exegesis scorns the word in favor of the idea, while rabbinic exegesis sticks closely to the word and offers interpretation as commentary. Interpretation and commentary, however, are exactly what Paul offers in this passage. His reinterpretation is quite worthy of rabbinic ingenuity, and he proposes not an idea or a system of thought but an interpretation of Torah. His claim is not that faith in the crucified makes the Torah as text unnecessary, but that it enables us to read the text of the Torah according to its basic intention for the first time.

We have seen hints that Paul, in accord with the Jesus tradition, also identified love as the fulfillment of the Law. Love like faith must, therefore, be a rediscovery of the true purpose of the primal prohibition, and a reversal of the corruption of desire to violence. The traditional terms for the discussion of the nature of love are agape and eros. To these we now turn in an attempt to understand the positive content of the Pauline gospel.

7

Sacred Violence and the Reformation of Desire
Eros and Agape

Νυνὶ δὲ μένει πίστις, ἐλπίς, ἀγάπη, τὰ τρία ταῦτα· μείζων δὲ
τούτων ἡ ἀγάπη.[1]

1 Corinthians 13:13

From your neighbor comes life and death.

Apophthegmata Patrum: Anthony 9:77B

Sacred violence and deformed desire need to be redeemed. Eros is the desire that needs reformation and agape is the redeeming action of God. The dialectic of grace is the dialectic of eros and agape. Just as the deforming act of desire produced a system of violence based on rivalry, so the reforming act of God produces a system of nonviolence based on love. Although Paul does not use the term "eros" in this way, he is a chief source for the idea of agape, and the organization of the discussion in terms of eros and agape is quite compatible with his thought.

Eros and Agape: A Different Angle
on the Same Triangle

Eros and agape are two forms of the same basic human propensity, one alienated and the other integrated. Eros is desire deformed by acquisitive and conflictual mimesis; agape is desire reformed by generous and consensual mimesis. When

---

[1] "Now abide these three, faith, hope and love; but the greatest of them is love."

the model of nonacquisitive desire replaces the model of acquisitive desire, when agape replaces eros, mimesis does not progress to conflict and the system of sacred violence does not come into being. In terms of triangular desire, this replacement happens when agape takes the place of eros at the apex of the triangle.

To recast the discussion in mimetic terms, we must show that the analysis of eros corresponds to our analysis of acquisitive and conflictual mimesis, and the analysis of agape to generous and consensual mimesis as revealed in the Cross of Christ.

Eros

Nygren contrasts agape and eros as unselfish and selfish love, respectively.[2] In a classic study he argued that agape is, according to Paul and John, the divine love that creates and bestows value on the beloved, while eros is the pagan desire that seeks its own fulfillment first. The finest form of eros is the Platonic desire of the soul for the good, which infected Christian spirituality through the influence of Neoplatonism, and turned the gospel of the descent of the divine into the discipline of the ascent of the human, the humanization of God into the divinization of humanity. There is a sharp Protestant edge to Nygren's argument, that cuts away the Catholic idea of grace perfecting rather than replacing nature. By this argument even the most noble of human capacities, like the fine philosophical eros, are inimical to the divine grace. *Sola gratia* and without the synergy of nature God re-creates the divine image in us, while we were yet His enemies and long before our desire turned to Him.

The Greek tradition holds that eros is the child of lack, or as Diotima puts it in the *Symposium* (203 b-e), the bastard offspring of wealth and poverty. It also knows that eros is triangular. Anne Carson writes:

> But the ruse of the triangle is not a trivial maneuver. We see in it the radical constitution of desire. For, where Eros is lack, its activation calls for three structural components—lover, beloved and that which comes between them.[3]

She bases this judgment initially on the following exquisite poem by Sappho, which we quote in Carson's translation:

> He seems to me equal to gods that man
> who opposite you
> sits and listens close
> to your sweet speaking

---

[2] A. Nygren, *Agape and Eros.*
[3] Anne Carson, *Eros the Bittersweet,* 16.

and lovely laughing—oh it
puts the heart in my chest on wings
for when I look at you, a moment, then no speaking
is left in me

no: tongue breaks, and thin
fire is racing under skin
and in eyes no sight and drumming
fills ears

and cold sweat holds me and shaking
grips me all, greener than grass
I am and dead—or almost
I seem to me. [Sappho Fr. 31][4]

"It is a poem about the lover's mind constructing desire for itself."[5] Sappho approaches her desired through identification with the man who sits "equal to gods" (ἴσος θέιοισιν) in her aura and is not consumed. Her desire is mediated and obstructed by this "divine" model/obstacle:

Thin lines of force coordinate the three of them. Along one line travels the girl's voice and laughter to a man who listens closely. A second tangent connects the girl to the poet. Between the eye of the poet and the listening man crackles a third current.[6]

Mimetic theory is particularly interested in the nature of this third current. The line from the poet to the girl runs through the man. It is not the sight of the girl alone that gives wings to the poet's heart, but of the girl and the man together. He is the mediator of the poet's desire, and mimetic rivalry causes the line between them to "crackle." He is "equal to gods" because he is the model/obstacle and as such representative of the sacred victim. As model and obstacle he represents the double valency of the Sacred. He defines eros because as obstacle he provides the element of lack that keeps desire taut, fascinated, and unfulfilled. "The man sits like a god, the poet almost dies: two poles of response within the same desiring mind."[7] The sacred and violence, god and death: two poles of response in the aetiology of sacred violence. Jealousy as erotic deference brings death ("greener than grass / am I and dead").[8]

---

[4] Ibid., 12–13. Cf. Catullus's *Ille mi par esse deo videtur.*
[5] Ibid.
[6] Ibid., 13.
[7] Ibid., 17.
[8] Cf. O, beware, my lord, of jealousy,
    It is the green-eyed monster, which doth mock
    The meat it feeds on.
            Othello, Act 3, Scene 3

Eros in its scandalous need for the obstacle is the love of death. This has been documented by De Rougemont in his studies of the links between the courtly love of the troubadours and the Catharist heretics.[9] The Catharii rejected the material world as a burden on the spirit, and divided their followers, as the Manichees did, into the "perfect," who eschewed sexual relations, and the "auditors" who were sexually active. Out of this renunciation came the extraordinary phenomenon of courtly love and troubadour poetry that celebrated a forever unconsummated and extramarital passion. It is the "love of love," which De Rougemont, describing Tristan and Isolde, says:

> ... has concealed a far more awful passion, a desire altogether unavowable, something that could only be "betrayed" by means of symbols, such as that of the drawn sword and that of perilous chastity. Unawares and in spite of themselves, the lovers have never had but one desire—the desire for death. Unawares, and passionately deceiving themselves, they have been seeking all the time simply to be redeemed and avenged for "what they have suffered"—the passion unloosed by the love potion. In the innermost recesses of their hearts they have been obeying the fatal dictates of the wish for death: they have been in the throes of the active passion of Night.[10]

The passion of night seeks fulfillment by a self-denial that is an inordinate self-assertion. Instead of accepting the self as mediated by the beloved, it seeks the self beyond and apart from the beloved, by the deliberate invention of the obstacle (the drawn sword placed between them). Thus eros refuses the other's service and cherishes its own lack. Its denial of the body of the other is a denial of its own creaturehood and dependency, a form of the desire to be as God. It will not have its lack filled by another. In fleeing from carnal concupiscence, it commits the concupiscence of the spirit that is rivalry with God. "The soul lives by a perpetual renunciation of the finite because the finite fails to give it what it wants, and it cannot rest until it passes beyond desire, never to return, and embraces and is lost in the All."[11]

It achieves this mimetically by idolizing the beloved, turning the beloved into the perfect model/obstacle by assimilating the model/obstacle point of the triangle to the object point. This in effect transforms the beloved into the Sacred, with reference to which the self can love only its own love, desire its own desire, because as total obstacle the other no longer mediates but merely reflects the self, while as perfect model it binds the self to itself absolutely. This is what Kierkegaard calls the essence of the state of anxiety, to love that which one fears, to be attracted by the terrible, fascinated by the awful, obeying

---

[9] D. de Rougemont, *Love in the Western World*.
[10] Quoted in M. D'Arcy, *The Mind and Heart of Love*, 36.
[11] Ibid., 45.

"the fatal dictates of the wish for death." It is what Girard describes as the phenomenon of the "scandalon" in his "interdividual psychology."

"Falling in love with love" is the worship of the pure energy of mimesis apart from any object or content, the worship of sheer violence, the love of the absolute obstacle, which is really the love of one's own love. Thus the Gnostic renunciation of the creation by the renunciation of embodied love and the stable mimesis of marriage is the culmination of the mimetic spiral that scapegoats the beloved and isolates the self. It is the worship of the Sacred through the sacrificed mistress and as such the love of death.

Agape

Eros does not really wish that there should be two in love: one of them must cease to be, and this feeling is so strong as to seem irresistible and the working of destiny. But agape accepts the other and thus guards and foments mutual love, heightening that love by the promise of fidelity which boldly challenges evil and fate.... Moreover, married love wants the good of the beloved, and when it acts on behalf of that good it is creating in its own presence the neighbour.[12]

Eros is the bad mimesis that seeks to possess the self in the other by taking the place of the other; agape is the good mimesis that cherishes the other in the self, and thus creates "in its own presence the neighbor." In agape the other is not the model/obstacle that is both cherished and overcome so that the mediated self can be possessed immediately, but the neighbor who is no obstacle and whose mediatory service is accepted with gratitude and willingly returned. Thus one loves the neighbor as oneself because one loves oneself in the neighbor. Agape is the transformation of the other from model/obstacle into benign mediator.

There is, therefore, a proper love of self and a proper way of mediating that love through the other without reducing the other to the erotic service of the self. It is the love that "is patient and kind, not jealous, boastful, nor puffed up, that does not behave indecently, nor pursue its own interests, is not provoked to wrath, does not keep score of wrong, does not rejoice at unrighteousness but in the truth. It throws a cloak of silence over what is displeasing in another person, and it trusts, hopes, and has patience in all circumstances" (1 Cor 13:4-7). It is the "fruit of the Spirit" that comes to those who "belong to Christ Jesus and have crucified the flesh with its passions and desires" (Gal 5:24). It is the renunciation of mimetic rivalry and the grateful acceptance of the other's service in the mediation of desire. Rather than acquisitive or conflictual, it is consensual mimesis.

The propriety of this proper love is in its priorities; the other must be prior to the self because the self in its lack needs the other as the other needs the

---

[12] De Rougemont, in D'Arcy, ibid., 47.

self. One loves the other first by serving as mediator, and then as the other comes into being through that mediation, so the self comes subsequently into being. One creates oneself by creating the other, and the more one enhances the other, the more one enhances the self. This is the mimetic meaning of the gospel saying that he who seeks to save his life shall lose it, and he who loses his life in the service of the gospel shall save it (Mark 8:35). Faith is the trust that puts the other first, and hope is the confidence that by so doing one will receive from the other one's true self.

This act of faith is based on the prior experience of faith in Christ as the new creation by which we ourselves have been reconstituted by the divine other and now exist in him (Gal 2:20). Thus mimetic theory gives us a precise phenomenology of faith, hope, and love, and shows that love is the greatest because it is the whole of which faith and hope are parts. Love is the good mimesis of co-creatorship with God (Gen 1:28), structured as a triangle with its apex in the divine.

The Different Angle

Eros is triangular—lover, model/obstacle, beloved—and agape is triangular—lover, creator/God, beloved. In the latter triangle the different angle is the divine nonacquisitive desire instead of human acquisitiveness. The creator God in the place of the model/obstacle gives to the mimesis of desire its proper form as the constituting power of the self. Eros is desire structured by lack and the pursuit of death; agape is desire flowing from the divine plenitude that fulfils our lack. They are both triangular, but there is one angle that is different, and that distinguishes the nature of each.

According to Nygren, agape is essentially the divine love whose primary form is love of enemies (Matt 5:44; Mk 2:17). While we were enemies, God gave the son to us, who died not for the righteous but for the ungodly (Rom 5:6-10). "God's attitude to men is not characterized by *justitia distributiva,* but by ἀγάπη, not by retributive righteousness, but by freely giving and forgiving love."[13] Agape is spontaneous and unmotivated, indifferent to value, creative, and the initiator of fellowship with God. When the divine is the apex of the triangle of desire, acquisitiveness is unnecessary, because the plenitude of agape fulfils desire's every need, and thus sets desire free for consensus. The divine desire expressed in agape is not acquisitive but generous, not conflictual but consensual. When the self mimes the divine desire, it becomes generous and agreeable rather than acquisitive and conflictual. This mimesis threatens no vengeance, sacrifices no victims, and spins no myths.

The key element in the concept of agape is creative generosity, the opposite of acquisitiveness (2 Cor 4:6). It is the power of the creation and the new

---

13 Nygren, *Agape and Eros,* 70.

creation, which takes its cue from the first command in the Torah, to imitate God's creativity. The command in Genesis 1:28 to "be fruitful and multiply" is essentially a command to mime the creative activity of God as pro-creators of the divine generosity. Since the relationship between the creator and the creature is necessarily an unequal one in which the former gives and the latter receives, this mimesis can only be a dependent, secondary one, as expressed in the term "pro-creator," and structured by the primal prohibition on rivalry with the divine.

Since there is nothing in the creature that the creator desires, excepting that the creature should be, there is no ground for mimetic rivalry between the two poles, because there is no envy in the divine.[14] The creation is unmotivated excepting as a decision of the divine freedom to confer the unparalleled blessing of being upon a nothingness that by that very conferral begins to be as a thanksgiving to its source. This creative love is by definition indifferent to any prevenient value of its creature because it creates that value itself along with the creature, and it initiates a relationship with the divine by virtue of the fact that it initiates the possibility of any relationship at all and holds the creature in being by nothing other than relationship. The doctrine of agape is, therefore, a form of the metaphysical doctrine of the total contingency of the creation upon the creator, and an expression of the limitless generosity of God.

Agape is also the prelapsarian innocence of Adam, when the prohibition defended him from the knowledge of evil and kept access open to the tree of life, while eros is the knowledge of good and evil. Agape trusts the God of the prohibition, puts hope in place of rivalry, and thus fulfils the Law. Eros suspects the prohibition of excluding it from an entitlement and so has deformed itself into rivalry with the divine, and the prohibition into a principle of competition in the mimetic game.

Eros's misrepresentation of its lack and the divine plenitude necessitates the threefold structure of lover/rival/beloved. Without the rival there is no obstacle to perpetuate and exaggerate the lack by which eros lives. This is the sense in which eros is the worship of death; it is internally structured by a nothingness that it wants to perpetuate. Agape on the contrary is the creative power that brings something out of nothing and satisfies all lack. It is a proper

---

[14] Cf. Wisd 2:24 "By the envy of the devil death entered the world." On the general theme of envy in the divine, see Plato, *Tim.* 29e "He was good, and in him that is good no envy (φθόνος) ariseth ever concerning anything; and being devoid of envy he desired that all should be, so far as possible, like unto himself." This is the "supreme originating principle (ἀρχὴ κυριοτάτη) of Becoming and the Cosmos." Cf. Phaedr. 247a: "envy is excluded from the divine chorus" (φθόνος γὰρ ἔξω θείου χοροῦ ἵσταται), quoted by Philo in *Quod Lib* 13; cf. *Spec Leg* 2.249, *Leg All* 1.61, 3.7, *Abr* 203–4. That the gods need nothing is a commonplace of Greek philosophy; see the evidence cited by H. Conzelmann, *Acts of the Apostles,* 142, commenting on Acts 17:25. The generosity of the divine was, therefore, a commonplace of Hellenistic philosophic and religious thought.

mimesis of God, the desire to imitate the divine in creative generosity and so fulfil the first biblical command to be pro-creator (Gen 1:28).

Agape removes the lack that eros cherishes, because it is the fulness that precedes the lack that deformed desire attributed to the divine and then realized in itself by turning away from the divine plenitude to its own emptiness in the denial of ontological dependency by misrepresentation of the prohibition. In agape the creature accepts both its own need and the divine sufficiency; in eros it cherishes its need and rejects the divine plenitude. Eros chooses emptiness, and persists in it freely; agape manifests the divine plenitude and causes desire to rejoice in it thankfully.

There are, however, two possible objections to the sharp distinction between eros and agape, one from the human point of view and one from the divine. Approaching from the human point of view, D'Arcy takes the natural law position and argues that there is a proper lack in human love. This view has powerful support from Augustine, who claims that the desire of the creature is naturally for the creator and "our hearts are restless" until they rest in God. There is in the creature an ontological need for God and so even life in agape is constituted by a sort of lack.

This lack is very different from the other, however; not a void that must be filled but rather a dependency that evokes a trust. This must be affirmed phenomenologically and theologically. The restlessness of the unfulfilled creature is an observable phenomenon that stems from the root cause of the deformation of desire to rivalry. Nevertheless, it is a deformation of an original ontological dependency that can be discerned beneath its pathology, and which is expressed in the command to procreate. That ontological dependency is, therefore, mimetically structured. Human being is originally in a mimetic relation to God specified as being in the divine image (Gen 1:26).[15] Being in the divine image means being in a mimetic relationship of the kind Paul describes when he says that Christ lives in him and he in Christ (Gal 2:20), or that he imitates Christ (1 Cor 11:1). This means that eros must not be denied altogether but redeemed, by a proper identification of human lack and a restoration of mimesis to the form of the image of God in humanity.

The sinister element in eros is its making a virtue of the lack that it misrepresented by its self-deformation, by the turning of trust to envy. The mind of love is confused in self-assertion and sacred violence, and this confusion cannot be cleared up without the intervention of grace. Grace comes as the Cross of Christ exposes the deformation of desire and makes the act of faith possible. By faith eros is transformed into agape by a proper acceptance of ontological dependency through the restoration of the angle of the divine creative desire

---

[15] Being in the divine image entails having dominion over the other creatures (Gen 1:26) just as being fruitful entails dominion (Gen 1:28). The concept of dominion in both verses, therefore, identifies being in the image with being fruitful.

to the place usurped by human acquisitiveness. In this sense grace perfects nature and the *amor concupiscentiae* becomes the *amor amicitiae*. Agape, therefore, is also a form of desire: the ontological dependence of the creature expressed as the creature's mimesis of the creator through being in the divine image. In this way mimetic theory restates and corroborates D'Arcy's view that the two loves have the same structure by legitimating the ordered self-seeking of redeemed eros.

In what sense could agape, however, also be the desire of God for the creature? According to traditional theology the creator cannot be ontologically dependent on the creature and so the divine desire must be essentially different from the creature's, arising not from lack but from plenitude. Arguing from the point of view of the divine, D. D. Williams substitutes the "process" metaphysic for the traditional patristic one of the impassible God.[16] According to this metaphysic there is a mutual if not equal dependency between God and creatures, and God does not love without any hope of reciprocity, but rather needs the response of the creature. Indeed, the being of God as love is incomplete without this reciprocation. Essentially there is only one kind of love and it always presupposes a need in the lover, even in God.

Williams's insight needs to be restated and corrected in mimetic terms. The divine need arises primarily from plenitude, not lack, and is therefore, the need to give. Since there is no envy in God, the one need God has is to give and to share. It is essential to maintain this self-sufficiency of God as the antidote to the mimetic misinterpretation of the divine as envious and rivalrous. However, the relationship between the divine and the human is mimetically constituted and, therefore, the divine needs the mimetic reciprocity of the creature for the relationship to succeed. When the creature misinterprets the divine desire as envious and turns to mimetic rivalry, the loss sustained by the divine is not ontological but mimetic. The divine suffers not diminishment but violence, as the Cross reveals. Thus the divine suffering occurs in the divine desire, not in the divine substance. In this way we maintain both the traditional doctrine of God's self-sufficiency, and the concept of the necessary reciprocity of love.

This can be summed up in Paul's statement, "I no longer live, but Christ lives in me; and the life I now live in the flesh, I live by faith in the Son of God who loved me and gave himself for me" (Gal 2:20). There is no self-contained or self-sufficient self, only the violently mimetic self of deformed desire or the God-related self of the restored creature. And that restoration comes through the reorientation wrought by the mimetic identification with Christ's affirmation of me by my affirmation of Christ. He lives in me and I live in him; a perfect expression of the mimetic constitution of the self in creaturely contingency, which takes account of the interests both of D'Arcy and Williams, without invoking natural law or the imperfection of God. This happens when

---

[16] D. D. Williams, *The Spirit and the Forms of Love.*

the divine becomes the apex of the triangle of desire and the relationship of desire between the subject and the model is transformed by agape.

D'Arcy's proper self-seeking in the creature is the mimetic orientation to the divine other and Williams's divine need is the creator's reciprocity that holds the creature in being. The proper self-seeking is the orientation of the creature to the creator and the creator to the creature, and every other such self-seeking is a deformation. Therefore, Nygren is both right and wrong. He is wrong to deny the natural orientation to God and right to suspect desire's urge to cope with dependency by its own striving. The natural orientation is the creaturely contingency, while the striving is the attempt to escape it, to possess the self alone and defy the mimetic constitution by absorbing the divine pole.

However, within the structure of sacred violence based on Adam's sin it is highly probable, though not inevitable, that we shall seek to escape from contingency and thus deform our natural creaturely desire into mimetic rivalry. Therefore, the natural propensity to enhance the self that D'Arcy commends remains highly problematic. In principle it is desire's proper need for creative reciprocity; in practice it is desire's violent rivalry with all others for its own independence. This practice must be reordered, and that reordering requires faith and grace. At best, therefore, the natural self-seeking is the ground of the possibility of redemption, at worst the energy of sacred violence.

Therefore, the relationship between eros and agape is dialectical and they both confirm and deny each other in the dialectic of nature and grace. Eros confirms agape to the extent that it is incomplete in itself and open to the completion that comes from the mimetic relationship with the other, and ultimately from God. It denies agape to the extent that the mimetic relationship is rivalrous and attempts to possess the self in the other by displacing the other, and substituting the model/obstacle for God. Agape confirms eros in that it too is open to the other but denies it in that it seeks its own satisfaction by affirming, not displacing, the other. Agape finds its own fulfillment in the fulfillment of the other because it knows that it can only possess itself mediately and not immediately, and ultimately only in God. This is the truth both of D'Arcy's proper self-seeking and Williams's divine commitment to the human.

The human is not impaired but restored by grace, and the divine impassibility is not impaired, because the creative love that mirrors the human other lacks nothing. Agape is not contingent on the human response, but is unconditional and entirely adequate, the power that creates something out of nothing. Nevertheless, as creative love it is abidingly open to the creature, and in that sense it is vulnerable to the violence of deformed desire and the Sacred, but never in need, and always unchanging in its plenitude of grace. The divine agape is driven by one desire only, the need to give of itself generously, and that is the desire we mime in the triangle of restored desire.

The True Triangle of Desire:
Faith, Hope, and Love

Agape is creative and graceful, and brings forth joy ex nihilo. It is essentially the power of divine grace. Paul, however, uses the term most often to describe a way of being human in the world, a way to walk and fulfil the Law. Agape describes the ideal of reformed eros and, as such, it is triangular like all desire. It is the paradigm of desire as triangular, because the mediator of agapaic desire is God the creator. For this reason agape can never be rivalrous; the mediator is ontologically beyond comparison and agape is the desire to give, not to acquire. Faith and hope describe agape's relationship to the divine mediator in the trust and confidence that marked Adam's relationship prior to the deformation of desire.

Thus there is an alternative to sacred violence even within the violent order of the old world; it is the order founded on faith, hope, and love (1 Cor 13; Rom 5:1-11). These three are the poles around which Christian existence in this world and the next is organized. They are the benign counterparts of the poles of sacred violence, deceit, mistrust, and rivalry. They are, like their negative counterparts, individual attitudes as well as communal conditions, and function as parts of an alternative social system. They are the conditions of the original creation before its corruption by the deformation of desire to violence. In 1 Corinthians 13:13 they are said to "abide" (μένει) beyond this world and into the next—that is, they are the fundamental conditions of human existence, not temporary adaptations to life in the temporal order. We shall understand them better if we analyze them by comparison with their deformations as found in the Adam story, since they are the structural characteristics of the life of paradise before the fall.

Faith is the trusting acceptance of the primal prohibition as part of God's order for the well-being of Adam in paradise. As long as Adam observes it, he has access to the tree of life and is beyond the reach of death. The one requirement for this observance is that desire trust God and accept the prohibition without question, resisting the temptation to deform itself by acquiescing in the possibility of envy that arises along with its freedom. Faith is thus the opposite and antidote to envy, because it assumes that the desire of the other is innocent, not deceitful; to benefit, not to best, the self. Faith is freedom from envy, especially with reference to God, and joyous obedience to the divine command (Rom 5:19).[17] It is the opposite of deceit because it assumes that the prohibition is beneficent and not a ruse. Abraham's trust in the promise of God is the exemplar of this faith (Rom 4).

---

[17] V. P. Furnish, *Theology and Ethics in Paul*, 182–87.

If we are confident that there is no envy in the divine, then we may trust that whatever God does will be for our benefit even when that is not immediately evident. This is the attitude of confident dependence appropriate for the relationship between the creature and the creator, not only here but also in eternity. The gain in knowledge that occurs (1 Cor 13:12) does not reduce the need for faith, because faith is not a substitute for knowledge but a fundamental attitude of trusting dependence that defines creaturehood. The creature is not and never will be self-sufficient, and faith accepts this fact without anxiety. Faith accepts the mimetic nature of the self and affirms the good mimesis of the *imitatio Christi* (cf. Phil 2:6-11).

The opposite of faith is an unbelief posited on the suspicion that God is trying to deceive desire through the prohibition. This unbelief takes the form of a striving to defend one's own interest. In terms of the Adam story it is the transgression of the limit in order to gain the knowledge of good and evil, which is the ability to run one's own affairs and so no longer be dependent on the divine in the game of rivalry. This is precisely the attitude of the zealous Jews that Paul resists in Galatia and Rome; they take matters into their own hands, because they do not trust God. Prior to the transgression Adam was in the state of innocence knowing only good and depending on God; subsequently he had in his own hands the power to dispose of himself morally, to do either good or evil. In that state God could not allow him continued access to the tree of life, because there can be only one immortal disposer over good and evil. To regain immortality we must regain innocence in the sense of trust in God.

Hope is the expectation of good from the one whom we trust (Rom 5:2-4; 8:24-25). It is essentially the same as faith in that it is a modality of creaturehood's dependence on the creator. Whereas faith contemplates the fact of existence, hope contemplates its promise. Faith marvels at the fact that I am rather than am not, while hope takes that fact as the basis for the expectation of a good future, especially for the confidence that the one who brought me into being did not do so just to let me die. Hope trusts the creator for eternal life. In terms of the Adam story, hope is the access to the tree of life that was open to Adam as long as he approached in faith—that is, as long as he accepted the prohibition (Rom 8:18-25). If faith accepts the prohibition because it believes that God is true and not a deceiver, hope accepts it because it trusts the promise that those who eat of the tree of life will live. Since observance of the prohibition is the condition of access to the tree of life, hope like faith is structured by acceptance of the true intention of the Law.

Love is the greatest of the triad, but is not essentially different from its two partners. It is the confidence in God that grounds faith and hope, their presupposition and motive power. As faith believes God is no deceiver, and hope believes that God will give and not withhold the good future, so they express the love that is nonrivalrous imitation of the divine, the pro-creatorhood of the image of God (Gen 1:28). Love is the return to innocence that allows God to dispose over good and evil, and is content with the good alone as God gives it to be enjoyed. It is the basic reality of which faith and hope are modalities, because it is the life of God in the lives of men and women. Love is the imitation of the divine agape within the triangle of desire.

When we love we are in the image of God. D. Williams expresses this eloquently:

> If creation for freedom to love is the image of God in man, sin is a perversion of man's essential being. It draws its power from what man really is. There can be no sin without love, either love perverted, love distorted, or, and here we peer into a deeper depth, love destroyed by a revengeful unlove which turns against life itself.[18]

The image of God is the freedom to love, but this freedom takes place within the triangle of desire as the freedom to mime the divine apex of the triangle. Therefore, under the circumstances of the fall, the restoration of the divine image in the human begins with the faith that allows the divine desire to replace the desire of the human model/obstacle in the triangle of desire. Then as the human mimes the divine desire it takes on the lineaments of agape, until the point of mimetic doubling is reached and the image of God in the human is restored.

Christ as the Exemplar and Mediator of Agape

For Paul the chief concrete image of agape is the self-giving of Christ in the crucifixion. In Romans 5:1-11 the triad of faith, hope, and love points to the work of Christ as the substance of the idea of love. The essence of the divine agape is the act of God in giving the Son to die for enemies (Rom 5:10). In Galatians 2:19-21 the crucifixion is a demonstration of the fact that God "loved me and gave himself for me" (τοῦ ἀγαπήσαντός με καὶ παραδόντος ἑαυτὸν ὑπὲρ ἐμοῦ—Gal 2:20). In 2 Corinthians 5:14—"the love of Christ controls us because we are convinced that one has died for all (ὑπὲρ πάντων); therefore all have died"—expresses the same idea.

The essence of these statements is in the preposition ὑπέρ with the genitive: Christ died on our behalf, to do us good, to give us something of value. This inverts the insinuation of the serpent that God is envious. It demonstrates the divine generosity and thus disarms rivalry with God, replacing it with the proper mimesis of God's love.

---

18 Williams, *The Spirit and the Forms of Love,* 143.

The Church as a Structure of Agape
Based on the Imitation of
Christ Crucified

The crucified is the substantive content of the divine agape as it takes its position at the apex of the triangle of desire. From that point on, Christian desire should mime the divine model and act in imitation of Christ. This has consequences for the nature of the apostolic ministry, the Christian community, and Christian behavior.

"Be imitators of me, as I am of Christ"
(1 Cor 4:16; 11:1)

The apostolic ministry is an imitation of the crucified Christ, which the Christian in turn should emulate. The believer is to mime the desire of the apostle as he mimes the desire of Christ. Thus Paul is a model/mediator of Christ, not a model/obstacle. He is not an obstacle because he deemphasizes his own importance by comparison with the relationship between the believer and Christ (1 Cor 2:2-4; 3:5). He does this by means of irony.

His chosen mode of self-presentation is irony, which is well suited both to his theological and historical situation. Theologically he represents the power of the Cross that is made perfect in weakness (2 Cor 12:9), and historically he faces a group of "boasting" opponents whose boasting compels him to use the same kind of rhetoric, which he can only do ironically. Irony, therefore, undercuts the obstacle in the apostolic model, and provides a framework for the argument about status that is going on in the Corinthian congregation.

The most vivid example of ironic self-presentation occurs in the so-called tearful letter.[19] "One must boast" (2 Cor 11:30; 12:1) is a slogan of the opponents that Paul repeats sarcastically. After an ironically boastful introduction (2 Cor 11:16-23a) he recites a list of his sufferings of the kind we know from Cynic and Stoic sources under the name "difficult circumstances" (περιστάσεις)[20] (cf. 1 Cor 4:9-13; 2 Cor 4:7-12; 6:4-10). In the boasting passage (2 Cor 11:16-23a) that introduces the *peristaseis* list (2 Cor 11:23b-29) the term "fool" (ἄφρων and its derivatives) occurs five times in six verses, and as he begins his recitation of the grounds for his claim to be a superior servant of Christ, he interrupts himself to exclaim, "Now I'm really talking like an idiot!" (2 Cor 11:23b).

---

[19] 2 Cor is a conglomerate of shorter letters. According to C. K. Barrett (*A Commentary on the Second Epistle of Paul to the Corinthians,* 11–14) they are the following: (1) The tearful letter (2 Cor 2:4) = 2 Cor 10–13; (2) the "triumphal" letter (2 Cor 2:14) = 2 Cor 2:14—6:13, 7:2-4; (3) a travel letter = 2 Cor 1:1—2:13; 7:5-16; 9:1-15. The rest of the text we may leave unclassified for our present purpose.

[20] Conzelmann, *1 Corinthians,* 89.

The list that follows must, therefore, be taken ironically; such lists were used by the missionaries of other gods, and perhaps by the opponents, to show their hearers how many difficulties their god had saved them from, as proof of the power and care of the divinity. Paul, on the contrary, uses one to show how many difficulties Christ *did not deliver him from,* as proof of the dialectical power of the Cross, and as a parody of the status claims of his opponents. The comical escape from Damascus in a basket sets the seal on this burlesque of status (2 Cor 11:32-33), and the conclusion "When I am weak, then am I strong" (2 Cor 12:10) summarizes the whole point of the irony.

The theme of strength through weakness is the dominant theme of the "tearful" letter, and it presents the apostle both as the scapegoat whose sufferings bring advantage to the church, and as the one who understands agapaic mimesis. Rather than enter into the rivalry by imitating the opponents' desire for power and prestige, he enters ironically by imitating the weakness and humiliation of Christ, and identifying with the weaknesses of his congregations. "Who is sick and I am not sick? Who is made to stumble and I am not furious?" (2 Cor 11:29). In weakness the power of Christ to diffuse mimetic rivalry is most effective; so it is not despite his affliction that Paul is a successful apostle of Christ, but precisely because of it (cf. the dialectical role of Israel in the plan of salvation). "Therefore, I am content with weakness, contempt, persecution, deprivation, and frustration, for Christ's sake: for when I am weak, then am I strong" (2 Cor 12:10). This strength is precisely the power of agapaic mimesis, of the imitation of Christ crucified, to dispel the erotic mimesis of rivalry for status. This is the specific content of the exhortations to imitate him that the apostle makes to his rivalrous congregation.

The calls to imitate the apostle are closely tied by their contexts to the substance of agape. In 1 Corinthians 11:1 the call occurs in association with several exhortations to loving humility. "Let no one seek his own advantage but rather the advantage of the other" (1 Cor 10:24), and "be without offense to Jews and Greeks and to the church of God, even as I seek to please all persons in all things, not seeking my own advantage but that of the many, in order that they might be saved" (1 Cor 10:32-33). This is what it means to imitate Christ through imitation of the apostle.

A second exhortation to imitate him (1 Cor 4:16b) explicitly identifies the apostles with the victims of sacred violence, and thus confirms our understanding that for Paul the antidote to sacred violence is identification with the victim. It comes at the end of a catalogue of adversities in 1 Corinthians 4:9-13 of the kind that we have already seen. The extended metaphor of victimage begins in 1 Corinthians 4:9 with the apostles in the arena as condemned criminals (ἐπιθανατίους). Condemned criminals are traditionally in the position of sacrificial victims, and in Latin the word *sacer* is used to describe them. The apostolic misfortunes produce the opposite good fortune for their congregations, just as the sufferings of the scapegoat secure blessings for the community. The passage culminates in the explicit identification of the apostles as scapegoats: "We have become like the scapegoats of the world, the noxious waste of all things, until now" (ὡς περικαθάρματα τοῦ κόσμου ἐγενήθημεν, πάντων περίψημα, ἕως ἄρτι—1 Cor 4:13).

He applies the metaphor of the apostles as victims and scapegoats as a moral exhortation to the community, to eschew rivalry and embrace humility. Since he is the father of the congregation (1 Cor 4:15), his children should imitate him in his humility and willingness to serve, and thus cease from "puffing" themselves up (1 Cor 4:6,18).

The apostles and their followers do not imitate moral examples from the life of Jesus, but the summary act of the crucifixion, the crucified Christ in his act of self-sacrifice rather than any specific pattern of ethics drawn from the memory of his life. The fact of the divine self-emptying is paradigmatic (2 Cor 8:9; Phil 2:5-11). "To imitate Paul and Christ means to be conformed to Christ's suffering and death in the giving of oneself over to the service of others"[21] (cf. Phil 3:10; Rom 15:1-3; Gal 6:17). The historical background of the concept of the imitation of the divine is something like the dramatic presentation of the cult myth in the cult of Dionysos, not in the details but in the major moments. Paul probably received this idea of imitation as part of the common Hellenistic culture of which he was a part, in the same way as Philo received it.[22]

Paul's use of the term μιμητής in general confirms its connection with mimetic theory. In 2 Thessalonians 3:7, 9 he tells folk to imitate the fact that he did not sponge off the community but worked with his own hands. This working is one of the "difficulties" that in 1 Corinthians 4:12 is the mark of the apostle as scapegoat. In 1 Thessalonians 1:6 mimesis is specifically the imitation of Christ, and in Philippians 3:17-18 those who imitate the apostle are contrasted with those who live as "enemies of the Cross of Christ."

The personal history of Paul the apostle as the model and mediator of agapaic mimesis is a critical link in the chain of theological argument. He makes his "difficult circumstances" paradigmatic of apostolic existence, but in so doing draws on conventional lists of hardships. However, in addition to such semistylized self-presentations, he does not hesitate to use his own personal experience as the basis for his theology. We have already seen how he made his conversion paradigmatic of faith as the transfer from the side of the executioners to the side of the victim. We must now consider the remarkable claim that he bore "the marks of the victim" (Gal 6:17).

The victim of mob violence is often singled out because of a physical peculiarity that becomes the mark of the victim. Any extraordinary feature— physical affliction, great ugliness, or great beauty—could be an invitation to victimage, as long as it was combined with vulnerability. There was something

---

[21] Furnish, *Theology and Ethics,* 223.
[22] H. D. Betz, *Nachfolge und Nachahmung,* 60, 86, 135–36.

about Paul that made him publicly contemptible from time to time. We believe that he suffered from an affliction of the eyes, as Galatians 4:12-20 suggests. Eye trouble is the most likely "thorn in the flesh" (2 Cor 12:7), because Paul was visibly stricken when the Galatians first saw him, in such a way as would tempt people to despise him and turn away. He came to them with the mark of the victim on him.

Galatians 4:12-20 begins with a reference to imitation that reveals the mimetic structure of the whole passage. "Become as I am because I also have become as you are, I beseech you brothers" (Gal 4:12). Betz says that this is a cliché from the courtesies of friendship, and if so it would confirm the mimetic theory of friendship.[23] Paul reminds the Galatians that they did not scorn or despise him. At this point the language recalls the traditional response of turning away from one possessed by a demon, but the Galatians did not do that. The link in the popular mind between demon possession and disfiguring affliction was close, but the fact that the Galatians did not follow custom but received him as Christ himself transformed the demonic into the divine by breaking the power of the scapegoat mechanism. By accepting rather than expelling the marked victim, the Galatians transformed rivalry into sympathy, and sympathy caused them so to identify with him in his sufferings that they were prepared if it were possible to exchange eyes with him! The conflictual erotic mimesis was transformed into consensual agapaic mimesis that accepted rather than expelled the marked victim and so identified with him that it desired to lift the mark from him onto itself. Rather than sacrifice the victim, agape wanted to sacrifice itself on behalf of the victim.

For Paul the zealous Judaizers, on the other hand, are full of erotic rivalry, as can be seen from the language Paul uses to describe them, especially the use of the term "zeal." They "pay zealous court to you" (ζηλόω—Gal 4:17), he says, and in 2 Corinthians 11:1-6, at the heart of the "tearful" letter, we find a similar erotic use of the term ζηλόω. However, the fact that he asks permission to play the fool (2 Cor 11:1) before he launches into the erotic confession of 2 Corinthians 11:2-6, shows that the confession is ironic. "I am zealous for you with the zeal of God" (2 Cor 11:2a) is probably a slogan of the opponents (cf. 1 Cor 6:12, 13; 10:23) that Paul quotes ironically. The true zeal is not erotic self-seeking, like Eve's and the opponents, but agapaic self-giving that mimes Christ.

The apostolic ministry is above all a ministry of reconciliation. This can be seen best in the "triumphal" letter, by noting the way Paul uses the two *peristaseis* lists (2 Cor 4:7-12; 6:4-10) in that letter to bracket the discussion of reconciliation, as if to say that reconciliation can take place only through knowledge of the mechanism of the scapegoat.

---

[23] H. D. Betz, *Galatians*, loc. cit.

In this Letter the note of rhetorical irony has been replaced by a straight-forward recognition that suffering is an integral part of the apostolic ministry. It is no longer necessary to use rhetorical irony because the conflict is over. The "triumphal" letter marks the resolution of the problem of rivalry and the reconciliation between the apostle and the congregation. Nevertheless, the theological irony of power through weakness does not abate.

The "triumphal" letter comprises the following sections: (1) the introductory thanksgiving—2 Cor 2:14-17; (2) letters of recommendation, and the relationship between the letter and the spirit—2 Cor 3:1-18; (3) this ministry is a treasure in earthen vessels—2 Cor 4:1-15; (4) a digression caused by the reference to "things unseen" in 2 Cor 4:18, on heavenly existence; (5) the ministry of reconciliation—2 Cor 5:11—6:13; (6) concluding summary—2 Cor 7:2-4.

The gravamen of the letter is in sections 3 and 5 on the nature of the apostolic ministry as a ministry of reconciliation. This stands to reason given that the letter celebrates reconciliation and the end of rivalry. The *peristaseis* lists bracket these passages on reconciliation. The first list (2 Cor 4:8-12) states the scapegoat theme explicitly: "always bearing in the body the death of Jesus, so that the life of Jesus might be manifest in our body. For while alive we are always being handed over to death on account of Jesus, so that the life of Jesus might be manifest in our mortal flesh. So death is at work in us, life in you" (2 Cor 4:10-12). The apostle suffers on behalf of his congregation.

In the second list (2 Cor 6:4-10) the scapegoat theme is closely linked with the imitation of the paradigm of Christ's humiliation as described in 2 Corinthians 8:9, "For you know the grace of our Lord Jesus Christ, that, being rich, he made himself poor for our sake, so that we might, through the poverty of that man, become rich." The apostle echoes this in the second list when he says that the apostles are "poor men who make others rich" (2 Cor 6:10).

Between these "scapegoat" brackets the description of the ministry unfolds as a ministry of reconciliation. The points of the argument are: (1) this reconciliation is the result of a new creative act comparable to the first creation (2 Cor 4:6; 5:17); (2) it takes place by means of the mimetic identification with Christ in his death and the translation of that into the mutual service of agape (2 Cor 5:14-15; 21); (3) agapaic mimesis is a way of knowing the other that is the opposite of the status-laden way of the "flesh" (2 Cor 5:16). Knowledge "according to the flesh" is knowledge from within the coils of mimetic rivalry (cf. Gal 5:20-21), and specifically for the apostle, from within the violent system of the Judaism he once represented as a persecutor.

We have, therefore, in these passages on the ministry of reconciliation, a good example of the reformation of eros to agape by the replacement of the model/obstacle pole of the triangle by the divine victim. The self-sacrifice of Christ as the model for agapaic mimesis reconciles the world to the creator and the creatures to one another by redirecting desire to the pole of true transcendence. The sin of Adam is reversed, the proper mimetic relation to the creator restored, and the prohibition reconstituted as the command to agape.

In all this the apostle appears as the representative of the divine victim, and the apostolic sufferings reveal and transform the scapegoat mechanism. From now on we are all scapegoats, and if we are all scapegoats, then nobody is a scapegoat. The rule of the surrogate victim mechanism is over and the new creation is here, "the God who said, 'Let light shine out of darkness,' has shone in our hearts to give us the knowledge of the glory of God in the face of Jesus Christ" (4:6). The Christian community is the vanguard and proleptic presence of this new creation.

The Church as the Body of the Crucified Victim

Love is a relational and therefore a communal category. It is inconceivable that love should be solitary or confined to one relationship. Miming the divine desire means loving all the creatures of God, and that means at least participation in a loving community. That is why the Christian community is essential to Paul's understanding of Christian existence, and why his deepest satisfaction comes from being the founder of churches. Love is phenomenologically the ideal quality of life in the Christian community (1 Cor 8:1; 12:31; 14:1; Gal 5:22; Phil 2:1-2), a life whose structure is faith and hope, and whose Spirit is love. The context of 1 Corinthians 13 is the problem of that strain on community placed by rivalry concerning gifts of the Spirit. The point of 1 Corinthians 13 is that love as the greatest of the gifts should be arbiter in the community, precisely because the gift that eschews the ambition to preeminence is the preeminent gift. Love, therefore, is a summary term for the structure of human existence in the Christian community.

The church is metaphorically the body of Christ, and 1 Corinthians 12 is the classic passage on that theme. The church under the sign of the Cross is the body of the victim and so the target rather than the source of sacred violence. The astonishing fact that some people thought that the cursing of Jesus could be inspired by the Holy Spirit can be explained only by the fact that they thought that the weak and crucified Jesus had been transcended by the powerful resurrected Christ (1 Cor 12:1-3). The cursers were not Gnostics who despised the flesh of Jesus, but mimetic rivals who despised his weakness, and his status as a victim. Against this Paul argues in 1 Corinthians 12 that the church in this world is the body of the crucified and that weakness and humility cannot be left behind or despised.

The context of 1 Corinthians is mimetic rivalry among groups within the congregation, and the argument against it culminates here in the metaphor of the body and the hymn to agape (1 Corinthians 12 and 13). The nub of the argument is that mimetic rivalry in the congregation misunderstands the significance of the Cross (1 Cor 1:18-31), and travesties the sacraments of eucharist and baptism (1 Cor 10:14-22; 11:17-34; 12:13) by construing the power of Christ as the power of the executioner rather than the power of the victim.

The nature of the sacraments precludes mimetic rivalry because they are essentially rites of identification with the victim. The celebration of the eucharist is the center of self-awareness for this community and it is a celebration of the death of Christ (1 Cor 11:26). They are all comrades of the altar (κοινωνοὶ τοῦ θυσιαστηρίου—1 Cor 10:18) and as such equal. In using this metaphor of the altar fellowship, Paul is not interpreting the death of Christ as a sacrifice, but merely using the metaphor to make the point of community solidarity. The altar functions in the same rhetorical way as the loaf in the statement, "because there is one loaf, we, being many, are one body" (1 Cor 10:17). The death of Christ unites them in a fellowship of agape; "let no one pursue his own interest but rather the interest of the other" (1 Cor 10:24).

Therefore, Paul's argument against rivalry is ultimately based on the significance of the Cross. There is only one crucified victim and so there can be only one community (1 Cor 1:13; 3:11).

The Ethical Implications of the Mimesis of Love

What does human behavior look like when the divine agape becomes the apex of the triangle of desire? Mimesis as such cannot be avoided, because it is constitutionally human, but it can be nonrivalrous. The Christian community is founded on that possibility of nonrivalrous mimesis, and in two places Paul gives us a description of the behavior that should flow from it.

From the point of view of our theory, which links mimetic violence and idolatry, it is remarkable to see that Paul makes the same linkage in his argument that agape is the way to deal with conflict and rivalry. In 1 Corinthians 10 we have a midrash on the wandering in the wilderness, from a mimetic point of view. All the signs of mimetic violence are present under the rubric of idolatry—desire, sacrifice, and eroticism. These signs recall the current rabbinic analysis of the progress of sin from desire to idolatry. "Craving" (ἐπιθυμία) leads to discontent with God's providence, which leads to the testing of God, and finally to apostasy and idolatry.[24] Paul's aim in this passage is to warn against moral overconfidence in the controversy about eating meat sacrificed to idols (1 Cor 8:1-13), but the deeper argument is against mimetic rivalry and sacred violence, of the kind exemplified in the story of the wilderness wandering. The moral point is that the "enlightened" ones should not idolize their freedom of conscience by treating it as an absolute right, but should curb it with respect to the demands of agape, which is the only absolute. In this

---

[24] B. Gerhardsson, *The Testing of God's Son.*

case agape takes the form of the demand to "build up" the church (1 Cor 8:1). To insist on the absolute freedom of conscience without concern for fellow members of the church is to practice the mimesis of sacred violence that is idolatrous.

Under the rubric of Romans 13:10, that love works no wrong to the neighbor and therefore love is the fulfillment of the Law, there follows in Romans 14 and 15 a discussion that illustrates what this means in practical terms. Romans 14:13-23 is a good example of the structure of Paul's good mimesis in the form of a nonlegalistic ethic. It begins by identifying the wrong form of mimesis precisely as a scandal (τὸ μὴ τιθέναι πρόσκομμα τῷ ἀδελφῷ ἢ σκάνδαλον—Rom 14:13; cf. 1 Cor 8:9), and says that rather than condemn the other, one should resolve not to put an obstacle or a scandal in the way. The mimetic sense of scandal is precisely the model/obstacle of the triangle of rivalry. In our terms, therefore, Paul warns his readers not to become model/obstacles to the desire of each other but rather to renounce rivalry, even if it means foregoing actions approved by one's own conscience.

In historical terms the obstacle or scandal in this case is to eat nonkosher food because one's own conscience allows it, in the presence of somebody who considers that to be a sin. The effect of this behavior is the activation of rivalry in its more obvious forms. The eating tempts those who do not eat for the sake of conscience to imitation, and they, in turn, mobilize the resources of resistance. The eaters display superior enlightenment that calls forth the superior piety of the noneaters. The community is wracked by mutual recrimination (Rom 14:4, 13) that threatens its unity. There is mutual scapegoating.

Instead of regaining unity through unanimous scapegoating, however, the eaters are in imitation of Christ (καὶ γὰρ ὁ Χριστὸς οὐχ ἑαυτῷ ἤρεσεν—Rom 15:3) to renounce this right for the sake of agape. Jews and gentiles within the congregation are to accept one another as Christ has accepted them (Rom 15:7). In renouncing this right and accepting in effect the constraints of the Mosaic Law, the eaters will be imitating Christ specifically in his submission to Jewish Law, as a "servant of the circumcision for the sake of the truth of God" (Rom 15:8). Rather than defend their right of conscience, they are to forgo it for the sake of the unity of the community. This is agape as good, nonrivalrous mimesis, because it mimes the self-sacrifice and renunciation of Christ.

The position Paul takes in Romans 14–15 is the opposite of the position he took in Galatia. There he was adamant that his Christians not compromise with Jewish custom; here he actually urges them to respect the scruples of their Jewish fellow Christians in the matter of food, not just theoretically but actually by observing their taboos. This shows that Paul does not intend to erect a competing structure of sacred violence. This reversal of position is the ethical counterpart of the disclaimer with which he ends Galatians, that neither circumcision nor uncircumcision is ultimately important, but new creation (Gal 6:15; cf. 1 Cor 9:19-21). This is what it means for agape to build up the community (Rom 14:19; 15:2; 1 Cor 8:1b), as a group in which there can be diversity of behavior and observance, and in which the mimesis of the divine love is the only ethical absolute.

Thus the transcendental fact of faith in Christ can have several different ethical outcomes in this world as long as they all can be fitted under the rubric of agape. Such faith renders the specific differentiations of culture and custom nugatory by comparison with the unifying imperative of agape, and undermines the possibility of the church being another closed sect.

Conclusion

The hermeneutic of the Cross has turned out to be doubly fruitful in the sense that the Cross has been both the *interpretandum* and the *interpres*. As we have interpreted the Cross we have been interpreted by it. Within its narrowest horizon the Cross showed Paul that he had been the servant of sacred violence. At the next horizon it exposed the Judaism that Paul served as an expression of sacred violence. Along the widest horizon it exposed the generative role of the primitive Sacred in all religion and culture. The double transference has been decoded and the victim, slain from the foundation of the world, lies revealed in plain sight.

The note on which the previous chapter ends seems to put in question the whole argument I have been making. If the solution to sacred violence is the renunciation of rivalry, and if faith can take different forms, each of them valid as long as they can be classified under the heading of agape, why have I endorsed Paul's attack on Judaism? Have I not been engaged in precisely the rivalrous behavior that I have been criticizing, rivalrously condemning rivalry?

In a sense there is no escaping this accusation, because all criticism is rivalrous; but that sense would be sophistic if it did not take into account the different levels of justification for criticism. The Pauline criticism of Judaism is precisely that the aspects of it he experienced cannot be classified under agape. Clearly, a religious system that kills innocent people "righteously" has less rational and moral justification than one that cherishes all in love. The former must be criticized and, more than that, withstood; the latter must be supported. For this reason, if in the course of criticism one points out that violence is the result of pathological desire escalated to rivalry, that criticism

is not automatically hoist on its own petard. It is not itself the result of pathological desire but of the insight given by revelation into the generative role
of the primitive Sacred.

The sophistic taunt that Paul scapegoats Judaism is, therefore, unworthy
of serious consideration. We have seen several ways in which he specifically
undermines the possibility that his theology and his churches might become
instruments of the primitive Sacred. To the extent that subsequent generations
have allowed them to be used for that purpose, they have been misused.

I believe that the theory of sacred violence has proved its cogency by deliv-
ering a convincing interpretation of the Pauline texts. It has explained: (1) the
psychological and theological dynamics of Paul's conversion, and his shift
from the Jewish to the Christian community; (2) the socio-psychological intentionality behind the Jewish persecution of Christians and the Judaizers'
persecution of gentiles; (3) the nature of sin as desire, using the primal prohibition to deform itself to rivalry and idolatry; (4) the marks of this sin in
religious communities as exclusionism and scapegoating; (5) the proper role
of the prescriptive element in religion and morals, to forbid mimetic rivalry
and thus forestall violence; and (6) the possibility of the healing of desire in
the transformation from eros to agape through faith as the restoration of the
divine to the apex of the triangle of desire.

Sacred violence succeeds as a hermeneutical thesis in terms of the internal
logic of the argument. Whether it is accepted as a plausible reading not only
of the tradition but also of the present times remains to be seen. It holds that
the tradition properly understood gives critical insight into the present, and
therefore it amounts to a claim for attention to the tradition.

There are formidable obstacles to the modern acceptance of the tradition
no matter how skillfully it is restated. The two most formidable are belief in
the divine transcendence and belief in the possibility of a new community.
Secularism has no use for the idea of God, and the claim that we can escape
mimetic violence into a new community of agapaic cooperation by restoring
the divine angle to the triangle will not be widely accepted. Indeed, one may
anticipate the accusation that I have analyzed the present situation with a view
to a divine solution and therefore that my analysis is merely an apology.

I cannot refute this accusation, but I can remind accusers that, while I acknowledge my preunderstanding, they are in the same hermeneutical plight,
committed to a preunderstanding that for the most part must be pragmatically
justified by its success in interpreting the signs of the tradition and the times. I
have asked my questions in the light of my intuition of the answer, and I can
point to the traces of violence on our common horizon to justify asking the
questions I have asked. We can also invite the accuser to join the conversation.

To the objection that faith in God rather than in one's own capacities to deal
with the problem weakens one's resolve and leads to laziness or carelessness,
I may point to the exposition of faith as precisely the taking of responsibility
rather than scapegoating others. To the accusation of obscurantism I might

point to the interpretation of the Cross as the decoding of the double transference. The one accusation that remains unanswered is that I have been too
pessimistic about the human order. To approach an answer to this would require a long conversation about history and the possible motivations behind its
tumultuous narrative. I offer the foregoing analysis as a contribution to such
a conversation.

Belief in the possibility of a new community can be catastrophically mis-
construed. I have argued that the church betrayed this possibility early on in its
history when it became just another religious community, and as such a structure of sacred violence. This I believe was because it neglected the Pauline
gospel in favor of an institutional self-understanding patterned on those aspects of Judaism that Paul so severely indicted, and on Roman bureaucracy.
The Pauline indictment of Judaism cuts both ways, of course. It criticizes religion as such and so undermines its own dynamic for religious self-definition.
The church as another exclusive religious structure is undermined by its own
gospel of the Cross.

This raises the questions of what the community of faith, hope, and love
might look like, and whether it is possible at all in this world. To the first
question the answer is that we have some idea, and to the second, more or
less. I must answer in this way to avoid the violence of utopianism, which is
simply the old sacred violence in new garb and all the more dangerous for the
disguise. Nevertheless the hope for a new order is essential to the necessary
distance that we must keep from the present order. One may not be able in this
world to get beyond sacred violence, but one need not pretend that violence
is peace, security, patriotism, and the moral way to be. One can relate to it
hopefully or cynically, but one cannot relate innocently.

In the tradition the question of the relation between the two systems took
the form of the relation between the communities of Judaism and the church.
The horizon of that form of the question stretches to the present and is still
full of the traces of violence. Paul's way of posing the question has caused
modern interpreters difficulty because of recent history, and in order to preserve
Paul's reputation they have tried to present him as more favorably disposed
toward Judaism than usually believed. One of the reasons sacred violence will
find difficulty in being accepted is that this presentation of it will probably be
interpreted, despite all our disclaimers, as anti-Semitic, if not by Jews then by
some Christian interpreters. For this reason I conclude with a brief discussion
of recent interpretations of Paul that have sought to minimize the conflict
between his thought and the Mosaic interpretation of Torah.

The question of the relation between Christ the victim and Israel the vic-
timizer must be approached within all three of the horizons of interpretation.
We must resist premature generalization to be sure, but we cannot avoid generalization altogether if we are to interpret at all. It is merely a question of finding
the appropriate horizons of generalization. I believe that I have shown what
the appropriate horizons are, by means of a movement back and forth from

the horizon of sacred violence in general to the horizon of Paul's individual experience of conversion, through the intermediate stages of the controversy between Jew and gentile over the meaning of the Cross.

Paul really does regard the Judaism of his time as more or less a system of sacred violence. The distinction between Judaism based on the Mosaic Torah and Pauline Christianity is sharp. Paul's vision of the inclusion of Israel in salvation is eschatological; the inclusion is hidden in the mystery of the future, and therefore essentially irrelevant to his day-to-day activity. This means that the dialectic of Israel's rejecting Christ is not overcome in this world, excepting in hope, which is not yet evident (Rom 8:24-25). In the meantime only the negative side of the dialectic is apparent and the clash between Israel and Pauline Christianity includes, in principle, the ambition of each to convert the other. When he thinks on the macro-level Paul sees the eschatological inclusion of Israel, but when he acts on the micro-level he tries to anticipate the eschaton by converting Jews to Christ.

This is the traditional interpretation of Paul that interpreters like Gager and Gaston wish to change.[1] If I have brought to the text a preunderstanding from the thought of Girard, they bring the well-known theory of Franz Rosenzweig, that Jesus is not the Messiah of Israel but only the Messiah of the gentiles. While this is a perfectly reasonable accommodation to suggest in the present religious situation, albeit misleading because it skirts the question of violence, it cannot be imputed to Paul. Their exegesis fails at virtually every critical point, and their interpretation of the exegetical findings that they cannot change is for the most part unlikely.

The claim that Paul did not consider Jesus to be the Messiah of Israel is only the most flamboyant of a series of conclusions that stretch credulity beyond the cracking point, and the logic of the position is confused at the level both of abstract and historical reasoning. Gager says that for Paul, Torah and Christ are "mutually exclusive categories. But the relationship between the two is such that neither invalidates the other."[2] Mutual exclusion means by definition that one invalidates the other. Furthermore, by the logic and evidence of the historical situation it is impossible to maintain that the Jewish reading of Torah and the Pauline reading of Torah lay side by side noncompetitively, because of a clear distinction in their spheres of interest. Mutual exclusion in the proper sense is too strong to describe the relationship, because Paul is not a Marcionite, but its sense in this context does indicate a sharp conflict about the meaning of the Torah. Pauline Christianity claims to fulfil the Torah; the Mosaic Jews make the same claim. It is these claims that are mutually exclusive, and as such

---

[1] J. C. Gager, *The Origins of Anti-Semitism: Attitudes Toward Judaism in Pagan and Christian Antiquity;* L. Gaston, *Paul and the Torah.*

[2] Gager, *Origins,* 247.

they could not fail to provoke the controversy that virtually every page of the Pauline corpus attests.

Gaston's claim that those who wished the gentile Christians to observe the Mosaic rituals were chiefly other gentile converts and not Jews is both intrinsically unlikely and false to the specific evidence of Galatians upon which the case rests most heavily. There the only Judaizers mentioned specifically are the Jews Peter and Barnabas and the people from James, who we might assume were Jews too and not gentile converts. It is intrinsically more probable that the Jewish Christians were the chief Judaizers, and that they did so both for reasons of internal conviction and because of pressure from zealous Mosaic Jews of the kind Paul had been.

These Jews would have understood that to refute the necessity for Mosaic observance in the case of gentiles undermines the authority of that observance across the board. If it is not necessary for some, it is not necessary for any. The Jews and the Judaizers saw this corollary clearly, being more attuned to what threatened their class interest than Gager and Gaston. One gasps at the boldness of an argument that admits on the one hand that Paul considered observance of the Law in the Jewish way to be a curse and condemnation,[3] and on the other claims that this curse and condemnation applies only to gentiles who wish to be observant. Common sense and exegesis dictate that once the Jewish observance of the Mosaic Law has been identified as a curse, it is a curse for all, which keeps the Jews from coming to Christ and lures the gentiles away from Christ.

Gager thinks that the fact that the church was not identified as the new Israel before Justin Martyr in the second century should be taken to mean that prior to that it did not think of itself as displacing the old Israel.[4] He is right, but for the wrong reason. At least as far as Pauline Christianity is concerned, there would have been no displacement theory because the church was not yet a system of sacred violence. Pauline Christianity was uninterested in displacing Mosaic Judaism not because it understood itself as strictly for the gentiles but because it understood itself as the community of the new creation for which the distinctions of the old creation, especially those between Jew and gentile, were irrelevant. The moment at which the church identified itself as the new Israel marks the moment at which it reveals its fall from grace and the deformation of its self-understanding as part of the new creation to a structure of sacred violence within the old. Along with the name of Israel the church inherited the veil of Moses and became just another exclusive religious structure. At that moment the church became the mimetic double of the synagogue, and the two have been scandals to each other ever since. The hermeneutic of the Cross should help the church to break out of this system of rivalry.

---

[3] Ibid.
[4] Ibid., 228.

The Pauline hermeneutic of the Cross causes a break not just with Judaism but with the world as the prevailing order of reality. It is an alternative to the dominant interpretation of reality. That is why it cannot be in a relation of both/and with the Jewish interpretation of Torah or any other exclusive religious construction. It is the either/or, the true heretic hermeneutic that deconstructs the dominant text of culture. To make Pauline Christianity into "Moses for the masses," as Gager and Gaston do, is to miss the most interesting thing about it—namely, its radical critique of culture. As just another religion Christianity is a more or less satisfactory amalgam of Greek philosophy, Jewish moralism, pagan enthusiasm, and Roman bureaucracy, misappropriated and reapplied. Its record as a religious machine is the same mixture of self-deception and sublimity as other great religions. But as the hermeneutic of the Cross, it is the first and most radical insight into the pathos of the human enterprise, credible precisely because of its incredulity.

Therefore, one should not distort the interpretation of Christian origins in order to combat anti-Semitism. It would be more honest simply to jettison Paul than to turn his attack on Judaism into a minor misunderstanding. His attack on Judaism is the spearhead of his attack on the structures of this world. In terms of his argument, one must either endorse the hypocrisy of human life and so reject Paul, or vice versa, but one must not turn him into a hypocrite, as if his agony over Israel's rejection were not real, but merely a momentary solecism in a serene vision of Jewish well-being in the long run, in a world where God's saving activity observes a religious apartheid. One can, of course, reject the whole argument root and branch, but in any case the decision must be either/or not both/and.

Paul stands in the prophetic tradition of Israel, affirming the plan of salvation that includes the rejection of Israel for the sake of the salvation of all the world including Israel. His prophetic hermeneutic decodes not only his time but ours, and since prophecy is essentially a reading of the signs of the times, I have taken his theology to be an interpretation, mutatis mutandis, of our times.

Hermeneutic is concerned initially with signs. It is the technique for the decipherment of signs, based on the assumption that signs are encoded and need to be deciphered. For Paul the master code of the world is the double transference, and the signs that have to be decoded are the signs of sacred violence. There are traces of this hidden violence on the horizon of the world. In his time the Cross was such a trace, in ours they are the retrospect and prospect of mass death. For this reason he should be readmitted to the serious conversation going on in our culture about the possibility of meaning in an age of limitless violence, as one of the more astute interpreters of the signs of the times.

Appendix I
Some Critical Responses
to the Theory

René Girard's theory has considerable interpretive power, but does it really account for the origin and deep structure of culture? The general accusation leveled against Girard is that of reductionism; he reduces the many causes in the socio-cultural system too quickly to the one mimetic desire. Furthermore, his analysis of desire is not nuanced enough, and even if one were to accept only one cause, the surrogate victim mechanism is too flimsy to be it. Pieter Tijmes makes these points sympathetically in the course of proposing a "minimalist" version of the theory.[1]

Mimesis and the Subject

First Tijmes questions whether desire is the sole energy of the self as it moves out to the other. In addition to desire he proposes love and learning, giving us a trio of basic motivations that are in turn vital (desire), affective (love), and discursive (learning). Love and learning, however, are forms of desire, and we are acquisitive before we are inquisitive and altruistic. The idea of desire as the sole moving force of self-consciousness seems to me to be adequate to the phenomena and to common sense. It does not require great insight to see how what passes for love and learning can be interpreted as transformations of acquisitiveness.

---

[1] "De twee hypothesen van Girard," *Mimesis en Geweld* (ed. W. van Beek; Kampen: Kok, 1988), 28–52.

Secondly Tijmes proposes that we recognize that there is in fact nonrivalrous relationship with others. He gives as an example learning from another what is edible and what not. Such imitation does not involve a third party as model and obstacle, but is direct and nonrivalrous. Clearly there are such relationships, but that fact is not significant, because the theory does not hold that all relationships are always actually rivalrous, but only that they are potentially so and that in fact culture is structured by the realization of that potential in a general sense.

This nontriangular imitation—which Tijmes calls "mediation"—is in effect the same as the external mediation of the mimetic triangle when the angles at the base are large and the plane of the mediator far from the plane of the subject. The concept of external mediation seems to account for everything Tijmes brings to our attention, and to have the added merit of showing how mimetic rivalry is a potentiality of human desire from the beginning.

Furthermore, the fact that mimetic rivalry can be observed among the animals means that it cannot be classified simply as a pathology, but must be seen as a constituent part of human desire from the prehuman through the moment of hominization to the cultural level. Indeed, if mimesis is only a pathology that occurs in the unfolding of desire, it must have occurred at the prehuman stage, because mimesis is an essential part of the process of hominization in the first place.

In a rereading of Freud, Borch-Jacobsen vindicates the mimetic explanation of the subject from within the context of psychoanalysis, although his discounting of its acquisitive nature leaves his version unable to account for the phenomenon of the obstacle.[2] In a sense his mimetic subject is simply a repristination of Hegel, the shortcoming of whose account I have argued below,[3] and shows the extent to which Freud was simply carrying on the great project of the *Phenomenology of Mind* by the method of psychoanalysis. Borch-Jacobsen, in turn, carries on the project of the deconstruction of the subject from within the psychoanalytic tradition and in the course of it pays some attention to mimesis.

The focus of Borch-Jacobsen's attention is the Freudian understanding of the subject, which, he argues, Freud illegitimately reified. For Freud the subject is what remains identical with itself beneath its various representations (sub = under; jectum = placed). The nub of the problem is the subject in the unconscious. Freud gives it the status of a subject within the subject, contrary to the evidence of dreams and symptoms that he himself collected. The Freudian unconscious is unlike any of its predecessors in that it is utterly inaccessible to consciousness excepting through transfigured representations. The content of these representations is a wish that has been repressed because, being sexual, it cannot be reconciled with the order of the conscious ego. This repressed wish

---

[2] M. Borch-Jacobsen, *The Freudian Subject.*

[3] See Appendix II.

is the "ideational representation of an instinct,"[4] of the libido. In this form the contents of the unconscious are homologous with the contents of consciousness and the same processes of thought go on in both. In principle, therefore, the processes of the unconscious can be understood; the fact that they come to us disguised does not mean that they are irrational.

Dreams are the *via regia* to the unconscious since they are always the disguised fulfillment of the repressed wish. They are not the only mode of access, however. The unacceptable thought is distorted in dreams, converted in hysterical symptoms, transposed in obsessive ideas, and rejected in hallucinations. Dreams and symptoms are together, therefore, the chief modes of access to the unconscious, but not all the contents of the unconscious present themselves in these disguises. There are thoughts that never present themselves in any way. Psychic life overflows the bounds of consciousness understood as the certainty and presence of the self in representation. There is a thinking that goes on in me without me. "This thinking thinks without me, without ceasing to think, moreover (as we see, for example, when it calculates, or makes a joke). It thinks, then—and it thinks."[5]

The question now is how we are to understand the thinker of these inaccessible thoughts. What is the relationship between the conscious and the unconscious thinker? Borch-Jacobsen states the problem as follows:

> In short . . . the otherness called "unconscious" no longer designates, rigorously speaking, that part of myself about which I wish to remain ignorant, but rather designates *my identity* or my very sameness *as that of another* . . . the *starke Gemeinsamkeit* that connects me with an other that I am "myself."[6]

To clarify this, Borch-Jacobsen gives a close reading of the texts of dreams in the light of the question "Who?," "Who is dreaming?," "Who is desiring?" The question "Who?" is the question about one's birth and origin. It reaches beyond the subject to another point, the point of the origin of my identity:

> The question draws me immediately beyond myself . . . to the point of otherness . . . where I am another, the other who gives me my identity. That is, who gives birth to me. My identity connects me with my birth. Hypothesis: the unconscious is that umbilical cord.[7]

The key to the role of the self in dreams is identification or mimesis. Dreams and fantasies present themselves as dramas rather than as single representations, and the self plays its role by identification with other characters in the drama.

---

[4] *The Freudian Subject,* 5.

[5] Ibid., 4.

[6] Ibid., 8.

[7] Ibid., 9.

It either hides itself behind another or hides another behind itself. In both cases it identifies itself with another. Thus the primary impulse in the dream is not the desire for an object or goal, but the impulse to identify with another, which, in turn, gives rise to desire. "The so-called 'subject of desire' has no identity of its own prior to the identification that brings it, blindly, to occupy the point of otherness, the place of the other."[8] The subject then desires not to have the object but rather to be the one who has the object; it is not a matter of having but rather of being:

> In order to achieve its own pleasure, the ego has to take a detour, one that causes its own pleasure to pass through that of another. And this detour is identification (mimesis), resemblance (homoiosis). One only enjoys, in fantasy, as another: tell me whom you are miming and I will tell you who you are, what you desire, and how you enjoy.[9]

A consideration of Freud's interpretation of dreams thus brings to light a split within the individual, between the conscious and the unconscious, that psychoanalysis regards against a background of a unified subject. Borch-Jacobsen argues plausibly that by its own logic psychoanalysis cannot maintain this unity of the subject, that it does so in order to safeguard fundamental interests, like the primacy of the libido, which must be given up. Freud could not accept the indeterminacy of origin that the logic of the unconscious as understood by Borch-Jacobsen demands.

At this point one is reminded of the well-known story of the Brahmin who was asked what the world rested on. "The back of an elephant," he said. And what does the elephant rest on? "The back of a turtle," he replied. And what does the turtle rest on? "Oh," he said, "after that it is turtles all the way." Freud could not accept the bottomless stack of turtles; like Descartes he required an Archimedean point, and like Descartes he finds it in the subject; not the subject of the *cogito* but rather the subject of the *libido*. In symmetry with the *cogito ergo sum* and the *libido ergo sum* we might propose *mimor ergo sum* as the correct point of origin, but that would be inaccurate, because there is no subject prior to the mimesis, and so the phrase should more accurately be *mimesti et sum*, "imitation happens and I am." The unity of the subject across the spectrum of conscious and unconscious activity cannot be maintained. There is a split within the self that is overcome only by the taking place of mimesis. The self is integrated by the force not of libidinous but of mimetic desire. It carries the other within, and is integrated as a function of the system of desire.

The next step in the exposition brings us to the level of the single other in the outside world, and the phenomenon that discloses the structure of this

---

[8] Ibid., 48.
[9] Ibid., 21.

relationship is narcissism. Now the self encounters itself as other not in the unconscious but in the concrete other. Having learnt its essential nature from the relationship within itself to the unconscious, it now recognizes the grim fact of its enthrallment by the concrete other in the external world. The phenomenology of this relationship passes through the stage of homosexual identification because the same sex is mimetically closest to the self. Even at the heterosexual stage the other is essentially a double. The double is the narcissistic double that inhabits the other and turns him into the I. I love myself in the other—and yet I hate myself there, because the other usurps my control and my space, by being "me" in the other:

> There is violence inherent in the very *appearing* of the other, a violence to which all empirical violence bears witness, and it has no "reason" other than desire (that is, *consciousness of self*), which seeks itself in the other and wants to be for-itself, independent, beside itself in its property. Desire is violence because it is a desire to be proper, a desire for propriation, and, as such, a hostile, murderous desire.... Desire is a violent mimesis then.[10]

The dire truth of this construction is that violence is inescapable, not because the subject chooses to possess a reflection of itself in the mirror of the other, a desire that could in principle be renounced, but because there is no subject except in the other. The narcissistic hallucinations, in which the self sees itself or hears itself in the other, bear witness to this state of affairs. Narcissism does not precede the relation to the other:

> So let us not dream, with Freud, of an ego whose existence would precede sociality (or—and it is the same thing—a sociality that would relate already-constituted subjects to each other). For narcissism is precisely that: the violent affirmation of the ego, the violent desire to annul that primitive alteration that makes me desire (myself) as the mimetic double.[11]

We have now arrived at the thesis of the radical sociality of the subject, and the problem of how to conceive the origin of the subject in the group, which Freud treats in terms of the relationship between individual and group psychology. Here Freud is at his most disingenuous, according to Borch-Jacobsen. He distinguishes the relationship of the group to the leader from the relationship of the group members to one another. The former relationship is libidinous; the members love the leader; the latter relationship is one of identification; the members imitate each other. Freud professes a deep dislike for the essentially mimetic—in the sense of spontaneous rather than free imitation—category

---

[10] Ibid., 90.
[11] Ibid., 93.

"suggestion," the "magical" word invoked by his contemporaries to explain the behavior of groups.

Suggestion comes from the realm of hypnotism and entails the subjugation of the subject to the will of the hypnotist. Instead of coercion at the heart of politics, Freud preferred to see freedom, and so made the essentially political decision against suggestion. Instead he explained group phenomena in terms of the psychology of the individual, in terms of libidinous desire and the identification of a preexisting subject with others. In order to achieve this free subject prior to sociality, he pretends that a freely bestowed desire constituted the power of the leader and a freely willed imitation the bond of the members. He could not, however, prevent the return of the hypnotist from the heart of the psychoanalytic process in the form of the analyst as the object of transference:

> The dependence of the hypnotized subject on the hypnotist; the establishment of an elective, exclusive, somnambulic bond; suggestibility, even thought transmission—all this had come back up, at the very core of analytic treatment, in the form of transference.[12]

The essential move in Freud's politics of freedom was to posit the existence of the presocial subject, of the individual essentially separable from the group. This is the function of the Oedipal explanation. It posits the existence of the primal father and son, and then explains the subsequent formation of the preexisting subject in terms of the Oedipal interactions. On this account the subject can, in theory, free itself from these bonds for an untrammeled individual existence. But from the heart of the analytic process comes the phenomenon of transference, which gives the lie to this ambition. The subject is irreducibly social, and the dynamics of the group are mimetic, not erotic:

> For this is no doubt the most impressive aspect of this chapter on identification: conceived by Freud as a sort of return toward the individual foundations of society, the text has, against all expectations, caused "social psychology" to resurface at the heart of "individual psychology," in the form of the identification of the ego itself.[13]

Freud systematically opts for Oedipal solutions in order to safeguard the subject and politics. He refuses to accept that there is violence at the very origin of both, for violence is the "political evil *par excellence*."[14] But his own logic has shown:

> Original identification with the other, if it is constitutive of the ego . . . is likewise a radical violence with respect to the other . . . a devouring mouth clamped down

---

[12] Ibid., 150.
[13] Ibid., 192.
[14] Ibid., 192–94.

on the alterity of others, an eye blind to what gave it light, an immediately destructive hand (grasping, grappling, appropriating) laid upon the breast. The birth of the ego, we might say in parody of Hegel's famous formulae, is the death of the other. It bears the death of the other in itself and it bears the other dead in itself.[15]

Borch-Jacobsen, therefore, shows that Girard's mimesis is a more adequate interpretation than Freud's of the phenomena than Freud himself discovered. It is not only better than Freud but also better than Borch-Jacobsen, insofar as it takes account of the acquisitive nature of desire in its initial orientation to an object. Mimesis begins as object-oriented and acquisitive, and only becomes "metaphysical" as rivalry proceeds. Borch-Jacobsen does not really progress beyond Hegel, nevertheless, his contribution shows the necessity of a mimetic reading of the subject, and therefore the subject's essential instability within a system of desire, its enthrallment to the system of sacred violence.

The Surrogate Victim and the System of Sacred Violence

Tijmes suggests that we also take a "minimalist" position with reference to this second moment of the theory, because there are other fundamental generative mechanisms, like sexual difference. This objection raises the question of the plausibility of Girard's description of origins in itself and in comparison with Freud's.

Girard's account of origins is a general model, not a historical account, but it does have a historic referent. In principle there was a "first time" while in fact the collective murder happened over and over again in prehistoric time, gradually turning into the ritual and myth. In this sense the theory is an alternative form of structuralism, one that combines structure and historical referentiality. Girard gives Freud full credit for having seen that a historical collective murder was necessary as a model for ritual sacrifice, but he faults him because a single event of this kind cannot explain the structured repetition of rituals—it is unlikely that we should get together regularly merely to remember the guilt of one primal murder.

We have already noted the second objection to Freud, that mimetic desire is more encompassing than erotic desire, because it accounts for the instability of the subject and gives a better explanation of the very evidence that Freud discovered. Here we may add that rivalry extends over a broader range than sex, that not all rivalry is sexual rivalry. A generally acquisitive mimesis rather than a focused sexual jealousy provoked the primal crime. The Oedipus complex is

---

[15] Ibid., 192–93.

too narrow an account of human relations and human origins. The surrogate victim mechanism, however, is broad enough to explain both the origin and the structure of culture. In this regard the surrogate victim hypothesis is a combination of Freud's idea of the collective murder as a structuring event at the beginning of culture, and Lévi-Strauss's idea of a plottable structure in myth that reflects the origin and progress of differential thought.[16] Sex as a founding mechanism is secondary to the surrogate victim.

Tijmes's "minimalist" proposal jeopardizes the whole theory by introducing other energies alongside desire, and thus destroying the symmetry of the system. One cannot question the primacy of acquisitive desire without bringing the whole system down. To be sure, it is a question of judgment rather than a matter of proof how one ranks the relative importance of the violent and benign elements in the process of the development of culture. Once one decides, however, that acquisitive desire is the primal energy one cannot avoid the systemic entailments that conflictual desire will follow because desire is mimetic, and mimesis violent, and violence the form of desire that drives the social system. A "minimalist" interpretation of the theory is attractive because it relieves one of the pressure to show how it accounts for everything. Nevertheless, its "maximal" claims must be maintained, and assessed as part of the systemic explanation as a whole, not in isolation.

The Christian Elements in the Theory

Tijmes questions the sharp contrast drawn between the gospel vision of nonviolence and the cultural condition of violence, as if there were two opposing worlds. He would rather locate the opposition within the one culture, between mediation, on the one hand, and mimesis on the other. Furthermore, he questions whether Girard really discovered the scapegoat mechanism by means of the Bible, because the Bible is as ambiguous about it as other great literature; there is little to choose between the Greek tragedies, the great novels, and the Bible, in this regard.

I hope to have shown that the writings of the apostle Paul do indeed reveal the surrogate victim mechanism, but without the Girardian theory we might not have seen it. This is the hermeneutical circle. Therefore it does not seem important to settle the question whether Girard discovered the sacrificial mechanism in the Bible or whether he merely found it disclosed there with exceptional clarity. We all come to the text with preunderstanding.

Tijmes proposes to locate the alternative between violence and nonviolence within the one system, rather than in terms of two separate worlds. The image of the two worlds, however, has good precedent in Augustine's two cities, and

---

16 *Things Hidden*, 124.

Girard's position is entirely Augustinian in this regard. The two worlds are not, however, sealed off from each other, but interpenetrate, so that the system of nonviolence takes place within the system of violence and vice versa. Tijmes's criticism represents the humanist conviction that human good is possible within the human world by human effort, while Girard looks for a divine intervention to rescue the human world. Tijmes is right to warn against too sharp a division between the two worlds that would result in an apocalyptic dualism.

It is not necessary, however, to use the two-world imagery; one could use the imagery of the system that can be radically transformed by a small intervention. The theory of systems recognizes the possibility that small inputs can have great effects. We might imagine the system of sacred violence transformed from without by the entry of nonacquisitive mimesis in the agape of the Cross.

In theological terms the basic assumption of the theory is the doctrine of original sin. The violence it describes is the result of a universal self-deformation of desire by its shifting its aim from God to itself. The instability of the independent subject has been recognized in Christian theology at least since Augustine,[17] and has in fact been known ever since the Bible. The self in the Bible is constituted by the call of God; humanity is structured by responsibility in the sense of the ability to respond to the divine call. The world is held in being by the call of God and the human response; the true human self exists only in God, who carries the self in himself and whom the self carries in itself. This is the desire for God that, theologically speaking, existed before the fall into rivalry. Paul describes this deformation of desire by means of the Adam story as he reads it again in the light of the Cross.

The stage of nonrivalrous desire exists, therefore, as a perpetual possibility but never, as far as we know, as a historical actuality. In the beginning the mob was not compelled to commit the fraud of the double transference, but was in principle free to take responsibility for its own violence and deal with it by self-restraint. The theological category of the fall designates the false step taken in the devising of the surrogate victim mechanism and the substitution of the primitive Sacred for the transcendent God. The original sin is the double transference that created sacred violence.

Burton Mack makes a more serious objection to the theory when he claims that the passion narratives do the opposite of what Girard claims.[18] Instead of revealing the surrogate victim mechanism so that it might be clearly acknowledged and repudiated, they take the cunning of the mechanism to new levels

---

[17] E.g., *Quoniam itaque et ego sum, quid peto, ut venias in me, qui non essem, nisi esses in me?; Conf.* 1:2 ("Since therefore I also am, how do I ask you to come into me, who would not exist were you not [already] in me?") Cf.*"tu autem eras interior intimo meo et superior summo meo"; Conf.* 3:6 ("You were, therefore, more intimate [to me] than my most intimate self, and higher than my highest self"). The latter text shows how Augustine anticipated the mimetic self.

[18] Burton Mack, "The Innocent Transgressor."

of malice. While pretending to reveal it they use that alleged revelation to obscure the fact that the mechanism is at work scapegoating the Jews.

Mack's basic argument is that the gospels are myths of origin invented some time after the events they purport to describe under the pressure of the current situations of the writers and with the purpose of vindicating the community in the face of its enemies.[19] Since the Jews were the enemies of the community, the myths of origin portray them spuriously as enemies of Jesus. The gospels are, therefore, myths in the Girardian sense of false accounts designed to cover up the anti-Jewish violence of the Christian community. Jesus was in fact put to death by the Romans on a probably valid charge.

While the evidence of the Gospels and Epistles does support the view of an increasingly bitter conflict between the nascent church and the dominant synagogue, there is no good reason to assume that the whole account of the Jewish part in the death of Jesus is a malicious fiction. And even if it were a fiction, it would still be a revelation of the founding mechanism, and then we would have to assume that the early Christians discovered it by some unknown means. It is easier to believe that they discovered it in the way that the Gospels and Paul say they did, from the fact of the murder of Jesus by the religious and civil powers of his time.

---

[19] Burton Mack, *A Myth of Innocence.*

Appendix II
A Girardian Reading of the Hegelian Problematic of Desire[1]

> Men are no longer enslaved by the sword but by the gigantic apparatus which forges the sword.
>
> Horkheimer and Adorno[2]

Central to the Girardian theory is the relationship between violence and desire. The problem of desire has been central to Western thought ever since St. Paul's reading of the Adam story linked desire (ἐπιθυμία) and sin. From Paul it developed via Augustine into the *amor amicitiae* and the *amor concupiscentiae* of the scholastics, culminating in the modern debate about agape (ἀγάπη) and eros (ἔρως).[3] Spinoza made desire (*conatus*) central to human nature in his *Ethics,* and Hegel made it *(Begierde)* "self-consciousness in general," in his *Phenomenology of Mind.*[4] Freud continued the Hegelian project by means of his new method of psychoanalysis, defining desire as the erotic instinct of the libido and contrasting it with the death instinct.[5] Finally, as Hegel's doctrine of internal relations decayed, desire:

---

[1] My sources are G. W. F. Hegel, *The Phenomenology of Mind;* A. Kojéve, *Introduction to the Reading of Hegel;* M. Heidegger, *Being and Time;* J.-P. Sartre, *Being and Nothingness;* Jürgen Habermas, *The Philosophical Discourse of Modernity;* J. P. Butler, *Subjects of Desire;* and H.-G. Gadamer, *Truth and Method.*

[2] M. Horkheimer and T. W. Adorno, *Dialectic of Enlightenment,* 233.

[3] A. Nygren, *Agape and Eros.*

[4] J. P. Butler, *Subjects of Desire,* 3, 7.

[5] P. Ricoeur, *Freud and Philosophy.*

increasingly becomes a principle of the ontological displacement of the human subject, and in its latest stages, in the work of Lacan, Deleuze, and Foucault, desire comes to signify the impossibility of the coherent subject itself.[6]

Girard's theory is scientific in the commonsense meaning of the word, and therefore far removed from the speculative idealism of Hegel. It is based on the evidence of literature, anthropology, and ethology, and offers itself for testing in the usual way. It does, however, interpret reality as a self-regulating system, and if one couples this with the generative role of desire in the system, then one must consider the points of contact between the Girardian and the Hegelian theories. Acknowledging that the metaphysical assumptions and starting points of the two reflections are quite different, we must nevertheless acknowledge that they both wrestle with the problematic of desire in ways that are remarkably analogous within their respective epistemological frames of reference. Accepting that Hegel is the idealist and Girard the scientific realist, I wish here to demonstrate in a preliminary way how the Hegelian speculation might be modified by a Girardian reading. What follows is a Girardian reading of Kojéve's reading of Hegel.

Desire and Violence

Desire begins as the consciousness of lack that looks outside itself for fulfillment. Desire constitutes the "I" as an acquisitive energy that goes out to an object and returns to itself. To say "I" is to say "I want." Desire, therefore, is the origin of the "I" revealed by speech. The intentionality of self-consciousness is the intentionality of desire, acquisitiveness rather than contemplation. I call this the epithymic constitution of self-consciousness.

No mere object can satisfy desire. Desire demands recognition by another desire; it needs to be needed, it desires to be desired. "Pay attention to me! Love me!" Recognition identifies me as the one who fulfils the other's desire and thus fulfils my desire. Girard calls this the "appetite for the neighbor's envy." Desire desires desire.

Desire is not only speech that says "I want" but also action to get what I want. It constitutes and then disquiets the I setting it in motion toward the object of desire. Every acquisition is to some extent a negation of the object— for example, eating transforms the object into the subject—and so desire affirms the self by negating the other. Therefore, since desire is acquisitive action by affirmation and negation, it is a becoming rather than a being—that is, it is historical and has time as its mode of existence. It is not what it is, and it

---

[6] Butler, *Subjects,* 6.

is what it is not.[7] History is the history of "desires desired."[8] It is a system of desire.

Humanly to say "I want" is to say more than "I have biological needs." The animal level upon which the human is based seeks only to meet the needs of the organism for survival. At this level there occurs only the "sentiment of self," not self-consciousness. This is because the positive content of the I is constituted by the not-I. At the animal level the not-I is the natural "thingish" object—food, water, etc.—so at this level the not-I can constitute only the natural "thingish" content of an I. For there to be self-consciousness, there must be a self-conscious not-I, and so desire desires desire. Anthropogenetic desire, as distinct from animal desire, is directed toward another desire rather than toward a concrete thing. "Real and true man is the result of his inter-action with others; his I and the idea he has of himself are 'mediated' by recognition obtained as a result of his action."[9]

Kojéve's description of desire needs to be expanded, specifically with regard to the way in which the I is mediated by recognition, and so at this point I introduce Girard's category of mimesis. There is a preverbal propensity for desire in the "sentiment of self " as a sentiment of lack, but "I" as "I want" is only spoken at the moment of desire's meeting with desire—that is, desire can come to self-consciousness only as a member of the group. As a member of the group the self is first part of the language tradition and only by participation in that tradition can it say "I want," because the tradition mediates the deposit of the desire of others from which the individual learns the meaning of the lack that it feels. Without the tradition the I would not be able to identify the other as the potential fulfillment of desire. Only when one hears the other say "I want," does one identify oneself as desire. For this reason a "thingish" not-I cannot constitute the self-conscious I, because it cannot speak or act communicatively. Therefore, the moment of recognition, in which desire discovers the desire of the other potentially desiring it, is a moment of imitation, in the sense of the identification of the self by means of the other.

The recognition of the self by means of the other is mediated by the object of desire. What desire wants is to be the object of the desire of the other; what it gets, however, is another desire wanting to be desired. Therefore it cannot satisfy its need directly. It cannot simply become the object of the other desire, because that desire, like itself, desires to be desired rather than to desire. Therefore the contest of desire for recognition has to be mediated. This mediation takes place through an object and so desire takes a triangular

---

[7] This is the recurrent theme of Sartre's *Being and Nothingness,* by which he means that although the self is constituted by its past, it is not bound to the past but exists as freely projecting itself into the future. In this sense desire is the essence of existential futurity.

[8] Kojéve, *Introduction,* 13.

[9] Ibid., 15.

form. The object becomes the substitute satisfaction for each of the struggling desires, and competition for the object becomes the substitute for the struggle for recognition.

When desire recognizes another desire, it does so in terms of the object of that other desire. To be sure, the ultimate aim of desire is to substitute the self for the object of the other desire, to attract the other desire to the self and thus acquire it by possessing not its possession but its possessiveness. But that substitution can take place only representatively through the object. Therefore, the struggle for prestige takes place as a struggle for possession of a material or symbolic object that represents the self in the struggle for recognition. Direct recognition is a limit; actual recognition is always mediated through an object. Desire is acquisitive, and acts through the representations of desire.

Desire is acquisitive from the start. The object does not enter the picture subsequently, but is present from the first appearance of desire. Through the object—as well as from the language tradition—desire learns the epithymic constitution of the other. When it finds that there is no satisfaction possible directly from the other, it turns to possess the object, and at that moment the other does the same. By this action desire confirms the tradition that the other is epithymically constituted like itself. Thus the two desires lock together in imitation; from now on, each causes the other to focus on the object, and rivalry for the object represents the struggle for recognition.

Thus the desire for recognition displaced from the other to the object takes the form of reciprocal imitation driven by a common attachment to the object in its surrogate status. So desire imitates desire and rivalry results. As the rivalry proceeds the object becomes less important and the rivalry more—that is, the surrogate status of the object fades and the hostility becomes unmediated violence. Desire rediscovers the desiring other as the only adequate object, and the struggle reverts to a fight for pure recognition or prestige. There is a crisis of relationship.

According to Hegel the struggle for prestige resolves itself into the relationship of the master and the slave as the winner overcomes the loser dialectically, sparing his life but taking his freedom, enslaving him by coercing his recognition. In the struggle between the master and the slave the former risked his animal life in action while the latter preferred animal existence to death. The master succeeded in taking possession of himself as his true self by commanding recognition of the other. By being able to coerce this recognition, his true self was no longer outside himself, he now had within himself the certainty of being recognized by the other. The social counterpart of this model is the relation between the ruling and the oppressed classes.

There is, however, a contradiction in this relationship that makes the class division based on it unstable. The I needs an equal I to recognize it, and the slave is therefore unable to sustain the free I of the master. "No man is a hero to his valet, not because the hero is no hero but because the valet is a valet."[10]

Furthermore, while the master has reached an impasse and cannot go beyond mastery, the slave has the master's autonomy over against him as a possibility of his becoming. The slave, therefore, has the beginnings of autonomy in himself because of the regard of the master, since even though he is regarded as a slave, it is a master who regards him as such, while for the master, even though he is regarded as a master, it is a slave who regards him as such. Since the slave has the example and the possibility of the master while the master is at the end of his possibilities, history is the history of the working slave who gradually finds the courage to risk his life for his humanity by breaking free of the givenness of his situation and engaging in human action. Thus the Marxist interpretation of Hegel in terms of the class struggle and the progress of history in favor of the slaves comes into view.

Since desire entails the other, the point of hominization is also the point of the first formation of community. For Marx hominization happened when we began to produce the means of subsistence by transforming adaptive behavior into instrumental action. Humanity and community were forged in the work place. For Freud the threshold was crossed when we invented an agency of socialization for our long-dependent young and transformed instinct-governed behavior into communicative action.[11] Humanity and community were nurtured in the family. There is, however, another way to translate the findings of the *Phenomenology* into social description, assuming that the notion of the absolute spirit is unacceptable. It is to observe the birth of society out of its religious institutions in the tradition of Durkheim and Girard. Humanity began when mimetic violence was channeled by the spontaneous emergence of the surrogate victim mechanism into sacrificial structures, and rivalry became piety. Humanity and community were conjured in the temple, when acquisitive mimesis became conflictual mimesis and founded the system of the Sacred.

Mimesis, therefore, stands at the threshold of hominization. The critical element in intersubjectivity is the power of desire to command imitation. At the prereflective level this power operates as a natural force arising from the same emptiness as the need for recognition. It is the result of the essential insecurity of the human subject, or, in terms of violence, one's essential vulnerability.[12] It results in violent rivalry, which must be contained if there is to be community. It could be contained by one desire conquering the other, and then we would have the master/slave dialectic; or we could discover a way of channeling this violence. The mechanism of the surrogate victim is such a way.

---

[10] *Phenomenology,* 673; *Reason in History,* 42–43.

[11] Habermas, *Knowledge and Human Interests,* 282. The unconscious is an induction from failures in communication, and so is not to be reified.

[12] P. Hoffmann, *Doubt, Time, Violence,* 118, equates this vulnerability with Heidegger's category of Angst.

In this alternative to the master/slave solution neither antagonist yields; each remains a master and they find a substitute for each other. Instead of enslaving or killing the other, which would defeat the purpose of the conflict, a third party is spontaneously substituted as the brunt of violence. This substitution is spontaneous, not studied, arising out of the dynamics of the struggle for recognition as a sort of postponement of the outcome, a temporary repository of desire's urge to dominate, which leaves the emptiness unfilled. Thus sacrifice is never more than a provisional solution to the problem of rivalry and violence, which leaves the need for recognition unfulfilled. That is why the sacrificial solution is inherently unstable and the sacrifice has to be ritually reenacted. What began as a competition for an object and became a competition for each other returns to its triangular form by the reintroduction of an object that is now the surrogate for each of the two protagonists, and by extension for the whole community.

The very first human maneuver was to substitute the object for the self and the other (acquisitive mimesis), and at this more advanced stage of the process the substitution ruse returns (conflictual mimesis). The representative object returns from the beginning of the process now in the form of the surrogate victim, to reinstate the mediatory function and return the struggle to the symbolic domain. Instead of one substituting for the object in the desire of the other (i.e., becoming the master), a victim is substituted for each of the antagonists in the desire of the other. Instead of desiring to possess the desire of each other by enslavement or killing, they transfer their violent desire to the sacrificial victim. By the double transference of mimetic rivalry and surrogate victimage—the victim caused not only our violence toward one another but also our need for further surrogate victims—the sacrificial order of human community is established.

At the prehuman stage mimesis is curbed by the formation of hierarchies or dominance patterns. In bands of higher primates the loser concedes before the rivalry results in physical violence and takes a subordinate place in the hierarchy. In hominid bands, however, the hunger of desire for recognition is so great that the momentum of domination does not stop until the other has been dialectically overcome—that is, enslaved (overcome but not destroyed). This process could continue until the group is divided into the classes of master and slave, as a Marxist account would have it, but such an account leaves the whole dimension of religion unexplained. Another force arises out of the situation of unbridled mimetic struggle for recognition, the mechanism of the surrogate victim. There is no dialectical overcoming at this stage; without the surrogate victim mechanism the rivalry would result in the death rather than the enslavement of the other. Dialectical overcoming is itself a form of sacrificial order, subsequent to the discovery of the sacrificial mechanism.

If my true self is in the other as his or her recognition of me, then by the same token the true self is represented in the victim. Thus, as we have seen, the device of representation comes into being out of the sacrifice through the ruse of substitution. In the case of the victim, however, the notion is extended beyond the idea that one thing can stand for another to the idea that one thing can stand for many, and that the part can stand for the whole; metaphor, metonymy, and synecdoche are grounded in sacrifice. The victim represents both the antagonists and by extension the whole community of competing desires. The victim is the slave that enables us all to pretend that we are masters. From the victim comes the spurious recognition that we crave, and that is one of the reasons why we identify the victim as a god.

The victim is transformed into the god by the double transference of mimetic desire and surrogate victimage. The victim (not the mob) causes mimetic violence and demands surrogate victims. On this double transference culture as false-consciousness is founded. Instead of acknowledging responsibility for our violence, we blame the victim. The victim is responsible for both the bad violence of rivalry and for the good violence of unanimity. Thus the fellowship of the lynch mob becomes the sacred community of the cult, tribe, and nation, and the sacred victim has a dialectical valence of threat and succor. The victim is a mechanism for transforming bad violence into good, and from the sacred emerge the three structuring transformations of violence— prohibition (law), ritual (religion), and myth (language)—which form the building blocks of the house of culture.

Prohibition prohibits situations and actions that might cause mimetic violence to break out again. Therefore, order takes the form of differentiation and the first difference is that between the sacred and the profane. The line of demarcation around the sacred precinct stands for the principle of differentiation. The first transference misrepresents the sanction of prohibition as the threat of the vengeance of the god. It is not that we shall fall again into our old rivalries should we transgress the limits, but rather that the god will punish us. We observe the limits because they define the prestige of the god rather than because they are the limits of our interaction.

Ritual reenacts in controlled circumstances the killing of the victim in the belief that repetition will repristinate the original power of unanimity. What is in fact a channeling of random violence out of the community onto the surrogate is understood as the appeasement of the wrath of the god for transgressions of the prohibition, or thanksgiving to the god for continued maintenance of order, or the feeding of the god so that the god may continue strong enough to maintain order. The fundamental ritual, therefore, is sacrifice, and it takes place in formal and informal ways, in the cultus and in the common strategy of scapegoating. The cultic functionaries partake of the prestige of the sacred, and together with the cultic institution they become the authorities in society. The prestige of kings, priests, and heroes is the prestige of the transformed violence.

Myth is the linguistic counterpart of ritual that recounts the founding murder in such a way as to cement the deception. Language therefore finds its first public function in the service of religious propaganda, and so it is no assurance against deception to substitute language for substance in the hermeneutical conception of the self. To be sure, language is in fact the common horizon of human being, and there is no ground for the reification of the subject apart from language. Nevertheless, the recognition of this fact does not materially improve our epistemological situation. The delusion of the truth of language, whether as semantics or discourse, is hardly less damaging than the delusion of the substantial subject.

The tradition as that which has been spoken (*fatum*) is mythic. I am not what I am, because fate is a lie. Language is the prison house of being because it occurs primarily as mythic tradition. There must, therefore, be a criticism of tradition. Noncoerced communication in the form of open dialogue, as recommended by Habermas, is probably the nearest we can come to such a criticism, but before we can achieve noncoercion there must be an exposure of the violent structuration of the linguistic tradition—that is, an exposure of myth.

The criticism of myths takes the form of an explanation of their genesis and progress as agents of the transformation of violence into language. When one finds myths in which the founder of the culture is accused of crimes and hounded to his death, one is in touch with the primal story. All other stories are transformations of this one.

Myth must be dialectically overcome, transcended but left in place. One must not substitute rational myths for primitive myths. The Enlightenment invented the myth of reason, which is even more deceptive than the primitive myths, and has been used to cover a multitude of modern malfeasance.

Violence and Dialectic

Hegel's insight that the core of truth is historical means that static order of traditional metaphysics has been held in place by violence. Violence freezes the dynamic of history in structures of self-subsisting being; but violence also propels history by the "determinate negation" that breaks up concentrations of being.[13] Negation takes the form of an iconoclasm and history is a process of deidolization driven by iconoclastic violence. Iconoclastic violence is still mythic, however, because it is violence controlling violence. Traditional metaphysics, on the one hand, is the mythology of iconostasis, while enlightenment metaphysics is the mythology of iconoclasm. Iconoclastic violence meets iconostatic violence, in the dialectic of enlightenment.

Hegel lapsed further into mythology when he identified the conscious result of the process of the dialectic as an absolute. Heidegger's call to return to the generative sources of thinking points beyond the myth of the absolute, but not beyond mythology. The way back to the generative source of thinking must go through the sacrificial violence of the absolute and the generative violence

---

[13] Ibid., 24.

of mimesis to a decoding of the double transference. The instability of the dialectic is the instability of a process in which violence controls violence.

This situation cannot be altered. There can be no nonviolent utopia within history. Therefore there must be no denial of the dialectic, and no attempt to eradicate the negative. The *simul iustus et peccator* of the Reformation and the memorable comment of de Maistre on the civilizing role of the executioner[14] express this insight. In this world there can be only the dialectic of iconostatic and iconoclastic violence, under the umbrella of the hope for eschatological nonviolence.

The myth of enlightenment is dangerous because it pretends to eliminate the negative rationally. The fascists made the Jews the historical embodiment of the principle of negation,[15] and in seeking to remove them sought to remove the threat of death and nothingness.[16] The attempt violently to change the order of sacred violence leads to an increase in violence because it removes the sacred constraints without changing the mimesis that makes them necessary.

Along lines like this, therefore, a rereading of the Hegelian tradition in terms of sacred violence might proceed until the violent origins of modern philosophy, especially in its Heideggerian mode, and modern nationalism and totalitarianism are exposed.

---

[14] "And yet all grandeur, all power, all subordination rests on the executioner: he is the horror and the bond of human association. Remove this incomprehensible agent from the world, and at that very moment order gives way to chaos, thrones topple, and society disappears. God who is the author of sovereignty, is the author also of chastisement: he has built our world on these two poles" (*The Works of Joseph de Maistre,* 192). DeMaistre's God is clearly the primitive Sacred.

[15] Horkheimer and Adorno, *Dialectic,* 168. Cf. Hannah Arendt, *The Origins of Totalitarianism,* 3–120.

[16] Cf. A. Megill, *Prophets of Extremity,* 303–4, where he argues that Derrida's attack on the mainstream Western tradition is inspired by the shadow of the Holocaust and his perception of Judaism as the "other" marginal tradition. Foucault's homosexuality makes him similarly marginal and inspires the radicalism of his critique. By comparison Nietzsche and Heidegger are still mainstream thinkers. This is questionable in the case of Nietzsche who can say that he owes all his philosophy to his sickness, and Heidegger seems to owe his "turn" to his encounter with Nietzsche and his taking with radical seriousness the death of God.

Bibliography

Anspach, M. R. "Penser la vengeance." *Esprit* 128 (July 1987) 103–11.

Arendt, H. *The Origins of Totalitarianism.* London: Allen & Unwin, 1958.

Atlan H., Dupuy, J.-P. "Mimesis and Social Morphogenesis." *Applied Systems and Cybernetics (Proceedings of the International Congress on Applied Systems Research and Cybernetics)* III (ed. G. E. Lasker). New York, 1981, 1263–68.

Barrett, C. K. *A Commentary on the Epistle to the Romans.* New York: Harper & Row, 1957.

———. *A Commentary on the Second Epistle to the Corinthians.* New York: Harper & Row, 1973.

———. *From First Adam to Last, A Study in Pauline Theology.* New York: Scribner's, 1962.

Barrett, W. *Death of the Soul: Philosophical Thought from Descartes to the Computer.* New York: Oxford University Press, 1986.

Barth, K. *The Epistle to the Romans.* London: Oxford University Press, 1933.

———. *A Shorter Commentary on Romans.* London: SCM, 1959.

Bataille, G. *Erotism: Death and Sensuality.* San Francisco: City Lights, 1986.

Beker, J. C. *The Apostle Paul: The Triumph of God in Life and Thought.* Philadelphia: Fortress, 1980.

Baumbach, G. "Die Frage nach den Irrlehren in Philippi." *Kairos* 13 (1971) 252–66.

Betz, H. D. *Nachfolge und Nachahmung Jesu Christi in Neuen Testament.* Tübingen: Mohr, 1967, 60, 86, 135–36.

———. *Galatians.* Hermeneia; Philadelphia: Fortress, 1979.

Bhaskar, R. *The Possibility of Naturalism.* Brighton: Harvester, 1979.

Borch-Jacobsen, M. *The Freudian Subject.* Stanford: Stanford University Press, 1988.

Borg, M. "A New Context for Romans 13," *NTS* 19 (1973) 205–18.

Bornkamm, G. *Paul.* New York: Harper & Row, 1971.

Bourdieu, P. *Outline of a Theory of Practice.* Cambridge: Cambridge University Press, 1977.

Brown, P. *The Body and Society*. New York: Columbia University Press, 1988.

Bruce, F. F. "The Curse of the Law." *Paul and Paulinism: Essays in Honor of C. K. Barrett* (eds. M. D. Hooker and S. G. Wilson). London: SPCK, 1982.

Bultmann, R. *Theology of the New Testament 1*. London: SCM, 1952.

Butler, J. P. *Subjects of Desire: Hegelian Reflections in Twentieth-Century France*. New York: Columbia University Press, 1987.

Callan, T. "Pauline Midrash. The Exegetical Background of Gal 3.19b." *JBL* 99 (1980) 549–67.

Carr, W. *Angels and Principalities: The Background, Meaning and Development of the Pauline Phrase hai archai kai hai exousiai* (*SNTSMS* 42). Cambridge: Cambridge University Press, 1981.

Carson, A. *Eros the Bittersweet: An Essay*. Princeton: Princeton University Press, 1986.

Charles, R. H. *Apocrypha and Pseudepigrapha of the Old Testament 1*. Oxford: Clarendon, 1913.

Clark, T. N. *Gabriel Tarde on Communication and Social Influence: Selected Papers* (ed. Terry N. Clark). Chicago: University of Chicago Press, 1969.

Conzelmann, H. *Acts of the Apostles*. Hermeneia; Philadelphia: Fortress, 1987.

———. *1 Corinthians*. Hermeneia; Philadelphia: Fortress, 1975.

Cranfield, C. E. B. *The Epistle to the Romans 1 and 2*. ICC; Edinburgh: Clark, 1975.

D'Arcy, M. *The Mind and Heart of Love*. Cleveland: World Meridian, 1962.

Davies, W. D., and Allison, D. C. *The Gospel according to St Matthew 1, Introduction and Commentary on Mtt I-VII*. ICC; Edinburgh: Clark, 1988.

Davies, W. D. "Paul and the People of Israel." *NTS* 24 (1977) 4–39.

———. *Paul and Rabbinic Judaism: Some Rabbinic Elements in Pauline Theology*. Philadelphia: Fortress, 1980.

———. "Law in First-Century Judaism." *Jewish and Pauline Studies*. Philadelphia: Fortress, 1984, 3–26.

de Maistre, J. *The Works of Joseph de Maistre* (ed. J. Lively). New York: Macmillan, 1965.

de Rougemont, D. *Love in the Western World*. New York: Pantheon, 1956.

de Waal, F. *Peacemaking among Primates*. Cambridge: Harvard University Press, 1989.

Derrida, J. "No Apocalypse, Not Now (full speed ahead, seven missiles, seven missives)." *Diacritics,* Summer 1984 (on "Nuclear Criticism") 20–31.

Dietzfelbinger, C. *Die Berufung des Paulus als Ursprung seiner Theologie*. WMANT 58; Neukirchen-Vluyn: Neukirchener, 1985.

Domenach, J.-M. "Voyage to the End of the Sciences of Man." *Violence and Truth* (ed. D. Mowchel) 152–59.

Donaldson, T. "The 'Curse of the Law' and the Inclusion of the Gentiles." *NTS* 32 (1986) 94–112.

Donfried, K. "Paul and Judaism: 1 Thessalonians 2:13-16 as a Test Case." *INT* 38 (1984) 242–53.

Doty, W. G. *Mythography: The Study of Myths and Rituals*. Tuscaloosa: University of Alabama Press, 1986.

Douglas, M. *Purity and Danger*. New York: Praeger, 1966.

Dumouchel, P. (ed.). *Violence and Truth: On the Work of René Girard*. Stanford: Stanford University Press, 1988.

Dunn, J. D. G. "Works of the Law and the Curse of the Law (Gal 3:10-14)." *NTS* 31 (1985) 523–42.

Dupuy, J.-P. *Ordres et Desordres, Enquête sur un nouveau Paradigme*. Paris: Grasset, 1982.

Eliade, M. *The Sacred and the Profane*. New York: Harper & Row, 1961.

Feminist Studies 14/1 (1988).

Fowlie, W. *Climate of Violence, The French Literary Tradition from Baudelaire to the Present*. New York: Macmillan, 1967.

Freccero, J. "The Fig Tree and the Laurel; Petrarch's Poetics." *Diacritics* 5 (1975).

Friedrich, G. "ἁμαρτία οὐκ ἐλόγειται ." *TLZ* 77 (1952) 523–28.

Furnish, V. P. *II Corinthians*. Anchor Bible; Garden City, N.Y.: Doubleday, 1984.

———. *Theology and Ethics in Paul*. Nashville: Abingdon, 1968.

Fussell, P. *The Great War and Modern Memory*. New York: Oxford University Press, 1975.

Gadamer, H.-G. *Truth and Method*. New York: Crossroad, 1988.

Gager, J. *The Origins of Anti-Semitism*. New York: Oxford University Press, 1983.

Gaston, L. *Paul and the Torah*. Vancouver: University of British Columbia Press, 1987.

Gerhardsson, B. *The Testing of God's Son (Matt 4:1-11 & Par.): An Analysis of an Early Christian Midrash*. Lund: C. W. K. Gleerup, 1966.

Giddens, A. *Central Problems of Social Theory*. Berkeley: University of California Press, 1979.

———. *The Constitution of Society: Outline of the Theory of Structuration*. Cambridge: Polity Press, 1984.

Girard, R. *Deceit, Desire, and the Novel: Self and Other in Literary Structure*. Baltimore and London: Johns Hopkins University Press, 1965.

———. *Violence and the Sacred*. Baltimore and London: Johns Hopkins University Press, 1977.

———. *The Scapegoat*. Baltimore and London: Johns Hopkins University Press, 1986.

———. *Things Hidden Since the Foundation of the World*, with J.-M. Ourgoulian and G. Lefort. Stanford: Stanford University Press, 1987.

———. *A Theater of Envy: William Shakespeare*. New York: Oxford University Press, 1991.

Gottwald, N. *The Tribes of Yahweh*. Maryknoll, N.Y.: Orbis, 1979.

Greenberg, I. "Cloud of Smoke, Pillar of Fire: Judaism, Christianity, and Modernity after the Holocaust." *Auschwitz: Beginning of a New Era?* (ed. Eva Fleischner). New York: KTAV, 1977, 7–56.

Haacker, K. "Paulus und das Judentum im Galaterbrief." *Gottes Augenapfel* (eds. E. Broche and J. Seim). Neukirchen-Vluyn: Neukirchener, 1986, 95–111.

Habermas, J. *The Philosophical Discourse of Modernity*. Cambridge, Mass.: MIT Press, 1987.

———. *Knowledge and Human Interests*. Boston: Beacon, 1971.

Hahn, F. "Das Gesetzesverständnis im Römer- und Galaterbrief." *ZNW* 67 (1976) 29–63.

Hamerton-Kelly, R. G. *Pre-Existence, Wisdom, and the Son of Man*. SNTSMS 21; Cambridge: Cambridge University Press, 1973.

———. *God the Father: Theology and Patriarchy in the Teaching of Jesus*. Philadelphia: Fortress, 1979.

———. "A Girardian Interpretation of Paul: Rivalry, Mimesis and Victimage in the Corinthian Correspondence." *Semeia* 33 (1985) 65–82.

———. (ed.). *Violent Origins: Walter Burkert, René Girard, and Jonathan Z. Smith on Ritual Killing and Social Formation* (with an Introduction by B. Mack and a Commentary by R. Rosaldo). Stanford: Stanford University Press, 1987.

———. "Sacred Violence and Sinful Desire: Paul's Interpretation of Adam's Sin in the Letter to the Romans." *The Conversation Continues: Studies in Paul and John in Honor of J. Louis Martyn* (eds., R. Fortna and B. Gaventa). Nashville: Abingdon, 1990, 35–54.

———. "Sacred Violence and the Curse of the Law (Galatians 3:13): The Death of Christ as a Sacrificial Travesty." *NTS* 36 (1990) 98–118;

———. "Sacred Violence and 'Works of Law.' 'Is Christ Then an Agent of Sin?' " *CBQ* 52 (1990) 55–75.

Hanson, A. T. *Studies in Paul's Technique and Theology*. Grand Rapids: Eerdmans, 1974.

———. "Vessels of Wrath or Instruments of Wrath? Romans IX. 22-3." *JTS* 32 (1981) 433–43.

Hardin, R., Mearsheimer, J. J. et al. (eds.). *Nuclear Deterrence: Ethics and Strategy*. Chicago: Chicago University Press, 1985.

Handelman, S. *The Slayers of Moses: The Emergence of Rabbinic Interpretation in Modern Literary Theory*. Albany: State University of New York Press, 1982.

Harari, J. V. "Critical Factions/Critical Fictions." *Textual Strategies, Perspectives in Post-Structuralist Criticism*. (ed. Harari). Ithaca: Cornell University Press, 1979, 17–72.

Harris, M. *The Rise of Anthropological Theory, A History of Theories of Culture*. New York: Columbia University Press, 1968.

Harrison, J. *Themis: A Study of the Social Origins of Greek Religion*. New York: World, 1962.

Hegel, G. W. F. *The Phenomenology of Mind*. New York: Harper Torch, 1967.

———. *Reason in History*. Indianapolis: Bobbs-Merrill, 1953.

Heidegger, M. *Being and Time*. New York: Harper & Row, 1962.

———. *Nietzsche 1: The Will to Power as Art*. New York: Harper & Row, 1979.

Hengel, M. *Die Zeloten: Untersuchungen zur jüdischen Freiheitsbewegung in der Zeit von Herodes 1 bis 70 n. chr.* A.G.S.U. 1; Leiden/Cologne: E. J. Brill, 1961, 151–234.

Hennecke-Schneemelcher. *New Testament Apocrypha 2*. Philadelphia: Westminster, 1965.

Henninger, J. "Sacrifice." *The Encyclopedia of Religion* 12 (ed. Mircea Eliade). New York: Macmillan, 1987.

Henrichs, A. "Loss of Self, Suffering, Violence: The Modern View of Dionysus from Nietzsche to Girard." *Harvard Studies in Classical Philology* 88 (1984) 205–40.

Hoffmann, P. *Doubt, Time, Violence*. Chicago: University of Chicago Press, 1986.

Hommel, H. "Das 7. Kapital des Römerbriefs im Licht antiker Überlieferung." *TheoViatorum* 8 (1961–62) 90–116.

Hooker, M. D. "Adam in Romans 1." *NTS* 6 (1959–60) 297–306.

———. "A Further Note on Romans 1." *NTS* 13 (1967–68) 181–83.

Horkheimer, M., and Adorno, T. W. *Dialectic of Enlightenment*. New York: Continuum, 1988.

Horsley, G. R. *New Documents Illustrating Early Christianity*. NSW: Macquarie University, 1987.

Horsley, R. *Jesus and the Spiral of Violence: Popular Jewish Resistance in Roman Palestine*. San Francisco: Harper & Row, 1987.

Hübner, H. "Sühne und Versöhnung." *KD* 29 (1983) 284–305.

Jameson, F. *The Political Unconscious: Narrative as a Socially Symbolic Act.* Ithaca: Cornell University Press, 1981.

Jardine, A. A. *Gynesis: Configurations of Woman and Modernity.* Ithaca: Cornell University Press, 1985.

Jewett, R. "The Agitators and the Galatian Congregation." *NTS* 17 (1971) 198–212.

───. *Paul's Anthropological Terms: A Study of their Use in Conflict Settings.* AGAJU X; Leiden: E. J. Brill, 1971, 95–101.

Jonas, H. "The Abyss of the Will: Philosophical Meditation on the Seventh Chapter of Paul's Epistle to the Romans." *Philosophical Essays: From Ancient Creed to Technological Man.* Englewood Cliffs, N.J.: Prentice-Hall, 1974, 335–48.

Käsemann, E. *An die Römer.* Tübingen: Mohr (Paul Siebeck), 1973, 187–88.

───. *Perspectives on Paul.* Philadelphia: Fortress, 1971.

Kaptein, R., and Tijmes, P. *De Ander als Model en Obstakel, Een Inleiding in het Werk van René Girard.* Kampen: Kok, 1986.

Keck, L. "The Law and the 'The Law of Sin and Death' (Rom 8:1-4): Reflections on the Spirit and Ethics in Paul." *The Divine Helmsman: Studies on God's Control of Human Events, Presented to Lou H. Silberman* (ed. J. L. Crenshaw and S. Sandmel). New York: KTAV, 1980, 41–57.

Kierkegaard, S. *The Concept of Anxiety.* Princeton: Princeton University Press, 1980.

Kim, S. *The Origin of Paul's Gospel.* WUNT 4; Tübingen: Mohr (Paul Siebeck), 1981.

Klassen, W. *Love of Enemies: The Way to Peace.* Philadelphia: Fortress, 1984, 28–71.

Klein, G. "Sündenverständnis und theologia crucis bei Paulus." *Theologia Crucis—Signum Crucis: Festschrift für Erich Dinkler zum 70. Geburtstag* (eds. C. Andresen and G. Klein). Tübingen: Mohr (Paul Siebeck), 1979, 249–82.

Kojéve, A. *Introduction to the Reading of Hegel: Lectures on the Phenomenology of Spirit assembled by Raymond Queneau.* New York: Basic Books, 1969.

Kümmel, W. *Römer 7 und die Bekehrung des Paulus.* UNT 17; Leipzig: Hinrichs, 1929.

Layder, D. *Structure, Interaction, and Social Theory.* London: Routledge & Kegan Paul, 1981.

Luhmann, N. *Soziale Systeme.* Frankfurt a.M.: Suhrkamp, 1984.

Lull, D. J. " 'The Law was our Pedagogue.' A Study in Galatians 3.19-25." *JBL* 105 (1986) 481–98.

Lyonnet, S. " 'Tu ne convoiteras pas' (Rom vii 7)." *Neotestamentica et Patristica: Freundesgabe O. Cullmann.* Leiden: E. J. Brill, 1962, 157–65.

Maccoby, H. *The Sacred Executioner: Human Sacrifice and the Legacy of Guilt.* London: Thames & Hudson, 1982.

───. *The Mythmaker: Paul and the Invention of Christianity.* New York: Harper & Row, 1986.

Mack, B. "The Innocent Transgressor: Jesus in Early Christian Myth and History." *Semeia* 33 (1985) 135–65.

───. *A Myth of Innocence: Mark and Christian Origins.* Philadelphia: Fortress, 1988.

Manson T. W. "ἱλαστήριον ," *JTS* 46 (1945) 1–10.

Martyn, J. L. "Epistemology at the Turn of the Ages: 2 Corinthians 5:16." *Christian History and Interpretation: Studies presented to John Knox.* Cambridge: Cambridge University Press, 1967, 269–87.

───. "A Law-Observant Mission to Gentiles: the Background of Galatians." *MQR* 22 (1983) 221–36.

————. "Apocalyptic Antinomies in Paul's Letter to the Galatians." *NTS* 31 (1985) 410–24.

————. "Paul and his Jewish-Christian Interpreters." *USQR* 42 (1988) 1–16.

McKenna, A. "René Girard and Biblical Studies." *Semeia* 33 (1985).

————. "Biblical Structuralism: Testing the Victimary Hypothesis." *Helios* 17 (1990) 71–87.

Marxsen, W. "Der ἕτερος νόμος Rom. 13:8." *ThZ* 11 (1955) 230–37.

Mearns, C. "The Identity of Paul's Opponents at Philippi." *NTS* 33 (1987) 194–204.

Megill, A. *Prophets of Extremity*. Berkeley: University of California Press, 1985.

Meyer, B. "The Pre-Pauline Formula in Rom. 3.25-26a." *NTS* 29 (1983) 198–208.

Moi, T. "The Missing Mother: the Oedipal Rivalries of René Girard." *Diacritics* (Summer 1982) 21–31.

Morris, L. *The Apostolic Preaching of the Cross*. Grand Rapids: Eerdmans, 1976.

Neusner, J. *Judaism: The Evidence of the Mishnah*. Chicago: Chicago University Press, 1981.

North, R. "Violence and the Bible: the Girard Connection." *CBQ* 4 (1985) 1–27.

Nygren, A. *Agape and Eros*. New York: Harper Torch, 1969.

O'Keefe, D. *Stolen Lightning, The Social Theory of Magic*. New York: Continuum, 1982.

Perkins, P. "Pauline Anthropology in the Light of Nag Hammadi." *CBQ* 48 (1986) 512–22.

Piper, J. "The Demonstration of the Righteousness of God in Rom 3:25, 26." *JSNT* 7 (1980) 2–32.

Räisänen, H. "Zum Gebrauch von ἐπιθυμία und ἐπιθυμεῖν bei Paulus." *StTh* 33 (1979) 85–99.

————. *Paul and the Law*. Philadelphia: Fortress, 1986.

Rhoads, D. M. *Israel in Revolution, 6–74 C.E.: A Political History Based on the Writings of Josephus*. Philadelphia: Fortress, 1976.

Rhodes, R. *The Making of the Atomic Bomb*. New York: Simon & Schuster, 1988, 104–13.

Ricoeur, P. *Freud and Philosophy: An Essay on Interpretation*. New Haven: Yale University Press, 1970.

————. *The Symbolism of Evil*. Boston: Beacon, 1967.

————. "Paul's Conversion and the Development of His View of the Law," *NTS* 33 (1987).

Röhser, G. *Metaphorik und Personifikation der Sünde: Antike Sündenvorstellungen und paulinische Hamartia*. WUNT 2.25; Tübingen: Mohr (Paul Siebeck), 1987.

Rorty, R. *Philosophy and the Mirror of Nature*. Princeton: Princeton University Press, 1979.

Rosenzweig, F. *The Star of Redemption*. New York: Holt, Rinehart & Winston, 1971.

Sanders, E. P. *Paul and Palestinian Judaism: A Comparison of Patterns of Religion*. Philadelphia: Fortress, 1977.

————. *Paul, the Law, and the Jewish People*. Philadelphia: Fortress, 1983.

Sartre, J.-P. *Being and Nothingness: An Essay on Phenomenological Ontology*. New York: Philosophical Library, 1956.

Sass, L. A. "Anthropology's Native Problems, Revisionism in the Field." *Harper's Magazine*, May 1986, 49–55.

Schmid, H. H. *Gerechtigkeit als Weltordnung: Hintergrund und Geschichte des alttestamentlichen Gerechtigkeitsbegriffes*. (BHT 40). Tübingen: Mohr (Paul Siebeck), 1968.

————. "Rechtfertigung als Schöpfungsgeschehen. Notizen zur alttestamentlichen Vorgeschichte eines neutestamentlichen Themas." *Rechtfertigung: Festschrift für Ernst Kaesemann zum 70. Geburtstag* (eds. J. Friedrich, W. Pohlmann, and P. Stuhlmacher). Tübingen: Mohr (Paul Siebeck), 1976, 403–14.

Schmidt, D. "1 Thess 2:13-16: Linguistic Evidence for Interpolation." *JBL* 102 (1983) 269–79.

Schmithals, W. *Paul and the Gnostics.* Nashville; Abingdon, 1972.

Scholem, G. "Revelation and Tradition." *Diogenes* 80 (1972) 164–94.

Schottroff, L. "Die Schreckensherrschaft der Sünde und die Befreiung durch Christus nach dem Römerbrief des Paulus." *EvTh* 39 (1979) 497–510.

Schwager, R. *Must there be Scapegoats? Violence and Redemption in the Bible.* New York: Harper & Row, 1987.

Schwartz, D. "Two Pauline Allusions to the Redemptive Mechanism of the Crucifixion." *JBL* 102 (1983) 259–68.

Schweitzer, A. *The Mysticism of Paul the Apostle.* London: Adam & Charles Black, 1931.

Scroggs, R. "Paul as Rhetorician: Two Homilies in Romans 1-11." *Jews, Greeks and Christians: Religious Cultures in Late Antiquity: Essays in Honor of William David Davies* (eds. Hamerton-Kelly and Scroggs). Leiden: E. J. Brill, 1976, 271–98.

Segal, Alan F. *Paul the Convert: The Apostolate and Apostasy of Saul the Pharisee.* New Haven: Yale University Press, 1990.

Shapiro, S. E. "Failing Speech: Post-Holocaust Writing and the Discourse of Post-Modernism." *Semeia* 40 (1987) 65–91.

Sontag, S. *On Photography.* New York: Farrar, Straus and Giroux, 1977.

Steck, O. H. *Israel und das gewaltsame Geschick der Propheten: Untersuchungen zur Überlieferung des deuteronomistischen Geschichtsbildes im Alten Testament, Spätjudentum, und Urchristentum* WMANT 23; Neukirchen-Vluyn: Neukirchener, 1967.

Steiner, G. *In Bluebeard's Castle, Some Notes towards the Redefinition of Culture.* New Haven: Yale University Press, 1971.

Stendahl, K. *Paul among Jews and Gentiles.* Philadelphia: Fortress, 1976.

Stuhlmacher, P. "Zur neueren Exegese von Rom 3,24-26." *Versöhnung, Gesetz, und Gerechtigkeit.* Göttingen: Vandenhoeck und Ruprecht, 1981, 117–207.

————. "Das Gesetz als Thema biblischer Theologie." *Versöhnung, Gesetz, und Gerechtigkeit,* 136–65.

Tannehill, R. C. *Dying and Rising with Christ.* Berlin: Töpelmann, 1967.

Theissen, G. *Psychological Aspects of Pauline Theology.* Philadelphia: Fortress, 1987.

Theobald, M. "Das Gottesbild des Paulus nach Rom 3,21-31." *SNTU* 6–7 (1981–82) 131–68.

Thomson, D. M. *The History of Europe since Napoleon.* New York: A. A. Knopf, 1961.

Thompson, R. W. "How is the Law Fulfilled in Us?" *LS* 11 (1986) 31–41.

Thrift, N. "On the Determination of Social Action in Space and Time." *Society and Space* 1 (1983) 23–57.

Tijmes, P. "De twee hypothesen van Girard." *Mimesis en Geweld* (ed. W. van Beek). Kampen: Kok, 1988, 28–52.

Tolbert, M. A. "Defining the Problem: The Bible and Feminist Hermeneutics." *Semeia* 28 (1983) 113–26.

Tomson, Peter J. *Paul and the Jewish Law: Halakha in the Letters of the Apostle to the Gentiles.* Compendia Rerum Judaicarum ad Novum Testamentum III/1. Assen/Maastricht: Van Gorcum and Minneapolis: Fortress, 1990.

Turner, F. M. *The Greek Heritage in Victorian Britain.* New Haven: Yale University Press, 1981.

Tyson, J. "Works of Law in Galatians." *JBL* 92 (1973) 423–31.

van der Leeuw, G. *Religion in Essence and Manifestation 1.* New York: P. Smith, 1967.

Verdier, R. (ed.). *La Vengeance 1 and 2: La Vengeance dans les sociétés extra occidentales.* Paris: Editions Cujas, 1980, 1986.

Verdier, R., and Poly, J.-P. (eds). *La Vengeance 3: Vengeance, pouvoirs et idéologies dans quelques civilisations de l'Antiquité* (1984).

Verdier, R., and Courtois, G. (eds). *La Vengeance 4: La vengeance dans la pensée occidentale* (1984).

Vielhauer, P. "Gesetzesdienst und Stoicheiadienst im Galaterbrief." *Rechtfertigung: Festschrift für Ernst Kaesemann zum 70. Geburtstag* (eds. J. Friedrich, W. Pohlmann, and P. Stuhlmacher). Tübingen: Mohr (Paul Siebeck), 1976, 543–55.

Waltz, K. N. *Theory of International Politics.* New York: Random House, 1979.

Watson, F. *Paul, Judaism and the Gentiles* (*SNTSMS* 56). Cambridge: Cambridge University Press, 1986.

Webb, E. *Philosophers of Consciousness.* Seattle: University of Washington Press, 1989.

Weber, R. "Die Geschichte des Gesetzes und des Ich in Römer 7,7—8,4: Einige Überlegungen zum Zusammenhang von Heilsgeschichte und Anthropologie im Blick auf die theologische Grundstellung des paulinischen Denkens." *Neue Zeitschrift für system. Theologie und Religionsphil* 29 (1987) 147–79.

Weder, H. *Das Kreuz Jesu bei Paulus: Ein Versuch, über den Geschichtsbezug des christlichen Glaubens nachzudenken.* Göttingen: Vandenhoeck & Ruprecht, 1981.

———. "Gesetz und Sünde: Gedanken zu einem qualitativen Sprung im Denken des Paulus." *NTS* 31 (1985).

Wendt, A. E. "The agent-structure problem in international relations theory." *IntOrg* 41 (1987) 335–37.

White, H. "Ethnological 'Lie' and Mythical 'Truth.'" *Diacritics* (Spring 1978) 2–9.

———. "Getting out of History." *Diacritics* (Fall 1982) 2–13.

Williams, D. D. *The Spirit and the Forms of Love.* New York: Harper & Row, 1968.

Williams, S. K. *Jesus' Death as Saving Event: The Background and Origin of a Concept.* Missoula: Scholars Press, 1975.

Wink, W. *Naming the Powers: The Language of Power in the New Testament, I. The Powers.* Philadelphia: Fortress, 1984.

Zeller, D. "Der Zusammenhang von Gesetz und Sünde im Römerbrief. Kritischer Nachvollzug der Auslegung von Ulrich Wilckens." *ThZ* 38 (1982) 193–212.

Index of Names

217

Index of Subjects

Agape, 161–70, 175, 181, 183, 184, 197, 199
  Christ as exemplar and mediator of, 173
  church as structure of, 174–82
  and the Law, 171
  See also Desire; Love
Akedah, 78
Analysis, 2

Baptism, 70, 85, 180
Bible, 38, 56, 59
  See also New Testament
Blood Sacrifice
  See Sacrifice
Buddha, 89

Catholicism, 9
Christianity
  and the Cross, 60
  relationship to Judaism, 144–46
  and sacred violence, 9, 52
  view of sex, 109 n.41
Church, The
  as body of crucified victim, 179–80
  as structure of agape, 174–82
Co-Crucifixion, 70, 92, 129
Community of the Cross, 83–87
Creation, 104
Cross, The
  and category of sacrifice, 77–81
  community of, 83–87
  and the Gospel, 65–71
  hermeneutic of, 183
  and plan of salvation, 81–83
  scandal of, 71–77
  and wrath, 102
  and zeal, 71–73
Curetes, 16 n.19
Curse of the Law, 71–77

Death, 99, 109–10
Desire, 158, 199–200
  corruption of, 98–99
  corrupt or pure, 116–17
  deformation of, 90–111, 113–14, 171
  forms of, 189
  function of, 69
  Girard on, 54 n.32
  and the Law, 97
  nature of, 19–24
  redemption of, 161
  reformation of, 118
  and sin, 88–90, 99 n.20, 147 n.16
  and violence, 193, 200–206
  See also Agape; Eros
Dominion, 168 n.15
Don Quixote, 17, 18, 19
Double Transference, 24–29, 79

Election, Doctrine of, 12, 106, 138–39
Envy, 88 n.1, 93, 100, 106, 146–47, 167 n.14, 171
Eros, 161–70, 184, 199
  See also Desire; Love
Eucharist, 85, 180
Evil, 105 n.34

"Failed Mind," 99, 103
Faith, 86–87
  and agape and eros, 168–69
  as fulfillment of the Law, 158–60
  and hope and love, 171–73
  and the Law, 105, 141
  and love, 145 n.13
  mimesis of, 117–18
  and salvation, 97
  and sin, 88, 95
Feminism, 47–48, 55–56

220

Index of Ancient Sources

HEBREW BIBLE

Genesis
1:26, *168, 168 n.15*
1:26-31, *105*
1:28, *166, 167, 168, 168 n.15, 172*
1:28-30, *105*
2:15-17, *90, 99, 100, 148 n.20*
2:16, *159*
2:16-17, *9, 92–97*
2:17b, *159*
2:24, *116*
3:1-24, *90, 92–97*
3:7, *91, 94*
3:8-19, *94*
3:17-19, *149*
3:22, *93*
3:22b, *159*
4:1-17, *96*
4:17, *34*
6, *91*
15:6, *74, 74 n.31, 75*
22, *78*
37:27, *123 n.13*

Exodus
4:21, *132*
6:7, *114*
7:3, *132*
9:12, *132*
9:16, *132*
10:20, *132*
32, *74 n.27*
34:29, *74 n.27*
34:33-34, *159*
34:34, *159, 160*

Leviticus
14, *78*
16, *78*

18:5, *76*
18:6, *123 n.13*
19:18, *9, 154, 155, 155 n.33, 156*
25:49, *123 n.13*

Numbers
25:1-5, *75 n.33*
25:1-13, *74*
25:4, *75*
25:11, *74*
25:12-13, *74*

Deuteronomy
6:4, *105*
21:22-23, *75*
21:23, *72, 72 n.17, 75, 75 n.33*
27:26, *76*
32:35, *151, 154*

Joshua
8:24-29, *75 n.33*
10:22-27, *75 n.33*

Judges
9:2, *123 n.13*

2 Samuel
5:1, *123 n.13*
21, *79*
21:1-14, *78, 79*

1 Kings
3:16-28, *26*

2 Chronicles
28:8-15, *154*

APOCRYPHA

NEW TESTAMENT

OTHER ANCIENT SOURCES